Barcode in Back

D1607425

Graphic Design
Worlds /Words

/

Nin

/

Itali

Refl

/

The

of C

Graphic Design and Page Layout
Andrea Codolo

Thanks to
Åbäke, Giacomo Covacich, Dexter Sinister,
for their layout designs
Manuel Joseph,
for permission to publish his text

Graphic
Design
Worlds
/Words

edited by
Giorgio Camuffo
Maddalena Dalla Mura

La Triennale
di Milano
Design
Museum

Electa

of C
The
/
Ref
Itali
/
Nin
/
Worlds /Words
Graphic Design

Graphic Design
Worlds /Words

/
Nin
/
Itali
Ref
/
The
of C

LA TRIENNALE DI MILANO

**FONDAZIONE
LA TRIENNALE DI MILANO**

La Triennale
di Milano
**Design
Museum**

**FONDAZIONE
MUSEO DEL DESIGN**

Graphic Design Worlds

TRIENNALE
DESIGN MUSEUM

26.01/27.03 2011
TRIENNALE DI MILANO

Director
Silvana Annicchiarico

Museum Activities Producer
Roberto Giusti

Collections and Museum Research
Marilia Pederbelli

Italian Design Archives
Giorgio Galleani

Projects Department
Carla Morogallo

Press Office and Communication
Damiano Gullì

*Triennale Design Museum
Kids Activities*
Michele Corna

Web Designer
Cristina Chiappini,
Triennale Design Museum
Studio Camuffo,
Triennale Design Museum Kids

Logistics
Giuseppe Utano

*Restoration, Research
and Preservation Laboratory*
Barbara Ferriani,
coordination
Alessandra Guarascio
Rafaela Trevisan

Founder Partners
Triennale Design Museum

General Coordination and Production
Triennale Design Museum
with
Triennale di Milano, Ufficio Marketing
and Ufficio Servizi Tecnici

Curated by
Giorgio Camuffo

Assistant Curator
Maddalena Dalla Mura

Production Assistant
Benedetta Crippa

Project Manager
Michela Miracapillo

Graphic Design
Andrea Codolo

*Graphic Design of the Walls
"Italian Graphic Designers"*
Giacomo Covacich

Video
Marco Camuffo

Web Production
Psegno

Set-up Works
Eurostands

The Curator wishes to thank
all designers and people who
made the exhibition possible.
Special thanks to Giovanni Anceschi,
Christian Braendle, Max Bruinsma,
Mauro Bubbico, Emily King,
Paolo Lucchetta, Marcella Matteazzi,
Alessandro Pedron, Stefano Pastorello,
and Sergio Polano, for their help
and support along the way.
Thanks also to Alessandro Mininno,
Claudio Grillone, Matteo Torcinovich

With the collaboration of

Technical Partners

PHILIPS

Media Partner

With the support of

Kingdom of the Netherlands

Institutional Partners
of the Triennale di Milano

CORRIERE DELLA SERA
PIRELLI

of C
The
/
Ref
Itali
/
Nin
/
Worlds /World
Graphic Design

**Graphic Design
Worlds** /Words

The Style of Signs

Silvana Annicchiarico

Director Triennale Design Museum

Turning graphic art into the theme or object of an exposition is not an easy task. Unsurprisingly, in the past three editions of the Triennale Design Museum, graphic art has nearly always solely been represented by a few *exempla*, no doubt of emblematic value, but certainly not exhaustive ones.

The fact is that graphic art cannot be dealt with hastily as an assemblage of manifestos, logos, characters and artefacts used for communication. Rather, it is a complex and harmonious universe, which foreshadows and implements a strategy, an artistic direction, probably an aesthetic, and perhaps even a philosophy of communication.

In other words, it is not limited to arranging a "page layout," the calibrated use of fonts, bodies, spaces, rhythms. It is, rather, a communicative act that results in immediate social, political and market-related implications.

In 2007, with *The New Italian Design*, we attempted to document the strategic core position of graphic art in the research developments and experiments of the newest generation of Italian designers. After that, in 2009, the *Spaghetti grafica* exhibition focused on a much-needed and deserving survey of the Italian graphic art of the new millennium, with close attention to its awe-inspiring creative and communicative developments. This time the Graphic Design Worlds exhibition, with Giorgio Camuffo as curator, aims at defining the state of the art at the international level by seeking out and valorizing the key experiences taking place on the contemporary communicative scene.

Can we really talk about a "style" of signs? About aesthetic that is first and foremost linked to the semiological materiality of communicative artefacts? Indeed, this is the basic question innervating and permeating this event, declined in a variety of ways by each of the thirty graphic designers chosen by the exhibition curator. Ever faithful to its vocation as a sort of seismograph of the present, as well as a stage for the past, by means of this initiative the Triennale Design Museum seeks to provide a wide open panorama, a multifarious one that evokes the heterogeneity of the many pathways being followed in the world in the processes of conceiving signs and the graphic representation of communication. All the Italian designers who have contributed their work are very young; the Triennale Design Museum has always been interested in discovering and helping emerging designers, and once again it has set itself the goal of offering credit and visibility to the new generations, in the belief that merit and talent must always be rewarded and valorized.

In a world where graphic art is everywhere, the *Graphic Design Worlds* exhibition suggests the idea that this genre is never merely a project in which to bestow a form on the world, but also, perhaps, the concrete and tangible envisioning of an idea of a possible future world.

Graphic design is
about something else
than yourself

Graphic Design Worlds

Giorgio Camuffo
Maddalena Dalla Mura

Graphic design is a territory that is difficult to take in with just one glance. Necessarily heteronomous, it presents itself not so much as a self-contained region with accurately defined confines, but rather as a nucleus from which and towards which different paths spread out as they relate to a variety of contexts, drawing a plurality of worlds. Although the history of graphic design is a short one, it bestows us with multiple identities, with a variety of experiences and names that have been shared to a greater or lesser extent, and that have gradually shaped the definition of graphic design as something poised between art and industry, between free expression and problem-solving, between creativity and the standard, between the banks of a professional sphere and institutionalized discipline, on the one hand, and those of amateur practice, on the other. Its current condition speaks to us of opportunities and challenges that call for up-to-date viewpoints and dictionaries. An ever-expanding landscape of products and places that fill our daily lives uses graphics to communicate and provide information on different scales and in different dimensions— from printed books to websites, from street posters to digital applications, from museums to shopping centers. Through them we are now surrounded by a wide variety of styles that brings together all the nuances, from good design to the "cult of the ugly," from the excesses of kitsch to those of minimalism, from *objets trouvés* to generative decorations. At the same time, easier access to the tools that allow graphic production makes not just the fruition but also the development and production itself of texts, images and signs more and more widespread and participative. In a scenario such as this, where "graphics" seems to be just about everywhere, graphic design's position is necessarily shifting.

Stimulated by big and small economic, social and technological changes—ranging from recurring industrial crises to the phenomenon of globalization by way of the digital revolution and the web—over the past decade graphic designers have explored and acquired different motivations and means to ply their trade: the acknowledgement as well as the assertion of having a non-neutral position; the attention turned towards the process and construction of experiences, rather than on the finished product; the stress placed on collaboration and participation beyond dyads such as question-answer, problem-solution, designer-client; the overcoming of disciplinary boundaries in favor of cross-pollination with other sectors and practices. And not just that. Supported by a growing awareness of their tools and called upon to move within contexts that are increasingly less certain and less linear, graphic designers, or at least some of them, have started to personally construct the opportunities and the conditions in which to intervene, design and communicate. This, for example, accounts for the growing commitment to lending their voice to contents and stories that lie beyond the market rationale by self-initiated projects; the use of graphic design as a form of research and inquiry; the interest in experimenting and connecting closely related activities such as graphics, writing, curatorship, editing and publishing, for the purpose of reaching a diversified audience. Similar experiences and directions—certainly not unprecedented and not wholly exclusive to *graphic* design—have not just contributed to redesigning the reference map for graphic design, broadening its scope of action, but have also attracted other visitors, as if towards a platform that will allow one to venture into different territories. Hence, alongside graphic designers who use their knowledge and skill to cross through different disciplines, perhaps even ending up finding a place for themselves right there, one can even meet artists who work with graphic design methods and tools, or critics who employ them to give shape to their hypotheses and ideas. One might say that, while keeping at a fixed point the "disciplinary barycenter" (an expression coined by Giovanni Anceschi) that was established in the past century, the waves that spread around that center of gravity are what generate fruitful prospects today. Although such oscillations can be bewildering or create confusion, they inevitably bring the position of graphic design—or better yet, of the graphic designer—back into focus. Proof of this can be found in the thinking that has developed inside and around the field in recent years.

Rather than dwelling upon the definition of a technical or professional specialization, an important segment of critical discourse has increasingly focused on the interpretation that can be given to, as well as on the use that can be made of tools and methods, that is, on the role that the graphic designer can play through them, as a subject capable of starting up and building relations, and as *author, producer, entrepreneur* and *agent*, taking active part in society and contemporary culture. Besides the individual readings of the graphic designer's role—in relation to which, among other things, designers actually show very little fondness—the common denominator of such interpretations is the call for graphic designers to acknowledge the potential and implications that their knowledge base entails, beyond the limits of self-referentiality. Trained to move amid the different languages and media that pervade our daily lives, ever closer to controlling the various stages that go from the conception of signs and messages to their configuration and production, graphic designers actually find themselves in the ideal position to read, filter and channel a social and cultural fabric that develops by communicating itself. The challenge is an important one, and one that is still wide open.

Akin to what happens when we find ourselves in the midst of a change, it is difficult to outline definite predictions. Nonetheless, while it is true that graphic design is made up of many and diverse paths, it is equally clear that in order to define its direction and value, what becomes increasingly relevant is the capacity to observe and listen to the world, to knowingly interpret tools and languages to establish relations, to build "worlds."

This is the key to the interpretation, and the persuasion, that underpinned and guided the project for the *Graphic Design Worlds* exhibition organized and produced by the Triennale Design Museum in Milan, and for which this volume is a necessary complement.

Graphic Design Worlds means opening a window onto contemporary graphic design—proposing a close-up look at the very pluralities and potentials that animate it—by inviting over thirty graphic designers to present their approaches and interpretations. Although they are all different, sometimes even opposites in terms of education and attitudes—from the small team to the large visual communication studio by way of the individual graphic artist—what all the designers and teams invited to exhibit their work share is indeed the critical awareness of the opportunities that the tools of graphic design offer in order to act upon the world. The very space of the museum, in all its dimensions, seemed to be the ideal place and medium to allow these designers to unfold their "worlds" before the public, to give this audience the chance to enter therein and wear a different pair of glasses, and to perhaps use this same pair of glasses to go back and observe its day-to-day universe. Hopefully, this is also an opportunity to suggest models and reference points to those who aspire to entering the world of graphic design, to establishing here their position. Of course, the selection on display is only a small part of the multifarious landscape described above, which is the result of not easy choices; but it is a part that, all in all, is definitely capable of stimulating further reflection, as is documented by this book as well.

Graphic Design Worlds/Words brings together words and texts that have accompanied the great effort that has gone into organizing this event: an investigative pathway aimed first of all at a closer understanding of the stories, attitudes and ideas of the invited designers (*The Worlds of Graphic Designers*), but also interested in comparing different looks on these worlds through the voices of historians and critics who have been observing them, studying them and experiencing them for years (*Nine Looks*). A twofold perspective that has also allowed us to keep track of a particular moment in Italian graphic design (*Italian Reflections*). Finally, Sergio Polano's afterword, by leading graphic design back to its origins, offers an unexpected glimpse through a reverse telescope and shows us what is true today.

Graphic designers are
authors, catalysts, com
craftsmen, creative peop
curators, curious peopl
itors, entrepreneurs, fa
alists, independent, inf
tuals, interpreters, isol
penser, makers, manag
problems, philosopher
problematizers, produc
ers, researchers, resp
thinkers, translators, u

vertising artists, artists,
rcial artists, connected,
critics, cultural agents,
lesigners, directors, ed-
itators, geologists, ide-
nation, agents, intellec-
l, journalists, maîtres à
mediators, people with
oets, problem solvers,
professionals, publish-
ble, service-providers,
ists, workers, writers...

Graphic Design
Worlds /Words
/
Nin

NINE LOOKS

GIOVANNI ANCESCHI

We would like to take advantage of this conversation to tackle—or at least make a start towards tackling—an issue which only appears to be a matter of terminology. If, on the one hand, it may seem banal to say that in recent years there has been debate as to the precise domain covered by the term "graphics," that debate also seems a clear sign of the developments taking place. We would like to hear your opinion on this matter. Giovanni Anceschi I always say that words are as solid as stones; terminology is fundamental. It is words that "call a thing into life." The word "graphics," for example, clearly bears the mark of its origins: it comes from the Greek word *graphein*—"I scratch," "I incise," "I engrave"—therefore, "I write." Giovanni Lussu would say that graphics is writing. I am not so categorical; however, it is still true that graphics is concerned with transforming things into "signs"—or rather, into "traits" rather than "signs" as they are understood in semiotics. Having said that, the term "graphics" does define a rather restricted domain. But when we form combinations such as "graphic design," we move beyond a more or less complex system that one might describe as purely notational. In fact, in Italian we do not even have the word "design" (that is, we didn't use to have). One might use the word *progettazione*, but that does not have all the same nuances. To tell the truth, I would have no problem pushing things to the point of using the expression "communication design" rather than "graphics" or "graphic design." However, I also think it is interesting to maintain the term: "graphic" associated with "design" sets up a fruitful conceptual tension between what used to happen in this field and what is happening now. Frankly, I can't make my mind up. But, as I said, the use of "graphic design" means that we have a term which covers what we do today, when there is a constant expansion in the number and type of things which are "designed." Up until quite recently, graphic designers—in Italian, *grafici*—designed what appeared on a page; they worked predominantly in two dimensions. Nowadays things have changed. Graphic design as such has become a region within a larger map, where one can see that the very nature and quality of the intervention of graphic design has changed; in particular with the peremptory presence of the temporal in design. At present, design is concerned less with artifacts and more with events; and the artifacts themselves are becoming more and more like many props for something that happens, for events. One could give any number of examples; but the most compelling of all, I would argue, is the advent of electronic media. That is an area where one finds a lot of graphic design as previously understood and practiced, but it is also one in which the importance of time is clear. These days, what is communicated is increasingly mobile, metaphorical. This is why I think the design professions could teach a lot to other disciplines, even to architecture. Speaking today about space in isolation from time is simply naive. What we have to manage and design at present are sequences, atmospheres, processes and, above all, transformations—this is the area in which graphic designers too have to work. A leading role is played by time. This is why for some years now I have introduced the notion of "direction" (as in film direction)—into my interpretation of the profession of communication design. It is a notion that is intended to reflect the idea that such a professional is engaged in shaping the flow of time, in modeling the process of communication.

Would you say that this issue of the temporal is a specific concern of graphic design? **GA** The eruption of the temporal within our culture and civilization is a more general question. It does not only concern the field of communication, but it does have a very powerful effect there. To be precise, one can't argue that this issue of the temporal suddenly emerged out of nowhere. It has always been there, and its importance has been "transversal": think, for example, of the idea of "art direction" or the notion of a "campaign" in advertising. In the 1970s I myself started am art group that was called Gruppo T, with the T standing for Time; I already knew that this was something one had to work on. Of course, one can go back even further, to Husserl, Bergson, etc. But I don't want to get into a philosophical discussion here. Suffice to say that there is a frame of reference for this whole issue. However, what one sees nowadays is the total predominance of the temporal. Today, when one considers it in

I was never really
interested in visual things,
I am more
interested in ideas
–

Daniel Eatock

Graphic design
means nothing;
"graphics"
is my profession
–

Christophe Jacquet (Toffe)

spatial terms, the world has become tiny; we can see the whole thing in its to-
tality—all we have to do is use Google Earth. But we don't have anything like
such a synoptic vision of time, of the temporal. We have no dedicated temporal
sense organ—and this is what is interesting. For space, we have the senses of
sight and touch; but for time we have no such sensors. This is why temporal-
ity is so much more difficult to verify, to exercise control upon. This poses an
extraordinary challenge, even from the cognitive point of view: time is consti-
tutive not solely of the fact that everything takes place and is transformed, but
also of the fact that you know this—for knowing is a process in time.

*Apart from the idea of designer as "director," there is another notion that
you have recently introduced into the discussion of design and graphic design: that is, the idea of "barycenter." Could you explain how this fits in with
what you have been saying?*   **GA** It is a new concept, covering the entire map
of the various types of knowledge brought to bear in the disciplines of design.
This notion of "barycenter" arose as a sort of reaction—and not only my own
reaction—to the perspective opened up by the postmodern, by what we refer
to as "weak thought." It is a reponse to a situation in which some foundations,
or previously unquestioned certainties, are attacked and eroded from various
directions. To give you an example, let's take the rhizome as a gnosiological
model. A rhizome is a stem that develops and grows horizontally; that once
planted can be separated from the original plant. Now consider what I would
call the metaphor that was valid before—that is, the reference to "foundations." This is a solidly static notion, referring to the foundations upon which
a constructed edifice arises. Now there is no doubt that the rhizome and other
more plastic (not to say liquid) notions that have emerged over the past decades obviously raise interesting points. However, while on the one hand they
are undoubtedly very malleable and adaptable descriptive terms, on the other
I would say that they seem to express a sort of lack of courage, a defeatist attitude. Think of relativism, not in the strictly scientific sense but in the wider
sense with which it is used nowadays. This is a notion which says that all things
are mutually conditioning, bound up in relations with other things. One might
also cite some rather perverse developments in phenomenology, which lead to
an acceptance and justification of anything. While these models might often be
useful to explain and understand certain things, we cannot deny the fact that
nowadays there is great demand for foundations. It is a demand that I myself
become aware of directly, in my work as a professor dealing with students. I

would say there is a strongly-felt need for propaedeutics. People ask: "What should I know before, and what after?" This is why I am particularly involved in basic design,[1] as you know, because this is an approach that brings together teaching and knowledge, epistemology and pedagogy; it links them indissolubly with each other. When you do some exercise in basic design, you are not simply undergoing training, you are generating knowledge... However, I don't want to go too far into the details of that here. Speaking in more general terms, the demand for propaedeutics, for foundations, means for example that all of us involved in teaching should be open and receptive to all the transformations currently taking place. We must be able to understand and incorporate everything; we must be elastic and open, but we must also have the courage to put forward things ourselves, to take a position. In short, what I am stressing here is what we can call *modus ponens*—something Umberto Eco pondered about: you propose something, you make an affirmation... The very word "thesis" means just that, "to take a position." But why have I raised all this in order to illustrate the notion of "barycenter"? Let's for the moment bracket out what I have just said, to return to it later. Here, I would like to turn to another consideration that is more loosely bound up with the very issue of disciplines as such. In design, various disciplines emerged and developed within a hierarchical structure which is the one of the *diva architectura*. Leon Battista Alberti, who designed everything, even typefaces, said that the architect brings God's design to perfection. Everything was in relation to architecture: architecture contained within, or beneath, itself all the other disciplines, the *ancillae* over which it was predominant. But then the modern comes along, and what happens? Obviously I am simplifying here, but with modernity what one gets is the final diversification—separation—of disciplines. Urban planning, architecture, product design, communication design, information design, etc.—each one of these disciplines has now achieved the dignity of its own "faculty" (in civilized countries, at least). A precise area of competence has been defined for each one of them, or some such attempt at territorial definition has been made. This, one might say, is the second stage. The third is the one we are experiencing at the moment, when various things have happened and continue to happen that undermine many of the notions and points of references

1.   See the website of the New Basic Design research group at the University IUAV of Venice: www.newbasicdesign.it.

which used to apply. I have already mentioned the peremptory advent of the temporal. But, as another example, one could cite the collapse of the notion of scale, traditionally so dear to architecture. Perhaps such a notion collapsed some time ago but it is only now that we can no longer ignore its demise. Is a website, for example, on a small or large scale? And, in its own day, was a Model T Ford on a small, medium or large scale? What we have witnessed and are witnessing is the breaking-down of all the boundaries, barriers and limits between disciplines. A final question: what is interaction design? Where does it fit within the ordered range of the professions and disciplines of the modern? Between urban planning and architecture? Between architecture and product design? Between product design and communication design? It can, to a certain extent, find a place anywhere; and it takes up that place not as a distinct entity but with a certain amount of transversal overlap.

One sees this "breaking-down" of barriers at the level of professional activity as well: skills and disciplines interpenetrate, there is closer collaboration... **GA** Yes. There has been this sort of explosion in some way. However, to go back to what I was saying before, this has also led to a certain weakening; boundaries have become blurred. This is where the notion of a plurality of barycenters becomes important. On the one hand, this complete "rhizomatization"—this lack of boundaries and clear definitions of limits—is something one has to take onboard and to make the most of. On the other hand, it would be nonsense simply to throw aside all professions, specific areas of competence and distinct disciplines, to jettison that which makes graphic design, design, architecture, urban-planning, etc. what they are and no other. In short, what has gone is the idea that there are rigidly-defined areas exclusive to each discipline. But, there is still something constant and stable about each, and this is what forms the barycenter of each discipline. Nowadays we recognize that there are fields of interference, areas of overlap. Design is increasingly involved in the bringing together of disciplines.

When you talk about barycenters, we imagine poles fixed in water, each one generating waves that then expand and interact with the rings of waves from a different pole... **GA** Yes, the image one might use to illustrate the notion of barycenters is that of a stone thrown into water. If you throw two stones into a canal, they produce ripple rings that then form interference patterns. Or you might think in terms of antennae emitting force fields—rather like magnets—which influence everything around them and interact with each other. But one should not forget that there can also be clashes and conflicts between the waves from different barycenters. I think that this model, this way of reading the situation, enables one to strike a balance between the modern model of distinct disciplinary domains and a postmodern model that eschews such clear-cut distinctions. Or perhaps it makes it possible to go beyond both. I like the idea of *surmodernité* proposed by Marc Augé or François Ascher's *hypermodernité*. However, it is important to insist upon the fact that as well as recognizing intersections and overlapping relations, one must also maintain the courage to recognize and assert the existence of the constants which form the "backbone" of each discipline, the cognitive hierarchy and interdependency of concepts which are proper to it. I would see that requirement in what one might describe as ethical terms.

Let's go back to the theme of education. Speaking with graphic designers in Italy and abroad, we have encountered some who complain about excessive specialization and others who criticize a tendency to generalize, to dwell upon ideas rather than professional competence. Can the notion of barycenter also have its effect upon education as such? In what direction should one go now? GA The theme of schools and education is a very delicate one. If I think what the Italian universities are being put through at the moment... then it would be better to stop talking about that and go for a swim! The barycenter model is a very new one. The fact is that it can only find practical application within systems of education if one has the "material power" to change things—a bit like Tomás Maldonado (who was my own teacher) did when he introduced certain paradigm shifts at the Ulm Hochschule für Gestaltung. He introduced those changes because he had the power to do so, and obviously the changes he made reflected the modern notions we have already discussed. Maldonado worked to consolidate a more sophisticated and nuanced structure of specialist disciplines. In his reform, even Basic Design was organized on the basis of disciplines: there was "graphic-pictorial" basic design for those involved in communication, "plastic" basic design for product designers and a "structural" basic design for architects, etc. Now would be the time to seize the opportunity offered by certain important changes to alter the entire system, to create an educational framework within which there is an easy overlap of the teaching of specialist and basic—what I would describe as "barycentric"—knowledge and work that might best be called transdisciplinary (rather than interdisciplinary). Think, for instance, of the approach that envisages the creation of university faculties defined by theme—again an approach that comes from Maldonado. For example, not a faculty of urban planning or architecture but one dedicated to the theme of the city, another faculty that is not dedicated to hydraulics or climatology but to the environment; and another that is not dedicated to transport engineering but to the epoch-defining phenomenon of migration.

Besides what can come from educational establishments—which are certainly important—it is also interesting to look at how young designers, in Italy and elsewhere, are setting about things. To us they seem to reveal a clear degree of self-awareness, but also a determination to change their profession. They are no longer content to be good graphic designers, they want to get involved with the content of their work; they want to discuss, to engage with each other, to measure what they are capable of. What do you think of this development? **GA** One thing I find particularly interesting is the emergence of the lead role taken by groups, the fact that numerous young people decide to work together. The existence of groups reveals that there is cultural movement; it has always been like that. First come the groups, and then the personalities emerge. I say this because I myself had this experience in the field of art. When it comes down to it, the individual navigates by sight; it is the group that wants to change the overall context, change the world. To put it in very basic terms, it is by being together that the young people give each other the courage to "go beyond." It is very important that such a phenomenon has re-emerged—and I think this development concerns all forms of design, not just visual communication. The existence of groups is a very good sign. We became "Gruppo T" for a number of reasons. In part because there is no better training than an apprenticeship in collaboration with your peers—whatever the creaky, tough-minded ideology of competition might say. In part because by being part of a group you experience models of existence different to those prevailing in the social context around you. And on a planet that is becoming increasingly homologized and standardized, there is a real need for new worlds.

The Language of Design[1]

MAX BRUINSMA

There are so many signs—the world has become a text. Often, it seems that all these signs and objects and products are as many loose words without grammatical structure. We can read each word for itself, each isolated object has a meaning, or a function, for itself. But what do all these messages, all these words add up to? What does this text tell us? This is where design comes in—to organize the product's meaning. Designing is not just clothing the object with a nice looking shell. It is: giving form to the meanings that the product can acquire, beyond its direct function, and in concert with the messages other products communicate.

Messages and meanings concerning our relation to the world lie hidden in the objects with which we sense, experience and manipulate our environment. Designers have the possibilities to visualize these connections and contexts. They can charge objects with meanings that express the concerns of our culture.[2]

Every visual communication is now evaluated in terms of the underlying cultural and aesthetic code systems. Under this scrutiny, obvious meaning is

---

1. This text is an edited compilation of fragments from articles I have written for various magazines and other publications during the past fifteen years. The selection of fragments condenses two of the most recurring themes in my writing, that of design as visual language, and the responsibility of the designer in using this language for cultural purposes. Edited together, they amount to one of many possible readings of the hypertext that I have produced over the years. For the *Graphic Design Worlds* exhibition I collaborated with Thonik on a second digest, a summary paragraph based on a typographic statistics of the most frequently used terms in the articles used for this essay. Thonik's design represents both a functional and expressive typography.

2. From "A New Mentality in Design," lecture, Alden-Biessen, Belgium, September 1995.

obsolete, true and false are words from an old dictionary. There has emerged a new aesthetics that is not, as it traditionally was, concerned with the hierarchical division of clear-cut meanings within the object, but that challenges the idea of ordering—and meaning—itself. The premier task of this aesthetics of transience is to show that it is quite possible to embed meanings within the object that enter into a relationship with the world outside of it. This aesthetics renders the object "intertextual." Much of what today looks simple and well organized is so only at the surface. Underneath rages the complex network of contexts that results in the constantly shifting meaning of even the simplest combination of text and image—in the eye of the beholder. Like poetry, the aesthetics of transience invites the reader to read between the lines, behind the screens, beyond the object.[3]

In this narrative of products, which are communicating messages between themselves and among a world of users, it seems obvious that images are challenging the privileged status of words as the prime carriers of meaning. But there is still considerable confusion about the ways in which this challenge can be met most effectively. Not, I hold, by concentrating on the merely formal aspects of visual communication. In a world in which the visual consistency of the cultural environment is as ephemeral as in ours, the focus on superficial aesthetics is becoming a hazard. More and more, the term "designer" is becoming associated with the most eye-catching, but in essence also most transient aspect of the trade: style. In my view, however, the responsibilities of a graphic designer in times of visual overload gravitate more and more towards the rescuing of what is—or can be—culturally meaningful in public and commercial communication. A design should act as an "agent," linking together cultural contexts and individual contents, rather than be pretty on its own.

To "rescue meaning" from the crushing weight of the data-avalanche means that one has to communicate more than mere messages and self-referencing visuals. More data instead of less. Linking a design to the rest of the world of messages and images requires an editorial point of view. For this, designers should convey a vision of their own, an interpretation that may go well beyond the client's message they're supposed to serve. There are more ways to enhance a message than to just make it look different

---

3.   From "The Aesthetics of Transience," *Eye*, no. 25, Summer 1997.

from other messages, which is what most clients want. You can also try and make things look related.[4]

Meanwhile, if the merging of art, design and advertising that we see in today's visual culture indicates anything, it is that forms and formats have become "empty vessels," whose appropriateness and quality are judged more by the content that is poured into them than by their form. This indicates that graphic designers should become as proficient in structuring, editing and accentuating cultural meaning in communication as they are in decorating its vessels. For inspiration, they can look at advertising's growing awareness of mass communication as a cultural strategy, for instance in connecting serious concerns of a brand's constituency to the brand's image—and the art world's critique of these strategies in works that mimic advertising's seductive rhetorics.[5]

These rhetorics have become part and parcel of today's communication, and they bias any information that is designed into a communication product. Information today is no longer the stuff that evokes what the great 18th-century German philosopher Immanuel Kant called *Interesseloses Wohlgefühlen*— the kind of thing that is in itself valuable, a thing pleasing to the disinterested mind. These days it is hard to be disinterested. We are bombarded by information and we are compelled to do something with that information, to act on it, to deal with it. Designers today are information agents, much more than they are commercial artists, as they used to be called. They traffic meaning, they transport ideas and concepts and opinions, they visualize structures and contexts. In short: they condensate information into cultural content.

There are in this context strong reasons to argue that the practices of art and design are slowly but surely merging—and that design is becoming the main referent of the amalgam. Since the visual has become a language that speaks to interests, aesthetics has become less disinterested. This means that for both designers and artists it is now more a question of choice, context and concept than of principle that decides whether they are making art or design. They work in the same room, and they can choose the door through which they want to communicate their output. At the same time, and for the same reason, designers should become more conscious of the fact that they are not the only ones who communicate. Graphic designers are among the many who use the

---

4.   From "Rescue Meaning," *Eye*, no. 28, Summer 1998.

5.   From "Communication as a Cultural Strategy," *Eye*, no. 29, Autumn 1998.

currently available channels of mass communication. Their main contribution in this arena is to warrant the effectivity of communication products, which is today more a matter of "conceptual functionalism" than of formal virtuosity. The role of the designer is shifting from visualizing to conceptualizing.[6]

On the other hand, style is content too. Still too often, visual expression is considered by many, both designers and readers, to be merely a superficial matter, a stylistic glaze that should either remain subordinated to the "substance" of a message or just look good. But, considering the emancipation of the visual in relationship to the verbal in our culture, this condescending attitude towards visual expression negates the very real and valuable potential of visual languages, including the language of signs we call the alphabet. Therefore, typography, with its rich potential for both structuring and expressing content, remains a craft central to the making of communication. The typographer's characteristic scrutiny of the minutiae of formal expression cannot be ignored in a culture where crudeness is paramount. What we need, therefore, is a typography of the visual, which recognizes that form does not just follow function, as the modernists would have it, but that form = function.[7]

Designers are more than dressers, decorators or even the engineers of messages—they are editors. Gui Bonsiepe proposes that from now on we call all designers interface designers, arguing that in times of information overload it is more important to design the means of access to information and navigation through it than the form of individual messages. This is an editorial quality of the designer, which determines whether the design enables the recipient of the message to make meaningful connections with the information culture of which the message is, whether we like it or not, a part. For singular messages have ceased to exist. So too have unambiguous messages. Therefore, every design, in essence, is a criticism of the context for which it has been produced. A good design "activates" these contexts by offering an understanding of, a comment on, or an alternative to them. Designers must realize yet again that the core of their profession is editorial analysis: a critical eye.[8]

---

6. From "Design Interactive Education," in S. Heller (ed.), *The Education of a Graphic Designer*, Allworth Press, New York 1998.

7. From "A Typography of Images," *Eye*, no. 32, Summer 1999.

8. From "An Ideal Design Is *Not Yet*," in L. ten Duis, A. Haase (eds.), *The World Must Change: Graphic Design and Idealism*, Uitgeverij De Balie, Amsterdam 1999.

What counts here is the reason for using the available communication tools. Is it to sedate consumers or to activate citizens? Design can be a dangerous tool in the hands of demagogues, but it can also be a powerful weapon for those who oppose them. Designers are in a perfect position to channel critical notions and alternative views into even the most prosaic commissions. When working from this mentality, designers could activate a critical sensibility instead of merely triggering buying impulses. They should not accept that design's powerful and rich visual languages be used as "hidden persuaders," to lure an unsuspecting audience into blindly agreeing with the messages presented to them. Designers do have a responsibility in guarding against a dumbing down of their visual languages and of what is communicated through them. They can honor this responsibility by looking beyond the decorative effects of virtuoso visuals, at what all this visual exuberance boils down to in terms of cultural meaning. Is it to entertain consumers, or to empower citizens? Socially and culturally responsible design should aim at keeping not only the eyes, but more importantly the minds of viewers and readers wide open.[9]

All communication design obviously needs to answer specific questions and "solve a client's problem." That remains a central task of communication design. But it can do so much more than that. At best, a design will actively demonstrate how it is embedded in the ways people experience their lives, how they communicate and express themselves. This way, designs can act as catalysts, and communication design becomes an active energy in visual culture. Cultural references may be hidden in the design, but they are in the deepest sense of the word catalysts for cultural connectivity: they can trigger the awareness of the cultural meaning and context of the design's message. They can connect different levels of information. They can add information to other information. They can link.

Meanwhile, the masses are finally learning to speak out on their own accord, and they are using visual languages to express themselves. Obviously, the great breakthrough here is the Internet, with its potential for a seamless range of media address between mass-communication and what is now called "P2P," peer to peer exchange. The web puts this potential in the hands of each and every individual with access to a computer and the Internet, of which there are about a billion today. The results are dramatic,

---

9.   From "The Long March," *Adbusters*, no. 37, Autumn 2001.

from economical, social, political and cultural perspectives: the masses talk back—as individuals. In countless blogs and homepages, in a host of forums and online communities, SMS and podcast—by all media available.

In this new condition of all-embracing communication, the messages of design cannot be seen as "objective" or "neutral" anymore, but must be understood as "the sediment of interpretations." I am using the word "sediment" here to evoke the informed look of the geologist to a formation of ancient rock. To the rest of us it looks like any old cliff, but the geologist sees in it the result of eons of physical processes, of a specific dynamics of nature. In our information culture, we—and especially communication designers—are all geologists of meaning; we read layers of context and process into the information landscape before us—we read in it the specific dynamics of culture. Or so we should, lest we become unwitting factors of it, mindless components of the residue.

Through its history of radical change and professional establishment, of new forms and deepening insights, communication design has become a culture of visual languages in its own right. It has evolved into a graphic system of combined words, visual signs and images, spanning a wide range of media and styles—a cross-cultural language which by now is globally understood. Communication design today conveys more than the literal meaning of a message, much like traditional art communicates more than the literal meaning of what is depicted on the canvas. As in art, in design you rarely just "see what you see," to paraphrase Frank Stella; much of a design's message resides in the way it is told. A design may say "buy this product," or "go to this theater play," but it also says "this is our culture, share it!"[10]

10. From *Catalysts! The Cultural Force of Communication Design*, exhibition catalogue, Lisbon 2005.

We see graphic design
as attracting attention

–

Thonik

Graphic design allowed
me to distance myself
from the capitalist drifts
of the industrial system

–

Na Kim

We are interested in the form of side effects

—

Dexter Sinister

STEVEN HELLER

As you know, we have chosen the notion of "worlds" to investigate and present some issues and features of contemporary graphic design. If it were up to you, how would you describe the worlds or the world of graphic design today? **Steven Heller** The world of graphic design is a little like what might be in a science fiction film: a world on the verge of some great upheaval. What we used to refer to as "graphic design"—the composition of type and image for a printed platform to communicate ideas and messages—is no longer a complete definition. Graphic design (and the term may need to change) is still composition, still type and image, but today it is about sound and time, space and motion. It is on many platforms for many purposes. So either the world of graphic design will explode (or implode) and return as another discipline or it will evolve (adapt) to all the new media that has come and is coming. So, let's just say, graphic design is an expanding universe.

Graphic design is a phenomenon that is always related to contexts, to the world. The position of graphic design in the world appears to be more complex than it was in the past: what has changed in the last decades, why is graphic design today no longer "our grandma's graphic design"? **SH** My comments above relate to this. But I would add that the position of graphic design in the world, is now a balance between "service" and "authorship." The former is the traditional role—to provide aesthetic and/or technical design aid to businesses and institutions, and to organize and aestheticize everything from forms to exhibitions—, the latter is developing content for a client, not merely packaging or ordering that content. And by content I mean ideas! Sometimes these ideas contribute to a client's needs. Other times, the designer is his own client.

Graphic designers have been and still are variously defined. Why do you think that the "designer as author"—as the Master you co-chair at the School of Visual Arts, New York, reads[1]—can provide the most fruitful perspective to educate graphic designers who would be able to contribute to the world around them? **SH** I don't think that we provide the "most fruitful" but we do challenge designers to make things of their own conception. Almost every designer is an artist in some way. Some are better artists than others. Some artists are better designers than others. But we believe that, as the saying goes, there is a novel in everyone (although not everyone can write), there is an idea in every designer that can be turned into a product with an audience. The MFA Designer as Author program pulls the designer out of the rut of just being a service facilitator into the role of content developer. Of course, some are much better than others.

One of the aims of Graphic Design Worlds *is to show the richness of graphic design, not just in terms of aesthetics and style, but in terms of "attitudes" and approaches to the world in which we live. Would you say that graphic design and designers can offer good models in contemporary society and culture, especially in Western society, beyond the community of designers themselves?* **SH** Remember, graphic design is not an island—you may call it a "world" but the world is not independent. Graphic design is interdependent with many other things—business, culture, politics, and so on. With the exception of certain "designed" products, the other world doesn't buy graphic design for its own sake. It relates to graphic design in terms of how it frames, supports, builds, advances, and more, other integral things. Even the products produced in the MFA Designer as Author program are not like "l'art pour l'art," or design for design. The graphic design is the glue that holds an idea together, it isn't the idea itself. But without the design component the idea or product would not exist. I hope that makes sense. If so, to answer the question, graphic designers can contribute in large and small ways to communities beyond designers, and not just in Western societies. If you will recall the 1920s–30s era statistician Otto Neurath, he developed the ISOTYPE [International System of Typograhic Picture Education] system of pictorial linguistics to transcend the babble of the world's tongues.

---

1. http://design.sva.edu/site/home.

He worked hand in glove with graphic designers to make this language a reality. Its aim: to help the world.

Many designers who have been invited to participate in the show seem to have a mixed attitude towards the future. While they are rather cautious about making predictions, and definitely far from ideas of linear progress and absolute creation, they appear to have a clear sense of responsibility about what surrounds them and how the present may affect the future; some of them also use graphic design to advance models for the world in the future, or to question it. What do you think about these attitudes? **SH** The future is a hard place to visit. Lots of delays in the airport. I think it is important to keep the future in mind. But designing for today will ultimately influence the future. Graphic methods of communication will continue to be used ten, twenty maybe even 100 years from now. Designers need to figure out a means to make what they do today relevant for tomorrow. Other than that, my idea of the future is determined by our ultimate mortality. Let's all do some good stuff before we are selected for the hereafter.

The growing interest and engagement of graphic designers in self-initiated projects is a positive phenomenon. Yet, on the other side, one may also read it as an index of a missing dialogue, as a reaction to the absence of opportunities for graphic designers to play a role, of commissions that would acknowledge this role and require their contribution on the economic, political and social level. How do you read this tension? Do you think there is a risk of isolation for graphic designers? **SH** A *very* interesting question. An unintended consequence of "self-initiated" projects could mean more isolation. But then again, it could mean more involvement than the client-designer model. The fact is, while certain work for designers has disappeared, other areas have opened. So, I don't think that doing "entrepreneurial" work is a substitute; it is just an addition, and alternative. I think graphic designers who choose to be isolated will be. Those who do not, will not. I would say, however, the bigger threat is not "self-initiated work" but media that keeps people in their homes or offices. Once, I remember well, designers got together at clubs and salons to talk about many things. It still goes on, but there is also a lot of computer-based social living. Isolation? Or expanding horizons? Let's wait and see!

Designers
are the ones
who look
at the world
of culture
and see
how vast
it has become
–

Mieke Gerritzen

Without
an idea,
graphic design
becomes
graphic irrelevance
–

KesselsKramer

ELLEN LUPTON

What is graphic design, or how do you read graphic design?
Graphic design is art people use.
Graphic design is the spit and polish but not the shoe.
Graphic design is a tool.
Graphic design is production.
Graphic design is what communication looks like.
Graphic design is what you make of it.
Graphic design is the art and business of making content readable.
Graphic design is helping people find the information they want.
Graphic design is changing people's minds.
Graphic design is pollution.
Graphic design is a pandemic.

If it was up to you, how would you describe the worlds or the world of graphic design today, which are the main features and issues? **Ellen Lupton** The world of graphic design is changing. Print is shrinking; communication is expanding. Graphic design used to be about controlling outcomes; now it is about creating tools and possibilities for experience. The expertise of the graphic designer is slipping into the general population. The tools we use are no longer secret. They are everywhere, and anyone can use them.

How deep has your personal experience and life affected your critical reading of design and graphic design? **EL** I studied graphic design in the early 1980s, just before the personal computer began revolutionizing print production. It was a period of deep postmodern foment in art and design, an exciting time intellectually. As a young student, I was always interested in writing, and I immediately recognized that graphic design provided a powerful tool for the writer. My dual identity as designer and writer has been with me since the very start of my career. Also with me has been the notion of design as a tool, rather than an end in itself. Since my earliest days in the mid-1980s, I have been a "do-it-yourself" designer, using graphic design as a tool for self-publishing. When I became a curator at Cooper-Hewitt, National Design Museum, in 1992, I became a "do-it-yourself" curator, able to use my skills to actively produce exhibition layouts, catalogues, graphics and later web sites and other media.

One of the most renowned essays from you is "The Designer as Producer" (1998),[1] that was published in a period when the role of graphic designers raised lots of discussions. One of its strengths lies in the effective connection that it acknowledges exists between mind activity and physical labor; as well as in the light that it brings onto the collaborative quality of design. Could you add something more on these points? EL Graphic design is a tool for doing things in the world. Graphic design exists to make something happen: sell an idea, push a product, explain a concept, underscore a brand. I am drawn to the word "producer" rather than the more high-minded term "author" because it suggests physical labor and the transformation of materials rather than a life lived wholly in the mind. Graphic designers have always needed to know how to produce things, whether working with print, film, architecture, or digital media. The word "production" is often disdained within our field as low-level labor. We all aspire to be "creative directors" instead. And yet ultimately the success of design lies largely in how it is produced. I am also drawn to the idea of the producer as someone in charge of a large and complex process involving multiple players. The producer is thus a maker, a thinker and a manager.

Would you say that designers and design culture, in some way, may provide a social and cultural model beyond their community? EL I don't think graphic design is a model so much as a tool. Anyone with access to computers and

---

1. First published in S. Heller (ed.), *The Education of a Graphic Designer*, Allworth Press, New York 1998, pp. 159–62; republished online at www.typotheque.com/articles/the_designer_as_producer.

networks can access the basic tools of graphic design. Perhaps even a marker or spray can is all you need, but it is really the culture of software that has opened up the access to design processes beyond the profession. In school, our children are learning the same software as the professionals. Growing up as digital natives, they will always approach the world in terms of software and social sharing. Design is part of their lives in a way that it never was for me until much later. This situation is taking place across the developed world and beyond. Design is indeed empowering, whether on an intimate personal level (family photographs) or a bigger social level (publishing a book or website). Increasingly, professional designers are creating tools for their clients in addition to fixed end products.

From your point of view, being involved in education at different levels, from do-it-yourself books and workshops to master degree programs, what are the main challenges and issues for graphic design (and design) education? How do you face them? EL Keeping up with technology is a huge challenge for educators. Teaching software has become a big part of what we do, and the software keeps changing along with the cultural context in which it is used. Today's educator is under a lot of pressure to stay in touch with a rapidly changing world while also looking past technical matters to enduring concepts such as working with constraints, creating hierarchy, communicating with typography, and considering the user.

Being a curator of an important institution such as the Cooper Hewitt, National Design Museum, you are in charge of mediating towards the "general public." As far as design, and specifically graphic design, is concerned, what is your priority as curator? EL Curators have to consider multiple audiences when creating an exhibition. At the highest level, we have to think of scholars in our field (other curators). We must also think of the professional audience, who has seen many things and already has strong opinions about design. And we must think about the general educated public who come to the museum looking for entertainment and a place to shop, as well as small children who are dragged along on field trips from school or on a family outing. It is tough work to please all these people, but we do it by creating installations that speak to people visually while also providing a degree of detailed interpretive content for the more inquiring visitor. And, of course, you must always be prepared for some people to be dissatisfied. For the critics, this is their job, and we must keep them in business. Personally, I feel that as a curator I owe a debt to the designers. A big goal of mine is to raise awareness of the role of individual designers in the creation of our world, rather than merely looking at products and communication as some kind of passive effect of society or politics.

What does it mean to conduct research in graphic design, in and out of academic institutions? EL Research takes many forms: market research, scholarly research, visual research. Perhaps what matters is what you do with it. Does research have an impact? Pure visual experiments can have a huge effect on visual culture when they are published and shared among designers. Marketing can impact the products we have access to, for better or for worse. Scholarship can disappear into academia, or it can change the way designers think by creating new schemes and categories for viewing how we work. Research can also be wholly personal, an element of the design process that ripples along beneath the surface of things.

Graphic design
is a good training for life
–

Anthony Burrill

Graphic design
is turning language into objects
–

Experimental Jetset

Graphic design
is the skin of information
–

Norm

The designer is never the subject, but always the filter

—

Metahaven

ANDREW BLAUVELT

How would you describe the relationship of graphic design to the world: what are the main issues and questions that graphic designers should face today? How can graphic design positively contribute to the world? **Andrew Blauvelt** Historically, graphic design survived the technological challenges of the 1980s and 1990s, when desktop computing and publishing not only increased access to the tools of design to a much larger audience but also simultaneously expanded the opportunities for graphic designers, first with interaction design and motion graphics and later with web design. Perhaps it was too early for graphic designers. I think about the interactive CD-ROM period when graphic designers were exploring the possibilities of video, interaction, dynamic graphics and typography, which were more attractive than trying to exploit the early limitations of the Internet. I see now a resurgence of interest by print designers with the invention of the iPad and other tablet devices with access to greater bandwidth. This great period of expansion also opened up many possibilities including formal, or aesthetic, ones. More designers, more styles, more formats, more voices, more tools. All of this "more" makes everything more complicated and complex. How will designers handle this complexity, complication, and contradiction? What is the future of printed communications? How many new specialities of practice will emerge and how many will end? I think the most important role of any designer is as a bridge between clients and users. Many other professionals are paid to represent only the interests of the client. Many designers believe that they have a duty that extends beyond that kind of relationship. There is, of course, a transformation that has taken place even within the corporate sector, part of a larger paradigm shift we might call "the birth of the user." This philosophy has the potential to rebalance the equation. Of course, this is imperfect because we need to weigh individual needs and desires against collective ones—community or environmental ones, for instance. The moral implication of your question is much more difficult to answer. Positive value is relative. Graphic design, as a purveyor of messages, requires us to ask who is speaking and what is being said because it is mostly about sponsored messages. However, we need both sponsored and unsponsored messages to fully explore the potential of graphic design. Graphic design can play a role in social change, but it is rarely social change in and of itself.

In 2008 you wrote an influential article where you talked about "relational design."[1] Could you tell us something about this notion/paradigm? How does it explain the condition and the role of graphic designers? **AB** About five or six years ago, I was searching for an explanation of fundamental changes that were underway in the design fields—graphic, product, and architecture. These changes were unlike previous ones. There seemed to be little in common: formal innovation wasn't particularly a focus as it had been in previous generations. The sheer variety of approaches was difficult to understand using previous lenses or perspectives. Either not much was happening or a major paradigm shift was necessary to better understand this newer work. Basically, the thesis is that modern design has been through three major shifts in the last century: the first was the development of a formal or visual vocabulary that could be manipulated and explored, which takes us through the first several decades and "isms" of the 20th century; the second phase was also a formal experiment but one premised on the notion of finding meaning through form, it was preoccupied with content and symbolism and culminated in postmodernism; and the third wave is one that is guided more by context and where form is shaped more by conditions, constraints and relations. Relational design is as much about the form of practice as it is aesthetics. These "relations" might be tied more directly to users' behavior, fiscal or technological constraints (contemporary pragmatism versus historical utopianism), systems-driven approaches (the

---

1.   A. Blauvelt, "Towards Relational Design," March 11, 2008, http://observatory.designobserver.com/entry.html?entry=7557.

design of systems), or open or crowdsourced models—the relations of designers to others. In these situations, the designer is not the sole locus of activity,
but rather a node in a larger network.

*The title of your article is "Towards Relational Design." Beyond some cases,
which can be clearly read, as examples of relational design, has the paradigm
really changed? Or is it also to be meant as a guiding principle for the future?
How can designers, and in particular graphic designers, move "towards"
relational design?* **AB** Yes, I believe the paradigm shift is necessary to better understand contemporary practices and its resultant form. Of course,
all design—past, present and future—is relational to various extents. But
that truism doesn't explain what motivates, originates and initiates design
today, and how previous models and approaches were discarded or over-
turned in the process. For instance, one might say that the rise of ergonomics is an example of relational design because it looked at the relationship
between people and objects. Perhaps it is an early example, but today we
understand complexity of use in a much more nuanced way—not a metrics
of use but the complication of actual use guided by consumer behavior that
might or might not conform to expectations. It is the difference between
Niels Diffrient and Dunne and Raby. Relational design describes only aspects of the current situation and it isn't meant as a universal description
of all designers or even a description of most current design activity. I was
looking at work that didn't seem to fit any previous patterns of emergence,
so it describes the situation of a small slice of practice. There is a good
chance, however, that more designers as well as future designers will move
towards these more contextual driven agendas because they are also echoed
in the society and culture at large. One obvious example is the technological
change wrought by Internet culture, which has created or recast the most
pertinent and persistent metaphors ("interaction," "sociability," "participation," "crowdsourcing," and so on).

One of the aims of Graphic Design Worlds *is to show the richness of graphic
design, not just in terms of aesthetics and style, but also in terms of "attitudes" and approaches to the world we live in. Would you say that graphic
design and designers can offer good models in contemporary society and
culture, beyond the community of designers themselves?* **AB** Yes. Design
itself, in terms of its processes and practices, can offer an excellent example

of engagement with problems of all kinds and at all scales. Design's synthesis and reconciliation of conflicting positions, its blend of art and science, its pragmatic problem-solving focus as well as its speculative and imaginative consideration of possibilities make a powerful case in realms outside of design itself. Designers have a special role to play in our society. Although designers are hired by clients with specific agendas, they must always bridge this relationship with one shared by the public—audiences, users, or communities.

One would say that designers invited in the exhibition Graphic Design Worlds *may be defined "independent," in the sense that they have set up their own studio and work on their own. Still, one could also discuss what independence really means. Moreover, in the recent years, "self-initiated" has become a buzzword in the field. Although we do believe that this kind of project constitutes a relevant element of what graphic design is today, we cannot help asking ourselves whether the growing interest and engagement of graphic designers in self-initiated projects is also an index of a missing dialogue with some other figures in the world around—companies, institutions, politics etc. How do you read this phenomenon?* **AB** While I was in graduate school in the 1980s at Cranbrook Academy of Art, perhaps at the zenith of the program's reputation as an alternative vision of graphic design, there was a specific emphasis on self-initiated work. However, it was balanced by the need to complete required assignments and freelance work derived from clients. Of course, the self-initiated projects became the most well known and publicized because they were seen as the purest expression of an idea, a style or an approach. This was largely "client-less" work that used existing formats, such as the poster as their vehicle. Later, self-initiated work transformed into entrepreneurial activity as the technology and parameters of design expanded. For me, this entrepreneurial approach has created the most vital alternatives to traditional practice. For instance, you publish your own magazine or produce and sell your own fonts. This allows one to create a different sense of autonomy, to be more in control of one's destiny as a designer. Cheaper and more widely available digital technologies also offered new possibilities for designers to work on their own since the start-up costs are so minimal. It seems like the era of the large graphic design studios is over. At the Walker Art Center, I embrace the model of the classroom studio, which was the environment I knew the best as a design educator before becoming a fulltime practitioner. Although technically the Walker is an in-house design studio, much like a corporation would have, I think it functions to allow more individual voices to contribute to the overall studio language. You raise an interesting point by asking what "independent" means. It could mean on one's own—away from the larger structures of a larger office or a studio—or it might mean expressing an individual voice, or autonomous—away from the structures and strictures of certain markets.

In an article published in 1995 in the AIGA Journal of Graphic Design you and Meredith Davis called for education programs "not in service to current definitions of professional practice," and for a "research agenda" for education and practice.[2] We know you have already been asked this question in 2004,[3] but: "how do you feel the current state of graduate design education"? Has something changed since then? Are there in the US or elsewhere, interesting projects, institutions, initiatives worthy of mention? **AB** There are many more design programs today. It seems the better programs all undergo the same process of evolution, dominance and decline. There are specific traits that I admire in various graphic design programs as they have grown and changed over time: the reconnection to work and printing espoused by the Werkplaats Typografie; the eclecticism and rigorous critique at the California Institute of Arts; Dan Fern's "permissiveness" at the Royal College of Art, which produced a new generation of designers pretty much on their own terms; the enthusiasm I perceive at École cantonale d'art de Lausanne; the contextualizing impulse at North Carolina State University; Art Center's Media Design graduate program that doesn't limit itself to such narrow definitions of interaction design, and so on. Among the undergraduate programs the trend is toward more emphasis on so-called social design issues, of understanding design practice as it impacts communities, which supports this notion of moving towards a more relational approach to understanding and practicing design.

---

2.   A. Blauvelt, M. Davis, "Building Bridges: A Research Agenda for Education and Practice," then republished in M. Bierut et al. (eds.), *Looking Closer 2. Critical Writings on Graphic Design*, Allworth Press, New York 1997, pp. 77–81.

3.   Interview with A. Blauvelt, by J.A. Tselentis, in *Speak Up*, February 19, 2004, www.underconsideration.com/speakup/interviews/blauvelt.html.

Designing
is like
channeling

Graphic
design
strives to
initiate
a relation

Radim Peško

Mathias Schweizer

Lo-fi
December 12, 2010 / e-mail

MARIO LUPANO

As a scholar and curator whose interests range over architecture, fashion, design and art, you are a figure who seems to work where territories overlap; it is as if such a position enables you to see more, especially in periods of great change. What do you see nowadays—in particular, with regard to these disciplines and the relation between them? **Mario Lupano** I choose to stay in a borderline position not for reasons arising from theoretical preconceptions and convictions, but simply because I found myself here and it suits me. There is no doubt that occupying the borderline of academically-defined disciplines is very useful when it comes to establishing fruitful relations with the world beyond—even if it can "slacken" the focus one finds in traditional forms of academic output (which have their own validity and relevance). Such a position undoubtedly allows me to perceive changes; it suggests previously unnoticed connections. Both within the university and elsewhere, I am less interested in nurturing theoretical convictions than in helping those who are talented. I focus upon teaching as the creation and organization of (perhaps very different) events that can stimulate learning for oneself— events which must always take the risk of being experimental. This is the approach I continue to pursue. Universities are still a long way off achieving the convergence of different identities within a dynamic community—the sort of community that is capable of understanding the world from a variety of angles. With regard to the fashion and design disciplines, our position might be said to be ambiguous in three different ways. First of all there is the ambiguity of Western society itself, with its great wealth and great squalor, with its capacity to invent and its appalling ability to waste. There is the ambiguity of issues of identity, of the relations between oneself and society, between oneself and the world. And finally there is the ambiguity of art, of its purpose and significance. These ambiguities generate themes and obsessions that are central to the definition of languages and strategies—within art and design, within architecture and fashion. Some of the creative processes adopted in a specific discipline reveal great potential when there is a shift in their application and they come into contact with other disciplines. Even unexpected juxtapositions of themes and events relating to the modern world with those relating to the past can generate very productive short circuits. Intelligent design—in whichever field it operates—consists in the ability to create new links and connections between things that we all know, which are already to hand as well as consisting in the visionary capacity to establish relations between things that seemed very distant from each other. Another feature that is very common to a lot of contemporary design and art is the fact that theory is embedded in practice; words are substituted by bodies and actions. Furthermore, rather than being producers *tout court*, designers are designers of scenarios, of concepts and imaginaries—explorers of "critical" states. For the new generations of designers and artists, concept and theory are not something apart, something external; they are to be found within the work itself. Hence, for these people it is often very important to talk about the work they have done. This is vital if one is to fix some "internal rules"; otherwise everything would just be aleatory.

Do you see relations between the worlds of graphic design and what is happening in the world of fashion and architecture? **ML** Nowadays, it is increasingly the case that graphic designers work within a territory in which predefined rules do not apply. Instead, the rules of the game are continually being renegotiated, identified through approximation, through strategic considerations. The territory within which the graphic designer works nowadays is a shifting landscape in a state of flux, a territory subject to a variety of simultaneous movements. And graphic designers are quicker than other categories of designers in understanding and "connecting with." Sometimes, this lightness of touch enables them to intervene in situations that up to a short time ago were the exclusive domain of architecture. At times, the graphic designer can be as swift as some of the figures now working in the world of fashion: it is a question not only of the tools that are used, but also of the procedures that apply in the process of design. For example, the graphic designer is familiar with the notions of concept definition and marketing logic. Traditionally, the graphic designer is in an "in-between" position: his task is to create interfaces, vectors of conjunction, and to highlight and make explicit the various threads of previously-invisible relations. Recently, I was made even more aware that communication runs in a variety of directions. Precisely like those who work in fashion, the most interesting graphic designers are capable of moving between the world of independent production and the logic of powerful clients (those who make sizeable investment in research) and brands. The specific identity of the figure of the "graphic designer" or "fashion designer" lies not so much in the exclusive choice of one of these two positions, but rather in the dynamic oscillation between two extremes; it is this oscillation which often reveals how the aggressive dynamics behind brands and the processes of independent experimentation can both work to nurture research. This intrinsically "transdisciplinary" situation is that described, for example, by Peter Saville, Hedi Slimane and Thomas Demand in their conversation with Hans Ulrich Obrist and Cristina Bechtler, published in 2008 under the very significant title *Art, Fashion, and Work for Hire*.[1]

In recent years the term "graphic design" seems to have been going through something of a crisis, with new interpretations of both graphic design itself and of the role of the designer. Are these changes examples of those "low-definition" attitudes which your work has always explored? ML When I talk about design (and, therefore, also graphic design) as "low definition," or low fidelity (lo-fi), I mean it is a territory within which it is actually possible for fragments of high-technology design to flow together with other aspects of design taken from informal culture or street culture. Once one gets beyond the ideological stance which sees these different types of design as in total opposition to each other, such approaches can happily co-exist, combining to respond to specific necessities and needs. Many designers now seem to understand how effective this approach is. When I talk in terms of "low definition" I am not referring to results but to a specific process, to a specific approach to design. As well as generating suggestions ("low definition" means that things are beautiful because they are open to a variety of interpretations), this approach is also an assertion of work that is "open,"

---

1. *Art, Fashion and Work for Hire* - Thomas Demand, Peter Saville, Hedi Slimane, Hans Ulrich Obrist and Cristina Bechtler in Conversation, Springer, Berlin 2008.

that eschews any sort of avant-garde edict. Such a strategy avoids the paralysis which can be induced when design falls victim to *idées reçues*; adopting a non-linear, composite, approach, it can search out and discover interactions with objects and communities. I am interested in exploring this feeling for "low definition" in order to understand how it might also be applied in the field of architecture. Some very sophisticated results have already been achieved in artistic fields other than architecture—I am thinking of music, which was the first to coin the term "lo-fi" and to recognize its creative potential. These fields reveal just how possible it is to combine, for example, precision with improvisation, script and design with ad-lib execution and performance. Such ideas undermine a large number of the convictions and mental habits that still apply in the fields of architecture and design; they lead to an interpretation of each construct or product of design as a process that is never actually finished. Thus objects of design themselves become necessarily imperfect; they attain their full value precisely when they achieve a high degree of "openness." The design disciplines need no longer dedicate themselves to the assertion of self-contained objects. They can activate processes that generate new interaction and involvement with various interlocutors and clients; they can open up new territories of cultural "negotiation." When graphic designers and designers work in this way, taking care of something that takes form, they strive to find out suitable situations and associates, refusing to wait for the right client or project to turn up. They start from what is—from how it is—without delaying until conditions become ideal for them to set to work. There is no such thing as an "un-educated" client; one starts with what one is given in order to generate a virtuous cycle. I think that this is the right approach; and I think that a lot of young designers have seen this.

Graphic Design Worlds *was inspired by the desire to explore the role of designers as capable to initiate and construct relations, who act as agents that make fully-conscious (and responsible) use of the tools and languages that are available to them for communication. In your opinion, what is—or, if you wish, what should be—the social and cultural role of today's graphic designer?* **ML** Graphic designers should get rid of any sense of guilt about their own history and background. They should build a better identity for themselves precisely on the basis of that supposed original sin—that is, their subjection to consumerism, their relationship with the world of business and commerce. They should explore this origin—for example, accentuating an interrogatory stance that refuses to submit passively to the pedagogical, "progressive," theory of design. Using one's instruments of communication in a responsive and mindful manner means, for one thing, being aware that graphic design serves not solely to resolve the problem of effective communication but also to raise doubts and questions. To me, there is often something stupid about the figure of the designer who, with a smile on his lips, is always there with the ready solution to problems. Why should one leave the raising of questions solely to art (that is, art as enclosed within the boundaries of the art system)? The graphic designer should strive to be used in such a way that interlocutors are presented with "critical states" of communication and are made aware of the paradoxes implicit in that communication. And graphic designers should also invent and provide the tools that make it easier to find one's way through the immense quantity of data on the Net.

Another feature of your professional experience is your work as a curator. From that point of view, how do you see the role of design and of the graphic designer? Could you give some examples with regard to exhibitions or events you yourself have curated? **ML** Curating exhibitions and curating/editing books are very similar in lots of ways. I love exhibitions that bring together different material, perhaps risking clashing juxtapositions or even confusion (for example, between original and copy). Often the exhibitions that I curate are transitory; they focus on the emotional intensity arising from a temporary event. In my opinion, an exhibition is an improbable mix of objects and works, brought together to generate syntheses. The whole art of displaying things rests upon recognizing the primary importance of the order intrinsic to the objects themselves. And I deliberately use the verb "display" and not "exhibit." The latter is linked with the idea of offering a vision of something, of producing documents and information, of administering (and thus revealing) something. "To exhibit" is a unidirectional activity; indeed, it is often an arrogant form of communication, simplifying in order to have a striking effect upon the spectator, to impart a message, to educate and edify. Usually graphic designers are used precisely to reinforce this "exhibiting"; to guarantee that the message gets across. "Exhibiting" is a verb that suggests an exhibition illustrating a thesis, something to be explained in a didactic and/or propagandistic manner. On the contrary, what I like are exhibitions that display and unfold the materials in order to raise questions, without pointing to some predetermined answers. I like exhibitions that form shifting and multiple landscapes. Hence, that is why I prefer the verb "to display"; it defines an area of design in which the relations established might initially be chaotic, but from which one gradually sees the emergence of themes and logics. "Displaying" is a form of showing that is related with "play" and revelation; with the notion of both moving and indicating; with setting in motion—activating—a process; with playing a role, which might even be that of a gambler or a trickster. The verb "to display" is also used with regard to the peacock when it opens up its tail and generates wonder. The art of display often proceeds in a compulsive manner, and is inspired by a taste for some sort of "polysensorial" approach. It results in exhibitions that suggest ideas and generate complexity. In "displaying," one opens oneself to a sort of *vertige d'archive*, one initiates a dialogue inspired by the desire to both lose oneself in and scrutinize material. Such an approach favors a low-definition strategy, because that is best suited to raising problems, to regenerating issues. (While the concerns behind the high-definition approach often result in exclusion that renders things more opaque.) The graphic designer refines his tools for the display of images; he works to bring out the concealed relations between the various fields of energy that come into play between words and icons. In this sense, a book too can be similar to an exhibition—above all, when it mixes and overlaps the formats of atlas, mapped constellations and conceptual diagrams. I am also very interested in identifying the processes of design involved in curating an exhibition. In effect, curating sees itself as engaged in a sequence of actions concerned with the construction of "devices," which may be exhibitions but can also be other things. I think that such a process suggests instruments that may be useful in cultivating—and trying out—a new idea of design, finally transforming design into a critical process. Curating is a practice which is, on the one hand, linked with the production of culture, but on the other engages with the public; constantly changing, its identity is ever-shifting. Given that it occupies interstitial territory, that it is mutable by definition, it is an important point of reference for the contemporary disciplines of design.

How would you image an exhibition on contemporary graphic design, or what would you like such an event to be? **ML** I would like to see an exhibition whose rhythm was a natural rendition of the fully 3D world of graphic design. I would like each of the designers involved to contribute their own idea of display, making suggestions, contributing new ideas regarding the very grammar and syntax of "organizing an exhibition." I imagine an exhibition that would cover the individual research of graphic designers not solely in terms of language but also of process. It would be a place where their work would re-emerge as the fruit of complicity with other agents; where "co-working" would not be simply an issue of a youthful environment but rather a necessity, a splendid opportunity. It would be an exhibition in which fashion was not demonized, recognizing that this sexy, embarrassing and hyper-commercial sphere is also a locus of innovation. I see an exhibition that would serve to identify new roles for both criticism and self-criticism, within a framework where new forms of cultural mediation arise from the ashes of old modes of both production and consumption.

One should construct design just as nature constructs a plant. It should be adapted accordingly —since it is living and growing— to the needs of the moment and of the place

–

Kasia Korczak

The intelligence within the field of graphic design lies in its ability to make connections between different disciplines

—

Zak Kyes

Graphic design as a practice has the potential to be one of the most commanding forms of cultural engagement

–

Elliott Earls

On Demand:
The Rise of Micro Design Publishing

ALICE TWEMLOW

The design press as it has existed for decades is in crisis. Long-established graphic design magazines like *ID*, *Step*, and *Grafik* have imploded and those that are still in business are scrambling to put out iPad and iPhone applications and to build their online communities. What is less widely reported is the profusion of new graphic design books, journals and zines published in small offset print runs or one at a time using print-on-demand services and edited, designed, published, and distributed by designers. They are made with modest means and by teams with little training or experience in journalism or editing. Yet these tight composites of design and writing, driven by passion for the subject matter and the tangibility of print, evince a distinct attitude, and are quickly gaining traction in terms of global visibility. The magazines are distributed via print-on-demand websites, the designers' own websites or in sympathetic bookstores such as Motto and Pro Qm in Berlin, the AA bookstore and Artwords in London, and Dexter Sinister and Printed Matter in New York. Their existence draws attention to the insufficiencies of the traditionally orchestrated design media. "The conventional professional boundaries have eroded everywhere," observes Simon Esterson, the veteran British magazine designer and art director and co-owner of *Eye* magazine. "Take a picture, conduct a Q&A conversation, edit the text, retouch the images, make pages on your laptop and upload them to a variety of websites where you can post a pdf or print from one to thousands of copies. Bookshops and newsagents are under threat, so sell online. These are the techniques conventional publishers are trying to catch up with. The micro-publishers are already there."[1]

1.　Simon Esterson in conversation with Alice Twemlow, September 2010.

Graphic design is not a lifestyle product that can be purchased or aspired to in the same sense that a Mark Newson yacht or a Konstantin Grcic chair can, for example. Promotional, informative, explanatory and mostly ephemeral—most graphic design cannot be bought, nor indeed is ever seen, by the general public and therefore does not appeal to the consumer-focused concerns of mainstream publishing. This is just one of the frustrations that fuel the creation of so many new independent graphic design magazines. They set out to present design not as an object, but more as a process, a lens and a methodology with which to approach the world. This reflects a more general tendency in contemporary graphic design in which the designer's traditional role as "problem solver" has been destabilized and replaced with a more exploratory, questioning and authorial sense of purpose that might be characterized as "designer as problemitizer." *Task Newsletter*, for example, is an annual publication edited, published and designed by three globally dispersed designers—Emmet Byrne in Minneapolis, Jon Sueda in San Francisco and Alex DeArmond in Arnhem, Netherlands. Their editorial statement explains that the newsletter "uses design as a perspective, designed objects as evidence of larger systems, and designers as researchers."[2] Its first issues include features that are not so much about design as they are about seeing things through designers' eyes—collecting the visual and textual manifestations of a particular cerebral and anti-design sensibility that connects an interrelated group of international designers. The theme of the second issue, a small, dense publication with the complexion of a pulp paperback, is "mundane science fiction" and the editors asked their contributors—mostly designers—to react to the theme. London-based designer Paul Elliman wrote a short story about the sentience of songs; New York designer Rob Giampietro submitted the text of an IM conversation with David Reinfurt about the latter's science fiction novel; the Rotterdam design firm Catalogtree made a dart gun which they used to run tests on the notion of a predictable near future and then depicted the results on a limited edition silkscreen poster, available for order on the *Task* website. These pieces of content—they are not recognizable as articles in the conventional sense—are typical of those in other alternative graphic design magazines. Another format favored by these publications are long-form, often unedited, interviews with designers.

---

2. *Task Newsletter*, no. 1, Winter 2007.

Back Cover, the magazine generated by the French designers DeValence and published by their imprint B42 Editions, relies heavily on interview and conversation formats. Their latest issue (January 2009) includes a richly illustrated eleven-page conversation between British designer Richard Hollis and the collective Åbäke and another extended interview with jigsaw puzzle maker Sophie Ollé-Laprune. The primary reason for this is a pragmatic one: to a designer unused to writing and editing, the transcribed interview appears to be the most straightforward and approachable editorial format. Other reasons are more philosophical: as Ian Lyman, a designer and writer based in Tokyo and who has a particular interest in the recent efflorescence of graphic design self-publishing, says, "there is such a glut of short format writing on the web, that designers have the desire to see their long-format written work in print."[3] Whether it is mere expediency or something more purposeful, the transcribed interview—replete with throat clearings, tangents, non sequiturs, the sounds of laughter and slurping coffee—suits these new magazines where many of the editors/publishers feel uncomfortable inserting their own editorial voice and see themselves more as assemblers of pre-existing content, rather than shapers of a particular narrative within the covers of a magazine.

Blogs, like *It's Nice That*, which specialize in gathering and posting examples of graphic design projects of interest to their hosts, are extending into print publishing too. The blogs function as databases of raw material that can be repurposed in the form of exhibitions, events, or publications. *Manystuff*'s print publication, an offshoot from the popular website run by Charlotte Cheetham in Paris, for example, emerged as a natural extension of the blog. Like *Task Newsletter*, the *Manystuff* imprint seeks to explore design in its transitory, amorphous and in-progress state rather than to present it as a finished product. Cheetham calls the imprint "a laboratory of experiments and meditations released from formal and theoretical prejudices."[4]

One "formal prejudice" of traditional publishing is news-driven content. Today online publications, blogs and newsletters like *Unbeige*, *Creative Review*'s blog or *Core77*, are better equipped to present news about design

---

3.   Ian Lyman in conversation with Alice Twemlow, September 2010; see the text published in the blog of the exhibition *Graphic Design Worlds, A Diary of an Exhibition*: www.triennaledesignmuseum.it/adiaryofanexhibition.

4.   *Manystuff* website. Its latest issue, published in October 2010, is titled *About Your Process*.

in a timely fashion, and so printed publications are freed to be more contemplative. Without the anchoring urgency of breaking stories and scoops, however, visually these timeless publications can give the impression of floating. Furthermore, when they reject the traditional editorial hierarchy with its front-of-book shorter stories, feature well, and reviews section in the back, only the best of the new magazines manage to sustain lively pacing and visual texture; many end up with plodding sequences of similarly sized features, organized according to default systems rather than any nuanced editorial decision-making. At their best the new alternative magazines are able to present issues in more depth than commercial magazines and to address topics that are not pegged to news. That doesn't mean that they are able to do this better than academic journals, which have the backing of rigorous scholarship and quality control via peer review. What this new breed of magazines is able to do that is different from existing models both on and offline is to present the text exactly how they want, often at great length, use images in allusive or referential ways, provide linguistic translations, experiment with the cover and the shape of the publication, include inserts, fold out posters, varied paper stocks and deploy other assorted features calculated to appeal to their target audience of designers.

One of the main differences between these independent publications and their commercial counterparts, is in their treatment of advertising. Where in most design magazines, advertising pages both dictate and interrupt the editorial flow, a self-publisher can choose to have no advertising, to group the advertisements in one section, or to design them themselves according to a house style. In *Dot Dot Dot*, a self-consciously and tightly wrought anti-graphic design journal launched by Peter Bilak and Stuart Bailey in 2000, for example, advertisers submit text to the magazine and it is printed in varying degrees of boldness, according to how much is paid—from barely legible pale grey at the cheapest level to rich black at the most expensive. Similarly, *Task* sells advertising at $1 per point size and prints the text-only notices in Pica in a Classified Advertisements section. These treatments of advertising and editorial, added to the fact that graphic designers tend to want to reinvent, or at the very least bring their own slant to, the magazine format, give the magazines their own visual aesthetic that can at first be bewildering for a reader used to the architecture of a traditionally organized magazine. These magazines are not exactly non-commercial—their creators often sell advertising and hope through sales to at least cover production costs. Mostly, however, they are enabled by grants or driven by personal belief and funding, and are often encountered in art exhibitions; they exist outside the normal pressures of the publishing industry and so can be seen as *a-commercial*.

The phenomenon of designers editing and designing their own publications is not new—magazines such as *Octavo, Fuse, Emigre,* and *Baseline,* for example, were also created and controlled by designers and they were all complete objects in which design and content were seamlessly integrated. In many cases they began as specimens for type foundries enriched with articles and amplified by the 1980s desktop publishing revolution. The genre also has progenitors in the 1960s radical underground "little architecture magazines" such as *Archigram, ARse* and *Bau,* which together represented a dissatisfied riposte to the format, mission, writing and images of the glossy architecture magazines of the period. And of course, the designer-owned press extends at least as far back as the late 19th century and the exquisitely crafted hand-pressed publications of English design reformist William Morris through his Kelmscott Press. Another branch of the lineage goes back to more democratically oriented presses such as Nonesuch Press where in the 1920s and 1930s Francis Meynell had books designed using a hand press but reproduced by commercial printers, making them available at lower prices. He believed that "mechanical means could be made to serve fine ends," a sentiment echoed by some of today's designers' experiments with the practical potential of print-on-demand services such as Lulu and low-end reprographic technologies such as mimeography.[5] Perhaps a more apposite precedent can be found in *Ver Sacrum,* the late 19th century publication by Austrian designer Alfred Roller, which combined graphic artwork and writings into a complete designed entity known as *Gesamtkunstwerk,* or "total work of art," a concept initiated by the composer Wagner.

Today's outgrowth of independent graphic design publications is composted by a combination of supportive booksellers, niche readerships, technology that facilitates low cost printing and distribution, and a generation of designers trained to think of themselves as authors and entrepreneurs rather than service providers. These young designers are well versed

---

5.   The most well known print- or publish-on-demand company is Lulu, founded in 2002. Authors keep all the rights to their works and retain 80 percent of the profit they set when their books sell.

in online publishing; what is important to them now is to make a record of their online activity, to pin down the fleetingness of the web into more concrete documents, to write at length and in registers particular to print, to design into and against a centuries-old tradition of print publishing. Ian Lyman says that they don't mind if, by doing so, less people see their work; what they want is to "be part of a formalized canon, be that canon design publications or the lineage of self-published works with multiples agendas across the continuum of history."[6]

6. Ian Lyman in conversation with Alice Twemlow, September 2010.

Our books are like little worlds

—
Fuel

Part of being
a graphic designer
is also about
being able
to read the world
–

Geoff McFetridge

CHARLOTTE CHEETHAM
Manystuff

As it was stated in 2010 in the Sofia Design Week *website, we would say that "[w]e don't know much about Charlotte Cheetham" but that your blog about graphic design "is one of the most popular ones in the world."*[1] *Can you tell us something about yourself?* **Charlotte Cheetham** I studied Communications and History of Art. I have always been immersed in the artworld: my grandfather and my uncle were painters and sculptors, my mother is a painting restorer and was an art dealer for a while. I did internships and I have been working in communication, mainly in the field of contemporary art. At the moment, *Manystuff*—blog, publishing, curating—is my only occupation in Paris, where I live.[2]

Why did you decide to start Manystuff, *what were your goals and how do you work?* **CC** I became interested in graphic design by coincidence: my boyfriend is a graphic designer, and when I met him I started to become interested in what he was doing. It gradually turned into a passion over the course of my Internet research on the subject. Initially, I used to send e-mails to my boyfriend and friends, recommending interesting links. One day I started a small blog with a few links... and visitors rapidly increased. The name "Manystuff" comes from "many things/stuff," since at the beginning, every day, I used to publish posts mostly about different disciplines and fields, such as illustration and photography. My working method has not changed really:

---

1. http://sofiadesignweek.com/en_program/en_forum/en_manystuff.
2. www.manystuff.org.

all day long, most days of the year, I surf the Internet and share what I like. Basically I share my daily thoughts on a blog. I must confess that at the beginning I didn't have any specific goal with this project. However, since then the activity has become more serious, more dense, and I have started to run side projects, such as exhibitions, publications, etc. Today it is still a passion but also an occupation. As the blog "slogan" says, "Every morning I [the visitors] check *Manystuff*"; "Every morning I do *Manystuff*," as I am in charge of it.

Why does graphic design play such a major role in Manystuff? **cc** It happened gradually. Graphic design has become a subject that greatly interests me. I think it is a discipline that is really important in our contemporary world. If we consider graphic design as the formal translation of information and knowledge, we can understand to what degree graphic designers are important, as they are responsible for the reception of that information and knowledge. Graphic designers are placed in a crucial position. I also like the multidisciplinary quality of graphic design, since it can include relationships and collaborations with authors, artists, archivists, different media, etc.

Searching the archive of your blog, one can compare how it has changed since 2007: you started with pictures and links, while now more context is provided in each post. Would you say that your editorial position has changed in a way? **cc** Although, as I mentioned, the method has not changed, I would say my approach has shifted and evolved. As I am an autodidact in graphic design, I learn every day. More and more I rely on exhibitions, festivals, independent initiatives (editorial projects especially), multidisciplinary projects—that involve curating, graphic design, publishing, photography, etc.—rather than only on portfolios of graphic designers, as was the case instead during the first year of the blog. Today I am more attracted by projects that show interesting, developed and accomplished concepts; projects based on research and process that are intensive and extensive. *Manystuff* is certainly not a collection of beautiful images. Nor it is meant to be just a directory of graphic designers. I try to report news concerning contemporary graphic design by highlighting the underlying context of research and the current dynamics. Thus, visiting my blog is not an end in itself: it is the starting point for the autonomous curiosity of the readers. An example of this quality is the Parallel School of Art project. By looking at the posts I published during the week I spent at the Royal College of Art (RCA) in London, a student from Paris, frustrated with his school, was impressed by the effervescence of RCA and he decided to launch the Parallel School.[3] Students from schools such as the École Nationale Supérieure des Arts Décoratifs in Paris, the RCA, the Universität der Künste in Berlin, and the Rietveld Academie in Amsterdam all participate in this project. It deals with ways of self-education, of sharing interests, points of view, and creating projects through the web. The main goal is for students to learn while initiating projects outside of the academic context. I think this perfectly illustrates the purpose of *Manystuff*.

How do you research information? Do you have collaborators? cc I work alone. I do original research every day, without going on other graphic design blogs. I am not interested in collecting the best information found on several blogs, nor do I want to work with information that only comes to me via e-mail. My research involves starting from a graphic designer's name, from exhibitions, from contexts... passing from link to link, exploring related subjects. In the end connections more or less build themselves. Internet can be an incredible tool.

Did you expect so much popularity? What is the main reason for it, in your opinion, and what kind of readers check Manystuff *daily?* cc I can't explain the popularity. Maybe the fact that I am alone, honest in my daily selection, and really passionate. I think that I now have a graphic design culture but my approach to graphic design remains visceral ("it works or it doesn't"). Although, as I wrote, the blog is not meant as a collection of nice images; I think that my sensitivity for images plays a major role in my work and that images can have a great impact on the readers, as they have on me. The visitors of *Manystuff* come daily from everywhere in the world but I don't know who they are exactly. I guess there are a lot of students, graphic designers, and also people working in the publishing field, in galleries, etc.

In 2008 you started a publication, and you also began to curate and organize exhibitions and other events. Why did you feel the need to engage out of the web space? cc As I wrote, the blog is not an end in itself. *Manystuff* database (the blog), extensively and daily updates, and also provides the basis

---

3.   www.parallel-school.com.

for my curatorial and editorial projects. The raw material—graphic designers, projects, concepts, creation processes, contexts—is the starting point for developing projects exceeding the format of the blog—publications, exhibitions and so on. *Manystuff* is a catalyst, a stimulator. First of all, *Manystuff* is a catalyst for myself: it is in contact (be it virtual, on the Net, or real, via *in situ* "reports" and journalistic immersions) with this work (projects, books, prints, artworks, etc.), its actors (graphic designers, curators, editors, etc.), contexts, places (galleries, etc.). For the first two issues, I didn't have any idea of the kind of content I could collect: the publication was built gradually, as well as its graphic design. The magazine is meant to function as a laboratory, as a space of experimentation—written or graphic. The contents may thus seem to be of an uneven quality. But this is deliberate: they are not theoretical reviews, they are not a catalogue, they are not a manual. These pages of paper have fixed, at some point, graphic designers' answers on a specific topic, on a question; and the answers may be in different forms, such as interviews, articles, graphic designs, collected images. My intention was to respect the personality and the spontaneity of the invited designers. *Manystuff* also tries to be a catalyst when I work on exhibitions: for certain projects, the idea is to stimulate and enhance graphic designers' willingness to engage in projects that are different from their daily work, different from working on commission.

If it was up to you, how would you describe the worlds of graphic design today, what are the main features and issues, or what are the main changes you have witnessed in the recent years? CC My first observation is the fact that graphic designers—be they students or professionals—are more and more concerned with the creative process of research and with concepts, rather than only focusing on forms. I also appreciate the dynamics of collaborative projects, as well as the increasing involvement of designers themselves in publishing, in printing—as if there was a desire to keep a trace, or keep track, of things. Pluridisciplinarity and interdisciplinarity are other major trends today: and I think this is great. I love the idea of dialogues, exchanges and confrontations. This is the case today for many disciplines such as graphic design, literature, architecture, publishing, photography, art, history.

What is your opinion on the growing engagement of graphic designers in diverse formats—publishing and editorial projects, exhibitions, conferences? Is it an index of maturity, of critical awareness? CC I think it is natural and good that people are asking questions about their practice, their work, and that they take a fresh look at themselves, that they reassess their position, their role within the society in which they intervene. But, of course, these activities shouldn't be limited to graphic design only. One thing that is really relevant, and that I observe in speaking with graphic designers, is that graphic designers themselves, as a public, are more interested in publications or events about other disciplines—or a mix of disciplines—than in publications and exhibitions about graphic design only.

Graphic design is one of the broadest disciplines you can imagine

–

De Designpolitie

There is always a reason, an event, and thus a message involved

–

Harmen Liemburg

EMILY KING

Thursday is fish-and-chip day for the graphic designers of the London-based outfit GTF. Not all of them take part in the mid-week evening football session that justifies the more substantial than usual lunch, but that appears irrelevant. The ritual is an established part of the studio's collective rhythm. Meanwhile, in Paris, lunch for Michaël Amzalag and Mathias Augustyniak of the design studio M/M is more of a daily ceremony. Usually eaten at a local restaurant (it used to be literally the closest restaurant, but now, after an unfortunate change of management, they frequent a different place a couple of doors along) it involves more than one course, coffee at the end, and a proper length of time. Recalling fights they have had between themselves, Amzalag admits that the spark of one of their grumpiest episodes was a dispute, prompted by an interruption of their routine, about where to eat.

Graphic design studios, like most offices, are worlds in themselves, with their own customs and laws. For the last couple of years I have been writing a book about M/M that is being designed by GTF. Spending time in their Paris and London studios, observing both sets of designers in their own and each other's habitats in relatively comparable circumstances has offered a unique opportunity to undertake a miniature and entirely unscientific study. Although slightly distorted by M/M's role as client, the project has given rise to detailed discussions about the history and output of both firms and opportunities for watching the designers go about their day-to-day activities.

The differences in circumstance and temperament between the London and Parisian peers are marked. M/M and GTF were close friends even before they founded their studios at the start of the 1990s, yet, in the twenty years since they have created two graphic worlds that, while they do intersect at points, are quite distinct.

Followers of graphic design are often surprised that the principals of M/M and GTF even know each other, let alone that they have a strong personal and professional friendship. Looking at the formal qualities of the designers' respective outputs, the general assumption is that their makers could have nothing in common, the intricate layers of decoration that are typical of an M/M piece seeming entirely at odds with the restrained generic gestures associated with GTF. The designers are aware of this perception and, when asked to compare their work, emphasise similarity rather than difference. Pointing to a shared passion for pop culture, an interest in already existing materials and an understanding of graphic design as a 3D discipline, Andy Stevens from GTF argues that they have a joint mission to bring "what's interesting in the world to graphics." "When I look at an M/M job I can kind of pull it apart in my head," he says, "I can make sense of how they've got to that point—understand the components and the decisions."

GTF's Andy Stevens and Paul Neale first met M/M's Mathias Augustyniak at the Royal College of Art in London at the very end of the 1980s. Stevens and Neale were in the year ahead of Augustyniak, and, along with GTF's third founding partner Nigel Robinson, had colonised the Graphic Design department's best studio. Noticing that they had similar Roger Tallon-designed LIP watches (quirky timepieces from the early 1970s), Augustyniak struck up conversation with Neale and from then on he spent much of his time "loitering" in the proto-GTF studio talking about British pop music and indulging in graphic-boy banter. Once out in the real world, however, the first-year/second-year hierarchy seemed to somersault. On graduation Augustyniak immediately joined forces with Michaël Amzalag, a friend from his days at the École des Arts Décoratifs, and began working from a spare room in Amzalag's father's dental surgery in the 10th arrondissement in Paris. Quickly amassing clients and equipment—computers, cameras and so on—the newly founded M/M seemed to be up and running before the year-old GTF had left the blocks.

In the early 1990s the professional environment of graphic design was very different in France and Britain. While independent studios had become commonplace in London, they remained something of a novelty in Paris. GTF entered a world already defined by individuals such as Peter Saville, Neville Brody, and Vaughan Oliver and colonised by studios including

Assorted Images and Why Not. On the basis of these examples, they expected to find work in design for music and their first business plan was based on the assumption of two such jobs a month. This was not to be. The combined forces of a severe recession and high levels of competition effectively barred their way to the recording industry and they have done only a couple of small music jobs over the last twenty years. Denied access to the red-hot heart of popular culture, instead they developed slower-burn specialisms in furniture and interiors, exhibitions, architecture and more recently art. In many cases they have grown up in parallel with their clients, several of the most longstanding also being small firms or individuals who built their businesses in the ashes of the early 1990s economic downturn, and the benefits of increasing maturity have flown in and out of the studio.

In Paris M/M were launching themselves into a very different field, one carved up between large commercial outfits and a couple of smaller, politically motivated studios that were the legacy of the student uprisings of 1968. As a freshly-formed, culturally ambitious two-man graphic design team their role was undefined and this allowed them the freedom to find their own shape. Like London, Paris was in the grip of recession, but the resulting stasis in the established publicly funded art scene had given rise to a new generation of visual artists including Philippe Parreno, Pierre Huyghe and Dominique Gonzalez-Foerster who hoped to challenge the way that art was made and exhibited. Near contemporaries of M/M, their embrace of popular culture encouraged them to collaborate with the designers on a profound level, allowing Amzalag and Augustyniak a role in reconfiguring French contemporary art that is without parallel. Apart from art projects, they also found jobs in more conventional design arenas. Amzalag had spent the years that Augustyniak was at the RCA designing the popular music magazine *Les Inrockuptibles* and gaining a reputation in the recording industry, but even music design, possibly encouraged by their collaborations with artists, they forged unusually deep partnerships, most significantly that with Björk.

Reflecting on M/M and GTF's dissimilarities, Andy Stevens suggests, "Rather than any fundamental or stylistic issue, I would say the biggest difference that has evolved over the years is in our relationships with clients." M/M's intensively collaborative method has kept their practice small. Still working from the studio they moved into after leaving Amzalag's father's dental surgery, they have just expanded their numbers to three designers and a studio manager. They are extremely prolific, yet to an extent their work appears to be the product of a single internally driven force that sweeps their clients into its path for as long as a collaboration lasts. Discussions about projects tend to involve both Amzalag and Augustyniak and their joint authorial input is very visible across the studio's output.

Over the same period GTF have moved studio several times, each premise being larger than the last. They have lost one partner, Robinson, acquired another, Huw Morgan, and currently list seven designers and a studio manager on their website—although with interns and people drafted in to work on particular projects their numbers are often expanded. Morgan, Neale, and Stevens lead projects individually or in combination, but clients usually come into prolonged contact with only one of them. Their work is consistent, but not necessarily recognisable. As someone who has worked most closely with Neale, I feel I can spot his particular graphic traits, but I wouldn't feel 100 percent confident in my ability to identify all GTF projects.

Where GTF rely on commissioned photography from a small group of trusted colleagues, M/M, apart the context of fashion, use almost exclusively their own photographic images. And, while M/M's work is characterised by hand drawing and lettering, GTF delight in largely forgotten print techniques or materials. M/M's pieces tend to be seductively dense; GTF's disarmingly simple. Yet, set M/M's most fully-realised projects, say the catalogues they designed for Yohji Yamamoto between 1995 and 2000 or their ongoing series of posters for the Lorient theatre, alongside those of GTF, their continuing work for the Frieze Art Fair, perhaps, or their catalogues for Habitat, and, rather than any kind of competition, you get a demonstration of the range of the best graphic design of the last twenty years. In creating very different graphic worlds and operating within them in dissimilar ways, M/M and GTF have both found the means to function to their fullest.

For an exhibition of their work in the Japanese gallery DDD in 2006, GTF created a poster map of their network of clients and colleagues titled *50 Projects*. Arranged chronologically, the diagram starts with a few friends and relatives and then branches out into a dense thicket of more and less direct connections. Tracing the lines, what soon becomes apparent are the conjoined forces of fidelity and chance, qualities that are similarly important determinants in the career of M/M. If Amzalag and Augustyniak were also to make such a diagram, it would be interesting to see the two side by side.

ITALIAN REFLECTIONS

THE WORLDS OF GRAPHIC DESIGNERS

1.

Graphic Designers, People with Problems.
Some Thoughts from Italy

CARLO VINTI

"They call themselves graphic designers; others say 'admen.' Either way, they are people with problems." This is how graphic designers were described in an article that appeared in the Italian weekly magazine *L'Europeo* in Spring 1962,[1] at the very height of the "economic miracle." Then as now, it was rather rare to find such a publication dedicating space to graphics; and in packaging this group portrait for the general public, the author, Gianni Roghi, could find no better presentation than a confession of his own difficulties in understanding what graphic design was all about. Thus he concentrated upon the problems raised by the very people who figured in the article—masters of their craft such as Antonio Boggeri, Erberto Carboni, Franco Grignani, Giovanni Pintori, Albe Steiner and Armando Testa, plus various other graphic designers from around Europe.

Handling large-scale investment in advertising—and thus having a decisive influence upon the "visual taste" of their day—this first generation of graphic designers were playing a lead role at a very important time. However, as that period fades further and further into the past, the myths regarding these people become ever more numerous, preventing not only accurate understanding of that past but also a clear-sighted and frank appreciation of the present.

Can we be sure that the "founding fathers" of Italian graphic design—who even nowadays enjoy wider international fame than their successors—were

---

1.   G. Roghi, "Il tentatore di professione. Inchiesta fra i grafici della pubblicità," *L'Europeo*, April 15, 1962, pp. 41–46.

really establishing a discipline based on commonly-shared criteria? Faced with the differences in approaches, opinions, and background that he discovered, Roghi, the poor *Europeo* journalist concluded: "It would seem to be impossible to lump them together as a single profession." That is the first problem facing graphic designers—one that is felt with particular urgency by the Italian professionals working in this field. So, let's start from there.

1. The Definition of the Profession
For many, this is the fruit of a long and hard struggle; something to be defended tooth and nail. For others, it is yet to be fully achieved, because there are no forms of public recognition for the work performed. But there is also a group—and it does not only include the younger members of the profession—who see this whole issue as now a false problem.

In Italy as elsewhere, graphic design arose from the interaction of input from various different practices: typography and graphic art, illustration and poster design, advertising and industrial design, art and architecture. It is a profession that has drawn upon the most varied contributions; that has tolerated a range of different definitions. Many of those who are generally included within the history of graphic design often worked in other fields as well—as typographers, art directors, painters, poets and cultural firebrands of various kinds.

True, there was a phase of boundary definition, which usually proceeded by exclusion (graphic design is not advertising, is not art, etc.). However, while these efforts at definition were taking place, the actual practice of graphics was going in the most unexpected directions. Furthermore, a common denominator between many of the figures in the so-called Italian "school" is the ease with which they have transgressed the borders separating different disciplines.

Whether we like it or not, we are now in a period when the barriers among disciplines have become permeable. Alongside the more traditional exemplifications of the profession, there is a world of young designers who come together to create platforms for exchanging ideas rather than to set up the usual design studio; who may be tucked away in the Italian provinces but try to achieve international recognition: who may recognize the historical and technical-cultural foundations of their profession and yet prefer to see themselves as working outside any so-called "discipline."

One must take an unbiased look at all these new developments. Little is to be gained by hurling around anathemas.

2. *Absence of Institutional Structure and a Professional Culture*

The paradox does not only exist in Italy: while the products of graphic design are a pervasive presence in modern daily life, both academic culture and the mainstream media show little interest in graphic design as such. This has been accompanied by a somewhat excessive lamenting about the tendency of both public institutions and the public at large to slight the skills and services that graphic designers might provide society.

True, Italy is not Holland, and the opportunities for a graphic designer here to obtain professional as well as cultural recognition are much more restricted. But if Italy does not offer great opportunities, then perhaps the only way forward is to approach things from the other side: instead of waiting for clients, institutions, and the public at large to recognize how important graphic design is, one should strive to make the content of such design important and relevant to social and cultural life. How? That is not an easy question to answer.

Independent self-initiated projects may have their pitfalls, but are not necessarily to be dismissed as an easy short-cut. When accompanied by an awareness of the possible risks of self-indulgence, they can be a way forward, a way of regaining confidence in the future. This is why this path attracts so many young designers.

Regardless of the difficulties mentioned above, Italy has highly-gifted professionals working in the fields of publishing, corporate image, and in establishing the visual identities of cities and regions. Furthermore, there is interesting work being done in type design. Within this framework there is room for experimental approaches and a more oblique interpretation of the profession, for courageous proposals that can infiltrate a number of areas of cultural activity, for independent projects that embrace a number of social objectives. Indeed, one might say there is an urgent need—rather than just "room"—for such developments.

Things have changed since the 1962 article in *L'Europeo*, and Milan is no longer the undisputed "capital of Italian graphic design." Gianni Roghi talked about a "few hundred" graphic designers, most of them Milanese. Nowadays, there is a mass of professional designers, distributed in a more or less homogeneous manner throughout the country.

The graduates which Italian degree courses turn out every year are well aware of the problems they will face; they are constantly being reminded of them. In a period of supposed stagnation, it is reasonable—and indeed desirable—that some of them should strive to break the mold, even if only at a visionary, theoretical level. It has happened before in the history of Italian culture, and it is happening now in the world of international design—in response to various things (one of them being a crisis that is not solely financial-economic in character).

3. Criticism of Graphic Design and Critical Graphic Design

The last twenty years or so have seen frequent calls in Italy, as elsewhere, for a careful critical reflection on the profession.

Upon close examination, one sees that the period when the professional terms *grafica* and "design" entered the Italian language was one in which art critics, semiologists and writers did show a certain interest in such matters. Gillo Dorfles, Umberto Eco, and Leonardo Sinisgalli—along with numerous other figures of importance in Italian cultural life—had important things to say about graphics and visual communication. Then, just as disciplinary borders were becoming more established and professions more or less rigidly defined, graphic designers began to suffer what one might call cultural sidelining. Since then the profession has made useful efforts to reflect upon itself from within. Important studies and training manuals have been produced, and the first attempts have been made to write the history of the discipline.

However, at this point what is required is something different: historical/critical writing which can use the products of graphic design to speak of something "other," which takes the work of graphic designers as a starting-point for a discussion of historical issues or the important questions facing the modern world. In other words, what is required is a critical discourse, which is not intended solely for graphic designers; which can speak to a wider public by exploiting the crucial role and relevance of graphics within contemporary culture and economics.

What is interesting is that there is a certain type of designer who is undertaking something similar. Refusing to remain confined to the *presentation* of the message, these designers invade the area of *content* itself. Bringing together such activities as editing, writing and designing, they see graphic design as offering a special vantage point from which to observe the world.

In Italy, only scant attention has been paid to the ongoing international debate, which started some years ago, with regard to the designer as author and the use of design as an instrument of critical investigation. And yet a speculative approach is inscribed within the DNA of Italian design culture—look, for example, at the paper architecture of Archizoom and Superstudio and the critical reflections of such figures as Enzo Mari and Ettore Sottsass (to name just two). Many indeed look at Italian design history as providing some of the experiences that are at the root of a view of design not solely as mediation but also as reflection, as a practice that can have a provocative and challenging role.

4. Design and Advertising

The espousal of "critical graphic design" is in some way motivated by an implicit rejection of that which already exists, a questioning of what has become normal practice. The relation between all graphic designers and their commercial role has always been somewhat controversial, oscillating between enthusiastic participation in and radical opposition to the system. The former attitude has often been predicated upon a sort of aesthetic utopianism, striving for a "democratization" of taste; the latter, more often than not, has quickly led back to complicity with a culture of consumerism.

The origins of Italian graphic design straddle the areas of advertising and industrial design. Not many remember, for example, that the AIAP—the body that represents Italian graphic designers—was founded in 1955 to bring together "advertising artists" and that a large number of its members were also members of the ADI (Associazione per il Disegno Industriale). If architecture and product design have always been a fertile ground of dialogue and exchange for Italian graphic designers, it was in the area of their troubled relations with advertising that Italy's first professionals in this discipline struggled to assert their identity—as one can see from the heated debates that took place in the 1960s.

Now, of course, we are all clear: graphic design is not advertising (at least that is not all it is). Students are told this repeatedly. However, to achieve genuine critical distance here, one has to revise the old models of interpretation; one has to recognize that all graphic design—even that which appears to have the least to do with commercial purposes—plays a crucial role in the present phase of capitalism.

It is also true there is a growing divide between experimental and commercial graphic design. And without fertile exchange between these two areas of activity, there is the risk that critical design—that which sees research as its aim—will end up isolated in a rarefied world, with no connection to design as an everyday activity. Given the present-day blurring of distinctions between the public and private, between culture and the economy, the historical aspiration of design to "re-design" the world often finds expression in perverse forms. But this does not necessarily mean that it should be abandoned altogether.

In Italy as elsewhere, it is difficult to give a clear-cut reading of the various ways graphic design is understood nowadays. The present situation seems to be gravid with unresolved questions—unresolved in part because we ourselves are immersed within that situation. However, if we do not look to history simply for "founding moments," for examples to be held up to future generations; if we view the work of designers in a larger context, allowing the figures and commentators of prior periods to speak for themselves—then we will find the same sorts of problems in the past as well, and with the same level of intensity and complexity.

The author of that 1962 article in *L'Europeo* observed that every single designer gave a different answer to the question: "Where is graphic design going?" He found himself faced not only with graphic designers who were architects and "advertising artists" (as opposed to "pure graphic designers"), but also with such figures as Franco Grignani, who had no problem in talking about advertising but considered it to be "a new art, as complete and real as old art."

If it has ever existed as a discipline proper, graphic design has always been characterized by instability and "promiscuity." Indeed, the current tendency towards the interdisciplinary is not in itself an entirely new phenomenon: many of the leading figures of the avant-garde were deliberately interdisciplinary, and we distort things when we try to force them into the narrative categories adopted by the history of graphic design.

The identity and "visibility" of graphic design in Italy continues to be a problem. Just as—in Italy and elsewhere—it is a problem for designers to find good clients and spaces which allow for independent expression. Opportunities for real experimentation and research—or even just for the application of high professional standards—are not always available. But perhaps it is not worth dwelling upon this kind of difficulty.

The *real* problems lie outside graphic design. Graphic designers are in a postion to analyze those problems, to place them before the public, to view them from a radically different critical perspective, and even to try now and then—in accord with an old modernist princple—to actually solve them.

Parigi. Moïse Depond (che si firma Mose) è un grafico votato alla caricatura e al bozzetto. Ha pubblicato alcuni libri umoristici, in cui l'uomo del nostro tempo è amabilmente preso in giro.

ei inducono
a spendere
il nostro denaro?
Ecco le idee
di alcuni
dei più famosi
grafici italiani
e stranieri

GIANNI ROGHI

SARANNO cinquecento? Forse sono di meno. Dai muri delle strade, dalle pagine dei giornali, dalle copertine dei libri, sono queste poche centinaia di persone a disegnare nelle nostre teste, tutti i giorni, qualche cosa che vi rimane impresso e spesso vi esplode in emozioni. Poi si va a comprare il dentifricio, la benzina, il sapone. Loro si chiamano grafici, gli altri dicono pubblicitari. Sono comunque gente con dei problemi. In questo breve viaggio alla ricerca di coloro che, in Italia e fuori, determinano il gusto visivo del nostro tempo, ho riscontrato che almeno una cosa hanno in comune: la vocazione. Adesso hanno chiamato intorno a loro anche filosofi, specialisti di psicologia di massa, psichiatri. A volte, tutti insieme, danno l'impressione di essersi ritirati in una specie di chiesa con un proprio rituale e una propria mitologia. La loro speculazione dottrinale è partita da tempo in direzioni che essi chiamano delle ricerche motivazionali, un lungo viaggio nel profondo dell'uomo alla fine del quale ci saranno una mezza dozzina di scoperte decisive. Perché gli italiani preferiscono le bionde? Stabilito questo, è fatta. I nostri grafici ci faranno preferire i loro sali da bagno e le loro scatole di-conserva? Di sicuro c'è soltanto una cosa: che nel 1961 il lavoro dei grafici pubblicitari italiani è costato a chi il paga-qualcosa come settanta miliardi di lire, forse di più.

Il primo contatto con il grafico può risultare alquanto allucinante, per il profano, ma è stato detto: questa è un po' una chiesa e bisogna avvicinarvisi con un minimo di umiltà e con la speranza di poter capire.

Adesso, mi dice il grafico, comincia l'era del segno. Che cosa sarebbe il segno? Il mezzo moderno per comunicare e informare: un linguaggio simbolico, allusivo, sintetico, fulmineo. La segnaletica stradale: basta il segno per dirti « guarda che adesso arriva una doppia curva fatta più o meno così la quale è ovviamente pericolosa se presa in velocità dunque rallenta ». Oppure il cartellone pubblicitario, il cartoncino natalizio, la sigla (segno!) musicale, il marchio di fabbrica: un linguaggio che è diventato sempre più semplice, ma più ricercato. Sofisticato? Certo no: essenziale. Il grafico mi dà alcune definizioni, ne scelgo una: il segno è ars publica. Insomma pubblicità? Be', anche. Ma soprattutto « un linguaggio diretto, umano, universale, immediato », e poi « un'arte nuova, vera e totale come l'antica ». Non ho ancora capito che cosa sia il segno, abbiate pazienza. E allora cominciamo le visite. Non ci sarà da girare molto: i grafici nazionali non sono più di una decina, e tenendo conto degli innumerevoli distinguo, non più di quattro o cinque.

Anzitutto, mi spiegano, bisogna dividere i grafici puri dai cosiddetti artisti della pubblicità che possono essere bravissimi, ma che sono un'altra cosa. Il grafico puro eccolo qui: Franco Grignani. Ti aspetteresti un tipo ieratico (così almeno lo immaginavo io, dalle opere) e invece assomiglia a un grosso fanciullo. La sua arma, o il suo gioco, sono le lenti. Le lenti, mi dice, me le fabbrica una ditta famosa e si chiamano « zoppe » perché deformano l'oggetto in cento modi. Ne ha una serie, e mi spiega la sua tecnica: per esempio, prendo un pezzo di carta bianca, ci incollo liste di carta nera in ordine geometrico, statico, poi intervengo con le lenti, giro,

continua alla pagina 44

41

Il tentatore
di professione

Italia
sono spesi
el 1961
tre settanta
iliardi di lire
pubblicità
afica:

I am not sure it even exists.

Being in the World.
Some Approaches to Graphic Design
in Italy Towards the End of 2010

SILVIA SFLIGIOTTI

It is difficult to talk about the current state of affairs in Italian graphic design, because I am not sure it even exists. I don't mean that there are no graphic designers in the country—sometimes one gets the impression that that is all there is in Milan—but because the ways in which these designers work are so diverse that at times one might think they were not engaged in the same profession.

This is because our profession is one that undergoes continual redefinition; within Italy it does not seem to have achieved a state of one might call "consolidation." And this certainly does not seem the moment when it could do so. In defining the myriad approaches within our profession, one sometimes feels the ground slip away from under one's feet. Which are to be pursued and which are to be opposed? Every new generation of graphic designers encounters their predecessors either as teachers or as the figures responsible for their "apprenticeship" in the craft. However, they then seem eager to forget them as soon as possible.

Now—just as we are, with some difficulty, achieving a "definition" and "recognition" of this profession (both terms are in inverted commas because they lend themselves to ambiguous interpretations)—we realize that graphic design is not as relevant as we had thought. And this realization comes when various sectors are trying to establish the profession's field of action and ethical priorities, to obtain adequate remuneration for the work done; when great emphasis is being placed upon the strategic role of the profession in the age of communication.

"I am not a graphic designer"

In the crowded and ill-defined world of "communication" (a term which in Italy can be used to mean just about anything), many argue that for too long now it has been impossible to earn serious money with graphic design alone. The only way to get by, they claim, is to sell a whole range of things for which one still gets well paid: strategies, positioning, branding, etc. In all of this, design proper is a mere detail. Its domain seems to be the twenty proposals for a logo that the ad agency submits to a client; the "sketches" which many clients now expect to find enclosed with an estimate of costs. It really is not worth dedicating too much time to it if you want your books to balance at the end of the year.

Indeed, the very term "graphics" seems to have become a belittling slur, reflecting the fact that such activity is of so little relevance in an overall process where decisions are taken elsewhere. There are increasing numbers of people who respond to the question "Are you a graphic designer?" with the answer "No, I work in branding" or "in strategy development." The ability to give appropriate form to specific content appears to be almost irrelevant. What is being sold is the discourse built up around those forms—a discourse that operates at other levels.

It is interesting to note, however, that the communication business's clear lack of interest in the artifact of graphic design as such forms a symmetrical pair with the apparent lack of interest of those who have opted for a conceptual approach to design as "process." Clear opposites, the two attitudes reflect each other.

Still, there must be something special about graphic design. It is not a profession that is "better" than others, but it does enjoy (or has enjoyed) a privileged position, coming into play at some of the key junctures of contemporary culture. But now that so many of the tools of communication are directly available to end-users themselves, the graphic designer is no longer necessary for the creation of individual artifacts. In such a situation, one has to ask how graphic design can survive, how it can make itself a decisive presence.

Directions

In striving to answer this question, various—sometimes divergent—approaches have been adopted. However, these are not declared explicitly, in open statements of principle and manifestos. With greater or lesser degrees of self-awareness, each critical position is expressed in a mode of praxis, and there is little attempt to measure oneself against—and even less, clash with—those who have adopted a different approach.

Some of us are proud to assert the status of graphic design, arguing that the boundaries of the discipline do not have to be redefined but rather re-asserted. Such people strive for recognition, seeing it as a confirmation of their authoritative standing with both client and public. The result of this can be very different modes of behavior. For example, on the one hand there are those who see graphics as valuable in themselves, as a "product"—as something to be added to an object or space in order to make them "more significant," or as embodying the added value that comes from the association of an important "name." And then there are those who see graphic designers as fulfilling a role similar to that of *maîtres-à-penser*, critical observers of the contemporary world. It is a role previously occupied by certain architects, who are unlikely to relinquish it. Others simply want to work freely, with the enthusiasm and apparent *naiveté* of those who do not want to be held back by the weight of the past; who want to approach the present as a sort of *tabula rasa*. Deep down, perhaps, this blithe insouciance is something we all desire; we all want to stay in that phase of adolescence where designers do not raise problems but are simply "kids who know how things are done."

And in the midst of all this, I can't help asking: what happened to social design? Not that I feel any nostalgia for a certain type of design that, behind the shield provided by good causes, churns out commonplaces rather than real projects. But there is a type of graphic design that is conscious of the social value of what it is doing, and is willing to act accordingly—not striving to change the world, but knowing that it could have a positive influence on the mechanisms of change. Perhaps it is better that such awareness has not resulted in an explicit movement as such.

The way things are at the moment, there is the risk that it would have resulted in nothing other than an exhibition of posters, mixing together provocation and good intentions—while, given they no longer exist out on Italian streets but are only to be found in the protected environments of design competitions and design galleries, posters have lost whatever ability they may ever have had to speak directly to society.

There is one thing that we can perhaps count on: we are finally seeing the emergence of a generation whose entire educational background and training are in the field of graphic design. Something which was very rare ten years ago, this is now possible thanks to the creation of faculties of design within various Italian universities. These people—hundreds of new graduates per year—start their professional career after a course of study that lasts at least five years. But then their encounter with the world of work often brings them up against a "communications market" which is not ready to absorb them. Due to a shortfall in the quantity and, above all, the quality of demand, there is more room for efficient executors of other people's ideas than for independent designers.

In spite of this discouraging state of affairs, there are those among these newcomers who, with a sort of pioneering spirit, are engaging in a critical enquiry which aims to redress the absence of any wide-ranging discussion of the role of graphic design—a discussion which, I believe, has been hindered by that lack of "common ground" between designers to which I have already referred.

Ways Out

It is interesting how the practice of graphic design leads people to want to do something else. It may be that this arises simply from the difficulties and frustrations that one encounters. However, I am more inclined to think that it is the work itself which stimulates this desire for change: all of this working "between" things, putting things together, mediating in order to achieve a coherent form, establishing dialogue between very different ideas and contexts—all of this triggers a sort of chemical reaction that generates change. Thus one can find oneself wanting to be something more like an editor or a curator (two very fashionable terms at the moment). The truth is that this yearning to go beyond graphic design paradoxically owes something to graphic design itself. I get the impression that this phenomenon is endemic within the profession, and I believe it can be very fertile if accompanied by the necessary degree of self-criticism. Blending together the graphic designer and the editor (who decides content) in one figure may, to an outsider, seem an undermining of boundaries, a recipe for self-indulgence. One would perhaps have to admit that we graphic designers do not always have something to say, even if we are very good at saying it. But that is not the only path. At times, we deliberately choose to restrict our field of action, opting to work within contained niches. In part, this may occur because such specialization is reassuring for the lazier type of client. However, it can also be due to the fact that this approach makes our visibility solid, not extensive but authoritative; that by addressing ourselves to a restricted public which is close to us, we have a chance of achieving tangible results, immediate feedback. And such "closeness" clearly links together with an aspiration towards a type of communication that is not simply mediated by the digital media; that continues to exist as a physical form, an actual presence in people's everyday life.

Recently, I have become aware of the latent tendency to withdraw from the entire game of commissioned work to strive for an ideal world in which we become our own clients. This involves an aspiration to a truly "independent" work existence, freed from the purely commercial constraints within which one feels to some extent compromised. However, at times the distinction drawn between "independent design" and "commercial design" seems forced and, above all, ambiguous. Where exactly does the boundary lie? And what criteria is one to adopt in making such a choice: cultural value, prestige, earnings, "creative freedom"? It is all a bit self-contradictory that a profession which emerged precisely in an environment of commissioned work should now want to break away from such commissions because they could be a source of contamination. In this state of affairs, the role of self-initiated projects changes. No longer mere instruments of self-promotion, created to attract new clients, they become the means whereby a desire can be fulfilled. In part, this occurs because of the great problem facing graphic design in Italy: that is, the absence of truly important and challenging commissions. But at times it is also due to a refusal to engage (or struggle) with the limits and difficulties implicit in a design that has to find its place in the real world. What inspires such a stance is the ambition to show what we are capable of when we are not constrained by the need to adapt to the demands made by others. However, in the best possible cases, there is also the desire to reveal that we can make a wider and more stimulating use of the tools we operate with everyday; that we can initiate new processes.

I recognize that graphic design may at times require protected environments, where cultivation *in vitro* can reveal new possibilities of development and evolution. However, one cannot go on living within such "bubbles" forever: ultimately one would end up exhausting the available oxygen and nourishment. Graphic design is a profession that should live via observation, *via* dialogue and interchange; it makes sense not within the restricted world of a few protected niches but within the world proper, the place where people live and pose new challenges.

Benedetta Crippa This first theme, "The Worlds of Graphic Designers," is intended to offer an opportunity for you to talk about your background; about the course you have taken; about the work environment you have created for yourselves—"environment" in the sense of both physical space and the network of relations that you have established over time. The presupposition here is that there are no pre-established formulas. When one meets designers one becomes aware of the variety of environments and contexts within which they work. Every one seems to have found his/her own personal way of interpreting the profession and their life within it. And we also get the impression that graphic design is not something that lives in isolation; it continually interacts with a variety of figures both within and outside the field. We would like to see if what you have to say on the matter confirms this impression.

THE WORLDS OF GRAPHIC DESIGNERS

Tankboys As for the physical place, now, after five years, we have finally managed to get a proper studio. But what is a "proper" studio? The truth is that, since 2005, we have had to search out alternative solutions—for example, applying to the Bevilacqua La Masa Foundation in Venice for for an artist residency. However, even this necessity became an occasion to share space with other people, to create a network. Being in the same physical space with other people led to us undertaking projects that were different from the traditional commercial work. The term that is often used is "self-initiated project," which is frequently taken in a negative sense—that is, I produce things under my own initiative because my designs are not worth commissioning. But the truth is that such projects are those into which you really put your whole self, in which you take risks. Not for money, but for other reasons. They are projects which have no immediate commercial value; which would never be produced within the market. Then there is the fact that perhaps we only really know how to do a few things. This led us over time to search out other people who were better at doing some of the things we wanted to do. So the studio is made up of two of us, but there are a lot of people we work with, with whom we "engage." And this makes us feel more rich, in a way. **Crippa** I would like to add a note here. There is one thing all the designers invited here have in common: the fact that they are in some way independent, that they set up their own   × **INDEPENDENCE**

business. Probably this very fact leads one to create networks. **Francesco Valtolina** I would like to say something about that. I think it is dangerous to hide behind such "independence," the boundaries of which do not strike me as being so clear-cut. Is Christoph Keller "independent" when he directs a series of publications for JRP, when JRP is a publisher that exists thanks to financing and relations that go well beyond the condition one would identify with "independence"? I have no answer, but I want to re-propose the question. *Mousse*, too, is sometimes associated with an independent publisher. But when talking in terms of systems, when charting the chronology of a professional career, the definition of "independence" varies and shifts. For myself, I come from a background of experience primarily within agencies, in the 1990s. Then, together with some friends, I set up a studio that alternated strictly commercial projects with our own self-initiated projects, intended to enable us to define ourselves. A few years later, the publisher of *Mousse*, with whom I had already begun to work, asked me to work on that project more continuously, and—seeing the great potential for growth of the magazine—I accepted. Now, two years later, I work together with ten people; there is an editorial body that publishes a substantial amount of stuff. And this has made it possible to establish a series of relations. When, as a publisher and designer, one's work is concerned with a specific artist or an exhibition, the relation established may be with the artist him/herself. And that artist can in a certain sense be seen as a client: producing a catalogue for an artist is like providing a service for someone who wants to present himself—exactly like a company that wants a catalogue to communicate its products. It is in this creation of relations that the strength of our work lies; there is always a dialogue, a process in which each participant brings to the table their own specific knowledge and expertise. I like to think that the role of the graphic designer is to be at the service of that developing discourse. As Keller would say, I have nothing to say myself; my job is actually to provide someone who has a lot of things to say with the means to tell them.[1] **Studio Temp** We three have known each other for years. We followed parallel courses of study, then we met up again and began working together. As Tankboys said, there were not many opportunities, so we ended up withdrawing into an attic. Then we got a real

---

1.   C. Keller, "Nostalgie d'un enquiquineur. Les livres et l'art-quelques Smacks sur fond de crise relationelle," *Back Cover*, Spring 2009.

chance: a space at a prestige location in Bergamo. If in Italy there is no well-established visual culture, if there is a lack of "openness," of connections between different fields of activity, then Bergamo is a thousand times worse. So we stopped a moment and pondered: "What shall we do? Go to Milan? Leave Italy?" We considered the options for a time and then decided: "No. Let's stay here—precisely because there is nothing here, no developed culture of visual images and communication. That is our profession, let's exercise it

Brave New Alps We have been working together as Brave New Alps since 2005, when we decided to develop upon the graduate thesis projects we had presented at the Faculty of Arts and Design at the Free University of Bolzano. The starting-point for our work there was a theme in which we were both interested: the implications of mass tourism within the Alps. In 2008 we decided to continue our training in England, at the Department of Communication Art and Design at the Royal College of Art—because that was where a number of designers whose approach interested us had come from. Up to now we have never had a permanent studio. This is a choice that depends upon the way we develop and work upon our projects. Ideally, the ultimate end and content of our work take form during a prolonged "inhabitation" of a space and time specific to the object of that project. This is why we tend to adopt and adapt spaces within the sites associated with the main project we happen to be working on at a specific time.

here." And everything started from there. Of course, the way things went wasn't as rosy as it appears when you tell it now. However, we may be crazy, but we have the real impression that things have been changing over the last few years; that more attention is being paid in Italy to the way in which ideas are communicated. **FF3300** With reference to what was said about producing a catalogue for an artist, our experience × DESIGN AND ART means that we run a mile when an artist asks us to do something. Artists think they can also be artists of page layout. We feel close to the ideas of Giovanni Lussu. We feel a basic incompatibility with artists. However, we do manage to work within the cultural sphere. It is true that culture, too, is commercial in a certain sense; however, we have never worked for a company, but only for associations and cultural/public bodies. **Joseph Miceli** I think it is a question of positioning. I have worked with a number of artists and it has never been a problem. I don't know if that has to do with the quality of the artists; it has more to do with the dialogue that one establishes with them. That dialogue may be difficult, but I look upon myself as a translator—in the sense that the artist gives me material which then has to be translated into another form. This participation is important. **Giovanni Anceschi** On the issue of "design and art," I can't avoid saying something. I am caught between two or three roles here—and one of them is my role as an artist.

I will try to say what I think on the matter. Art and Design definitely have something in common: the fact that they give form to things, to communication. The ability involved here is the same. The substantial difference is that art is autonomous and design is heteronomous. In short, if there is no client, then you are an artist. Another word which can and should be associated with the designer as well as with the artist is that of "intellectual." We are more like "intellectuals" than "technicians"—or, better, we are "technical intellectuals." This is fundamental: we produce culture. And in the world as it is now, there is a great need for intellectual input, for culture. **Angelika Burtscher** Daniele [Lupo] and I opened up the "Lungomare" exhibition space precisely because we felt the need to produce content, to propose points of view with regard to the contexts within which we operate. Perhaps even here one can see the difference between Italy and the Netherlands. For example, in Italy design is rarely used as an instrument of research, to explore and discuss reality. For us, the construction of content is just as important as the organization of that content within form. This is reflected in our projects as curators. We are striving to open up a dialogue; thus, we start from the point of view of design to then open out to other disciplines—not just creative ones, such as sociology or political sciences, which do not usually fall within the category of "creative activities." **Invernomuto** We would like to cut away some of the romanticism surrounding art and artists. For example, it is not true that the artist works and creates within his studio solely for himself. Artists, too, work upon commission: you are commissioned to produce a work and, while you are obviously free, there are also limits and restrictions. So art and design may be different, but they border on each other. **Anceschi** Exactly. It is a question DEFINITIONS × of definition. It is when there is a commission that you become a designer. Michelangelo was an artist but he worked on commissions from patrons such as Pope Julius II, with whom he argued, because the work had to

Brave New Alps Personally we are very skeptical about those who distinguish between art and design, saying that—unlike the artist—the designer always and only works in response to the demands of a client. After graduating, we realized that the world outside the college did not seem to offer space for design as we understood it—that is, an independent, reflective, proactive activity. The two most important commissions—the ones that opened up new paths for us—both came from art institutes. However, we have always seen ourselves as communication designers. This is the field in which we trained and it is the area that we wish to help define. Even at the RCA it was often a struggle to make people understand that what we do is neither art nor curatorship, but communication design.

be done in a certain way. That is, he was also a designer. Over time, the associated skills, the professional figures became distinguished. **Invernomuto** The first job we undertook as artists was an editorial project, in collaboration with other artists, graphic designers and musicians. So we started with the publishing end, without thinking of ourselves as "graphic designers"—in part because we weren't: We had graduated from the multimedia department of the Accademia di Brera, which did not train you for any specific role, neither that of "artist" nor the professional role of "graphic designer" proper. But from within that confusion we drew the initial impetus to start. First we began working in other media: installations, video, etc. But in fact, right from the start, our idea was to create a small network. There was a compelling feeling of urgency. To return to the issue of the work environment for a moment, we come from Piacenza and we worked in very domestic settings, in small studios—the first was a loft, then came the former office of the father of one of us. After that we moved to Milan, where we now share a large building in the Lambrate area—a very peculiar situation in a city like this. Having grown up in rural areas, we felt the need first of all to work out in the provinces, to discover the visual characteristics of such a region; then came the need to establish a dialogue with the outside world. The idea was to stimulate movement, to discuss and impinge upon themes and areas of discourse that had not been subjected to clear-cut definition. Over time, publishing has become an instrument, which we could not possibly do without... even if, since 2005, we have not sold a single copy of our magazine *ffwd_mag*! **Studio Temp** We bought it! **Invernomuto** However, to conclude, with regard to the relation between design and art, we often find ourselves in an ambivalent position. So for us it is important not to give too strict definitions. In part because these very definitions are those which have in a certain sense sidelined us over all these years. **Daniele Lupo** I feel a little uncomfortable speaking about definitions, because it is not easy to give a straightforward univocal definition of our work. We have a studio that works on communication design and on 3D design; and we run a space for which we act as curators, organizers and sometimes fundraisers. We are "multifaceted" and have stopped worrying about how others might define us. We try to define ourselves in accordance with the needs we must meet. **FF3300** Instead, we think that words are important. We can't be both flesh and fowl. As teachers at the Politecnico di Bari, we tell our students: "If you are thinking of being artists, then there is the door!" × **EDUCATION** We teach communication design, not art. **Burtscher** But someone might want to learn communications design to then produce art—to take what you teach as a starting-point to be used in a different way.   **FF3300** In our opinion it is not an issue of defining categories. What is wrong is trying to enhance the profession of design by associating it with art. We think that the work of the designer should be treated as legitimate in itself, not through some identification of the designer as an artist.   **Valerio Di Lucente** Perhaps it is more a question of the perception of roles, which is not the same thing as defining them. In Italy, the art industry and the design industry have always moved along separate courses; the general public perceives artists in one way and designers in another. But then there are any number of examples of designers also being artists, such as Bruno Munari, or Anceschi himself… Even if words are important, definitions are still ends-unto-themselves to a certain extent.   **FF3300** But when you have to explain to a student of eighteen who is enrolling in a three- or five-year degree course, it is important.   **Di Lucente** Agreed. But many artists think like designers and there are designers who think like artists, in terms of methodologies and approaches to problems. We could use all the various shades of meaning to explain these things.   **Tankboys** Years ago I was a student under Giorgio [Camuffo]. Compared to other teachers of graphic design, there was one fundamental thing that he taught me: there are graphic designers who work as graphic designers, who study books, who do their job well, but there are also graphic designers who strive to do something else as well. And that something else is not "be an artist." Rather, it is what can be exemplified through the work of numerous graphic designers over the last few decades, who helped to change the way graphic design is meant; who began to draw upon input from other worlds without getting bogged down in the problem of definitions. Put simply, they are graphic designers who have a different type of sensibility; who feel the need to look at things in a different way. They do not merely think "I have to do this layout correctly," but "We are thinking beings; we are people who can put something of our own into this." This awareness has had a decisive effect upon our way of working; it has led us to explore, to adopt a certain attitude… and probably to enjoy ourselves more. It means we do not see our studio as an office in which one works from 9 in the morning to 7 in the evening. The issue is not one of definitions but of the approach one takes to graphic design.   **FF3300** We look upon ourselves as visual communication designers. Full-stop. And in designing visual communication we can, as occasion demands, draw on all sorts of different disciplines: science, linguistics, cognitive psychology, and also art. But within our field of work we have also encountered people who declare themselves to be "artists." We often hear that term bandied about, but with nothing behind it. That is why words are important. **Tankboys** In Venice one also uses the term *artista* (artist) or a skilled craftsman. You can call a good bricklayer an *artista*, which is wonderful! **Crippa** The relation between art and design is one that has already been the object of numerous debates on various occasions, and we are certainly not going to resolve it here. I would therefore ask you to move on to a description of your various worlds... **FF3300** So, we have marked down a few keywords. First of all "FF3300," which means "orange." It is a code and a declaration of intent; it refers to writing and notational systems. *FF3300* was founded in 2006 as an independent magazine—we produced it in the kitchen, a bit like they used to do in the 1960s and 1970s. Then in 2009 we opened a studio. FF3300 is a sort of platform or "hub," that is, it tries to establish relations between different fields of knowledge and know-how; we often engage people from outside the studio. Another word is "liquidity," because we try to keep the various roles interchangeable. Each one of us has specific inclinations and skills, but we try to maintain a constant interchange of knowledge and information with each other. And finally we have marked down the word "South," because we are well aware of being *terroni*, natives of the Mediterranean basin. We are not striving to ape the myth of the North, of "Milan, the capital city of Design"; instead we are striving for our own myth of the Mediterranean, of openness to × **REGIONS** "otherness." **Miceli** I too am from the South: I was born in Siracusa. My father is a painter and my family moved to New York when I was five years old. I grew up in a very creative and artistic environment, going to a state school that focused on the arts. In 1999 I came back to Europe and studied at the Rietveld Academie in Amsterdam from 2004 to 2007. This was a very important experience; thanks to the various models and examples

Nazareno Crea I was born in a small town in Calabria but grew up in Rome; then when I was nineteen I moved to Milan for a short time. I undertook my first studies in Lausanne, at the École cantonale d'art de Lausanne, where I also worked as a graphic designer and teaching assistant. Then I went to London, where I took an MA in Art and Design at the Royal College of Art; I still live and work in the city. I do not think I am cut out for long-term collaboration. In this job, such long-term collaboration is rare—as difficult to maintain as a marriage. However, I strongly believe in short-term collaboration on specific projects, when such things are necessary. I am often called upon to work with other people on commercial or personal projects, and it is always interesting.

it introduced me, it shaped my way of working. Recently, I have moved back to Italy; I currently live in Turin. At present I work a lot with art and printing; but that was not a deliberate choice. I am not one for a planned life; I always say that I follow the stars.   **Tommaso Garner** I came in late. I earn enough to get by working as a graphic designer; over time I have learned a method, how to use the tools of the trade. This is my studio: my bag. With inside a computer and a mobile phone. I am sorry not to have seen a single image so far. Perhaps by showing a few images, I could give you a better idea of what I do.   **Di Lucente** I am from Rome, where I studied at a small private school in Trastevere: the Centro Studi Comunicazione. I was taught graphic design in a very professional manner, but without any encouragement of a critical spirit. After Rome I moved to London, mainly because there was no alternative. I was looking for a work environment and atmosphere, or for a group—something that I hadn't found in Rome. There is a film, *La Guerra degli Antò* [by Riccardo Milani], which tells the story of four punks from Abruzzi who live in a small provincial town outside Pescara, Montesilvano. One of them decides to go to Amsterdam. Accompanying him to the train station, one of the others says: "You've got real guts going to Amsterdam!" The other looks at him and says: "Well, it takes guts to stay in Montesilvano." I heard that a lot. Everyone was telling me that I had guts… even yesterday the taxi-driver—Eugenio, a Tuscan—who took me to Milan Central Station told me I had guts. But I think it is you who have the guts. However, I went to London and worked for three years in a studio. In 2007 I went to the Royal College of Art, which embodies my ideal model for design work: people from various disciplines working together. Julia—the studio I founded with two other guys, a Brazilian and a Frenchman, is located in a building where there are fashion designers, illustrators and photographers, so there is a constant exchange of ideas. What I was searching for in London is the same thing that you are creating in your cities. In England there is London. In Italy things are much more fragmented: Bergamo, Bari, Piacenza, Venice… like Joseph [Miceli] I, too, continually look towards Italy. However, there is a tangible difference here with respect to other countries. In the Netherlands, for example—which I take to be the exact opposite of Italy—there is a cultural and social context for our work; there are social and economic structures that support design and the visual arts. In Italy that is the real problem. I remember a distinction, which Pier Paolo Pasolini drew in his *Lettere luterane* between development and progress. In Italy there has been constant, yet somehow fake, progress in industry and in infrastructures, but what is missing is cultural development.   **FF3300** On the subject of guts; we had the guts to move back down south, to Bari. We are from Benevento [Carlotta], Foggia [Alessandro] and Bari [Nicolò], and we studied in Rome, in Urbino [ISIA] and in Venice at the University IUAV respectively. We had guts because in Bari there isn't a lot. In fact, there's nothing at all.   …

THE WORLD OF GRAPHIC DESIGN AND GRAPHIC DESIGN IN THE WORLD

Silvia Sfligiotti First of all, I have to say that I am one of those who is mixing things up—in the sense that for years I looked upon myself as a graphic designer, then a French magazine I work with presented me to its readers as a "critic." True, I have been writing about graphic design for years—but that writing is, for me, a necessary complement to the way I practice my profession. With regard to what graphic design is, I would like to quote what was said a few years ago by Stuart Bailey, founder of *Dot Dot Dot*: "Graphic design doesn't exist." From the way I see it, graphic design doesn't exist because, by definition, it is a profession that arose in response to something, then it is a profession built on dialogue. So, if we want to overcome the various dichotomies against which we still keep stumbling—dichotomies such as that between "design" and "art"—we have to acknowledge that, without some form of dialogue, graphic design, visual communication, does not exist. It seems to me that some of the most interesting things that have been happening in the field recently arose as responses of various kinds to the question, "Is there such a thing as graphic design or not?" On the one hand there is a tendency to a more "scientific" approach, returning as much as possible to very precise foundations for the profession; on the other, there is a striving for ever greater autonomy, which means that graphic designers increasingly become their own clients. This happens because we are cultural agents, and there are projects we want to—and have the means to—do. Don't forget that independence here is linked to one factor above all else: nowadays we are closer and closer to being able to control the entire process of design, production and distribution. Thus there are a number of ways in which we can perform our role. One of these is to give voice to—to render public—a specific content; to get things moving. A few years ago there were those who thought design could change the world; nowadays perhaps the idea is more that design can make things happen. In the past, attention was turned on the political role of design, but it is its social role that is emerging nowadays. But while one can witness a number of very interesting developments, our professional world is one that at times does not enter into dialogue with the world beyond itself. One sees the creation of niches that NICHES × perhaps only engage with each other. True, our niches are our world; but do these niches engage in dialogue with the outside world or do they only talk among themselves? I think that the problem is not so much one of engaging in dialogue with other design disciplines—architecture, product design, urban-planning—but of establishing a dialogue with the world. What is involved is intervention upon reality—even if it is increasingly likely that any such intervention on our part will be small-scale. So, with regard to what has already been said concerning independence and commercial design projects, I would say that we should not be ashamed of the latter—precisely because it is they which enable us to engage with, to measure ourselves against, existing reality. In short, mine is not a question but a series of considerations, which are perhaps provocative in intent.

Anceschi I, too, had intended to say a few things not on the worlds of graphic design but upon the theme of design in the world. However, as you know, I never manage to follow discipline, even when I apply it to myself—Angela THEORY × Vettese [contemporary art critic and historian] has described me as "the undisciplined Anceschi." In other words, this is not going to be a nice and neat academic introduction. I would, however, like to draw your attention to a few points. The first is a theoretical issue. There is a word that has so far not come up: "theory." "Theory" does not only refer to theoretical formulations. In philosophy there is the notion of "theoretical shift," which applies very well to our profession. For example, the engineer who designed the Walkman for Sony made an extraordinary theoretical shift: first there was no listening to music when one was on the move, then there was. So, I don't think we should be frightened by terms like "intellectual" and "theory." Far from it! Theory is part of the way we live our lives. It seems to me that it is present in everything you have been saying, even if not openly. Secondly, I would like to point out that the fundamental issue in our work nowadays is the question of its temporal dimension, and this, too, has emerged from what you have been saying, when talking about producing "actions" and "events." And related to this temporal dimension is a third aspect: the action of design requires the adoption of a certain mode of behavior. Nowadays the word "strategy" is very popular, I prefer the term "direction." Our reference model is no longer the figure of the painter or sculptor, of the producer of artifacts and objects. These products are simply the "props" for the events we actually have to deal with; they are complementary to what is the truly important thing: cultural and intellectual action, practical action, taking action. We are increasingly commissioned to design events, to manage the temporal. We are no longer dealing just with space but also with time… or, better, space-time. Finally, I would like to quote a great friend, Shutaro Mukai, who studied with me at Ulm and is now Professor Emeritus at the Musashino Art University in Tokyo. Shutaro has written a very interesting text about the "science of design,"[2] observing that the peculiarity of our specific discipline—design—is that it is undisciplined. That is, design must have the intellectual level and quality of science but it must also allow itself to be non-disciplined, in the sense that it does not bow down before power. This raises the issue of the multi-disciplinary quality of design, which also figures in what you have been saying: "We do our work and yet we involve other disciplines, other figures." As another great—and greatly undisciplined—figure, Otto Neurath, once said: "Lads, remember to make sure you change your job every five years. Otherwise, it becomes fake!" (I can't remember whether he said it or wrote it; it was Tomás Maldonado who told me the story.) I would like to end with the theme of the disciplinary barycenters. It is clear   x BARYCENTERS that we are in a situation where the boundaries between disciplines are being undermined in various ways; the idea of distinct and separate disciplines—typical of the modern—is gradually disappearing. And thus what I call "barycenters" come into play, a notion which helps us to examine and explain a lot of things. The new landscape before us is a single field, a single sea in continual movement; it is not subdivided into regions, but one does see arise within it certain stable and unmoving "antennae," which are the barycenters of the traditionally-recognized disciplines. This, too, is reflected in what you have been saying, and I think one should explore its implications.

Garner I am a graphic designer simply because it is a type of work that suits me: there is a tool, the computer, and there is software that allows me to carry out the necessary editing. I am doing exactly what I did when I started   x EDITING

2.   See *Another Proposal for the Science of Design: The Need for a New Design Education and Prospects for Related Issues*, www.ssdsj.net/eng/sym/doc0/SM02_K30.html.

Crea For me, graphic design is a very simple discipline in which two entities come together to convey a message. (Once upon a time people talked about "information," now they talk about "communication.") These two entities are, on the one hand, the client, who makes a specific request, and on the other the graphic designer, who uses his visual ability and his knowledge to give visible and sensorial form to the message that meets that initial request. Good graphic design is always the result of the encounter between a good graphic designer and an equally good client. As for my own world, there are two aspects to my manner of producing graphic design—but the aim is always the balanced equilibrium of "ecstatic truth," to quote a phrase that Werner Herzog used when commenting upon Akira Kurosawa's film *Rashomon*. This truth always depends upon the essence and simplicity of the message matching those of the image. In my work—primarily in the field of image creation and editorial design—I strive both to respond to a precise brief and, at the same time, to pursue my own exploration of graphic design itself, of the way we perceive such design. What interests me most is perception, how our ways of seeing change continually depending on social and cultural context.

off designing t-shirts. I used to be given a theme, which could be anything, then I would go on-line to find a font, an image, a random association. Then I would put the numerous pieces together using the computer, finally illustrating them manually to give the digital collage a more "analogical" look. It was totally pointless research, with no content at all. Obviously, it was very boring. I do not even know that it can be classed as graphic design. But I understood that the truly interesting thing about it all was collecting fragments from off the web. I began to do my own research; to scrape together a load of digital fragments, a load of images. Now what I do is fundamentally editing. I look upon my job as pointless; it is not something I boast about... What I do is look at the things all around me and interpret them. In my personal works I like to take an image and then massacre it, completely destroy it. I like looking at things that are perhaps generated within inward-looking niches. I am fascinated by the ambiguity of the non-representational image, without any apparent composition; created through repeated manipulation. **Anceschi** There! When you say "I have discovered CREATIVITY × that the important thing is to go and collect small fragments," that is your theoretical shift! Each of us does these things. In the past it was foolishly mistaken for "creativity." And please do not start talking about the "creative" disciplines, because the idea that one can "create" something is an ingenuous one; our job has always been that of transforming things. **Burtscher** Design is an instrument that serves us to establish a relation with the world. This also answers the question of niches, which Silvia [Sfligiotti] mentioned. We often strive to establish a relation with the region within which we live, with the people who live there, trying to produce possible answers to the questions raised by that particular context. In 2008, on the occasion of Manifesta 7, we invited four graphic designers to Bolzano and we asked them to come up with forms of expression and communication that responded to the themes posed by that area—social, political and cultural issues. Bolzano is in an interesting position, because it is where North and South converge. On that occasion Luna Maurer & Roel Wouters intervened in various parts of the city, proposing a number of simple instructions whose aim was to modify the daily habits of passers-by. Kasia Korczak and the **× PARTICIPATION** collective Slavs and Tatars came up instead with a public celebration of controversy, in deliberate contrast to the consensual approach so often urged by those in power; it was all based upon a re-reading of the Gershwin song *Let's Call the Whole Thing Off.* We are increasingly interested in how one is to get out of the niche and find new means of establishing relations with different sorts of context.   **Lupo** One could limit oneself to the definition of graphic design as the organization of content. But if we do not become aware of our role in society, then our approach will be very reductive. I would agree with Anceschi that we are involved in some sort of "directing," putting together and

> **Brave New Alps** For us, graphic design is one of the many tools that we have at our disposal. It is something we use when we work on a project of communication design—that is, when we are planning a complex communication process that focuses upon a specific situation or theme. Communication design as we envisage it involves much more than the visual; it is a means of exploring the world and creating relations. We are interested in the cultural import of design, in its ability to question, explore and mold the reality within which we live.   As for the responsibilities that go with design, we believe these are substantial: we cannot expect to act in this sphere without our actions having political implications. Each design project we work on shapes the world and our perception of that world. We firmly believe that every designer should adopt a questioning attitude to the reality within which he/she operates; should ask himself/herself what his/her own values are.

nurturing different types of ability in order to create content, to define how that content is then to be conveyed into the public domain. As for the barycenter, we believe that ours should be as low as possible. The decisive force here is the gravity exerted by the real world rather than by other disciplines; it comes from how we engage with reality and the world in which we live.   **Tankboys** To explain how we work, we would like to go back to what Silvia [Sfligiotti] said with regard to commercial work. We, in fact, try to take an active part in all so-called "commercial" works; we try to interpret what the client wants but also to help the clients to understand what they want to do. We try to carry out that work of editing to which Tommaso

Silvana Annicchiarico

Giorgio Camuffo

Giovann

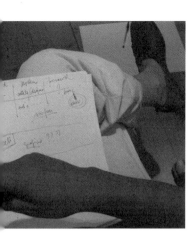

Damiano Gullì

Silvana Annicchiarico   Giorgio Camuffo   Giovanni Anceschi

Benedetta Crippa

CREDIA-
MO
NEL
POTERE
DELLE
IDEE,
DEL
METO-
DO,
E DELLA
CULTU-
RA

Lorenzo Mason   Marco Campardo

Fausto Giliberti   Guido Gregorio Damine

Giovanni Anceschi

Silvia Sfligiotti

Valerio Di Lucente

Tommaso Garner

Simone Bertuzzi

Francesco Valtolina

Simone Trabucchi

Nicolò Loprieno

Marco Fasolini

Daniele Lupo

Angelika Burtscher

Joseph Miceli

Alessandro Tartaglia

Carlotta Latessa

ITALIAN REFLECTIONS

[Garner] referred. It is a mental approach to our whole work, not just a practical matter. That is why we look upon ourselves as authors. We truly participate in each work we do; we take it so much to heart that we can get into heated arguments with some clients! This is partly why we always want to have other people—curators, copywriters, writers, illustrators, photographers, artists—working alongside us, because in editing we need to take various different points of view into account.   **FF3300** To explain our approach, we would like to show you three objects. But first a short introduction, which for us is important, which is our manifesto: "Communication is a question of design and language. We believe in the power of ideas, in method and in culture." Having said that, let us introduce the objects. I [Alessandro] brought little bricks because, in effect, we design systems. We are communication, we work with and upon processes. These little bricks can be used to construct designers, things by following specific rules, to link different pieces together, taking into account junctures, interactions, relations. Nicolò has brought a pair of glasses, as a quote from our teacher, Roberto Perris, who died this year. He taught us to see things through the lenses of design, to see objects as structures and structures as a combination of systems, to deconstruct, analyze and then design. Carlotta has brought a globe, her personal interpretation of a profession that arises out of continual curiosity. This job enables us to explore other worlds, other people's lives. It is something we could not do without. It means we never get bored. The question is: "Why must we be one specific person? Why can't I be a thousand different people?" Graphic design is a way of entering other worlds.   **Studio Temp** We would like to add something to what was said before, which we think was rather too academic in tone. Art, design—OK. But when it comes down to it, art is what BEAUTY × is in galleries, museums and institutions, and what the market decides that art is. So what are we talking about? As for the second point—what do we do exactly?—we have brought an object with us: it is a book that is also a teddy bear. Have you ever seen anything so beautiful? There has been talk here about what graphic design might be—exercising a profession? Applying a method? Being an artist to some extent? Looking around one? Well, this book sums it all up. There is form, typography… and it is really beautiful. OK, we are intellectuals, and there is a lot of philosophy behind the words one uses, a lot of thinking. But, in the end, there has to be something that makes us say a thing is beautiful. Perhaps more or less useful, more or less to the point, more or less fashionable—one can debate all that. But everything we have said—the

118

way in which each one of us works, our professional experience—produces our sense of taste. Knowing something about architecture and art, being in part artists, architects, product designers, painters, sociologists, politicians, etc.—all of this goes towards creating Beauty, with a capital B. In the sense that all of this makes us capable of seeing Beauty. **Tankboys** Perhaps what we call "beautiful" or "good" is what remains, what becomes sedimented: relations, connections… **Miceli** It appears to me that we are the sort of people who use certain techniques in their work, who are conscious and aware of certain processes. In this sense, rather than transmitting our idea of Beauty to others, I think it would be more useful to transmit interest in the process itself, because it is that which can perhaps be applied in other worlds and contexts. **FF3300** We believe that one should talk about × USEFULNESS usefulness rather than beauty. Conveying information is what we are about— for example, knowing how to use infographics to explain things. **Studio Temp** Perhaps we didn't explain ourselves very well. When we used the term "beautiful" it wasn't synonymous with "cool." If a thing is beautiful, it is a whole load of things: useful, beautiful, to the point… In this sense, the job of the graphic designer is both important and difficult, because knowing how to do it well means knowing how to do a lot of different things. And if you do not know how to do it well, you involve other people. **FF3300** In our opinion there is one very important thing that no one has mentioned yet—and that is that our work is one which bears an enormous respon- × RESPONSIBILITY sibility: we work with information, and information is the basis of all varieties of knowledge. The problem arises when we do not communicate infor-

Crea I do not think that graphic designers are particular in that they bear enormous social and political responsibilities—the sort of claim previous generations of designers used to make. Graphic design is nothing but a pixel in the complex JPG that makes up the image of our reality. However, like any other profession, we can make a difference by stimulating curiosity, stimulating the minds that receive our messages. Our role has changed radically in recent years. Technology now allows anyone to become a "weekend graphic designer"… But what still sets us professionals apart is our cultural knowledge of the use of images and the written word. This is why I see my artistic/cultural contribution as connected with a commercial contribution, not the other way around.

mation but "fake" it—we are quoting Marc Augé here. The true problem in our society, and not just within graphic design, is that fiction has replaced the collective imagery. We have to find space for the recovery of dreams. If we do not change the way we are going, then there is the risk that we will end up in a world that is worse than the one we are in now. **Invernomuto** We were very pleased to be able to take part in *Graphic Design Worlds*, in the first place because of the presence of that word "worlds" in the title. We have come here from various exhibitions and it strikes us that various terms are repeatedly abused—for example, "imagination," "archive." Here, though, the good thing is that we are all talking about the same thing but in different ways; we are getting back to that upon which we actually work—that is, the shared imagination, understood as the creation of worlds. That is what we see being done by the graphic designers we know—primarily Tankboys, Studio Temp and Tommaso [Garner]. The fact is that they have a world "behind" them, a world to which I can gain access through their designs. That is what interests us most: there is research here, and one can see there is—in everything, from the simplest thing they produce to those which are most personal to them. What we see is a specific attitude to design. **Valtolina** Here we are, telling each other the way things are. We have been talking about the types of design in which we are involved, which often however—it **INWARD-LOOKING** × seems to me—have a serious limit: they form an inward-looking circuit. I often wonder about the need for what we do. Are we pursuing this sort of research solely to show our results to those who are also engaged in its pursuit? True, everything we have been saying may be interesting; but we have to move beyond these walls. So, the exhibition *Graphic Design Worlds* could be an important occasion to raise reflections beyond the field. At the same time, it is very important that our work not be enclosed within the space of the museum; we must create a more open and extensive platform for communication. I think this is one of the goals we can set ourselves. **Sfligiotti** On the theme of recognition, of our profession's "visibility," I would like to add that I do not think it is that important we should be **RECOGNITION** × recognized as "designers." Without denying anything that has been said so far with regard to the instruments and tools at our disposal, I would point out that these are always instruments that relate to the world at large. A little while ago I was in the Milan Metro and there was a map of the entire system above which someone had written: "I can't make any of this out. Fucking graphic designer!" I thought: Finally, our profession has been acknowledged! The person who wrote that realized that there was someone working on that design, and that he could do a good or bad job of it. If a person can complain about something, it means that he can also expect something better. And that can only be good for us. **Di Lucente** My approach to graphic design is very simple. I do this job because it is a good excuse for doing the things that interest me, while maintaining the sort of distance that enables me to quit when I want or get closer and more involved when I want; to be in contact with other people. It seems to me that for many of us graphic design was a means of getting closer to the things that interest us, to explore. Graphic design is an instrument for mediation, and the graphic designer works as a mediator.   ...

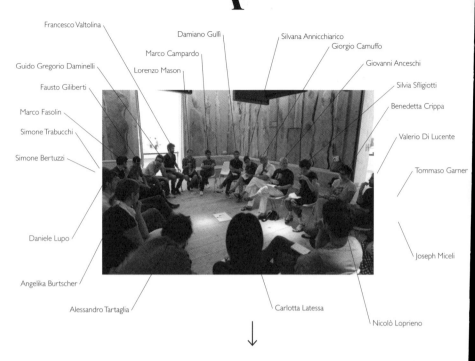

Francesco Valtolina
Damiano Gulì
Silvana Annicchiarico
Giorgio Camuffo
Marco Campardo
Guido Gregorio Daminelli
Lorenzo Mason
Giovanni Anceschi
Fausto Giliberti
Silvia Sfligiotti
Marco Fasolin
Benedetta Crippa
Simone Trabucchi
Simone Bertuzzi
Valerio Di Lucente
Tommaso Garner
Daniele Lupo
Joseph Miceli
Angelika Burtscher
Alessandro Tartaglia
Carlotta Latessa
Nicolò Loprieno

↓

HOW WE WERE TAUGHT
GRAPHIC DESIGN?

↙   ↖

WHICH IS THE FORM OF   *EDUCATING*   HAVING JUDGMENT
GRAPHIC DESIGN?   ABILITY

↓   ↘   ↗

THE IMPORTANCE   CONVEYING
OF DEFINITIONS   JUDGMENT ABILITY

↓   ↙

CRITICAL AND
SELF-CRITICAL THINKING

∞

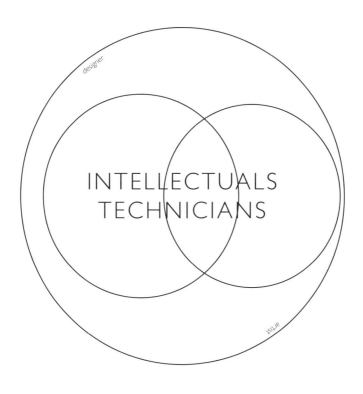

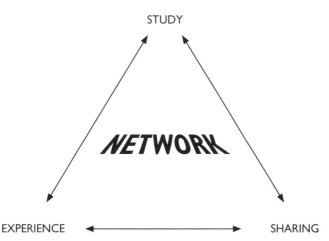

"DESIGN *AND ART*"

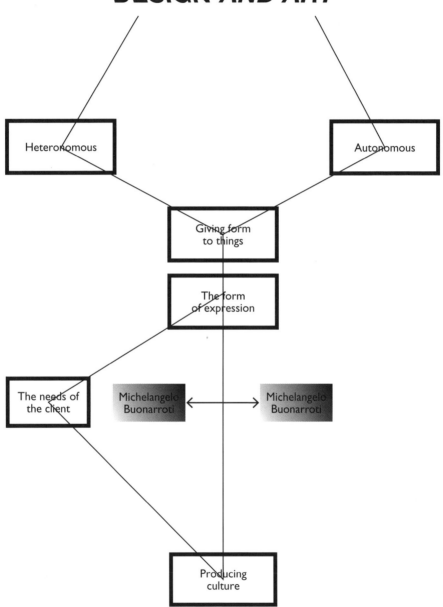

Heteronomous

Autonomous

Giving form
to things

The form
of expression

The needs of
the client

Michelangelo
Buonarroti ⟷ Michelangelo
Buonarroti

Producing
culture

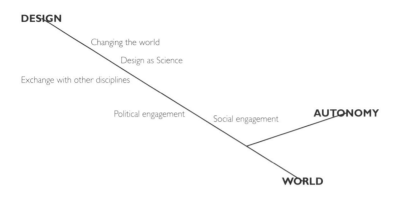

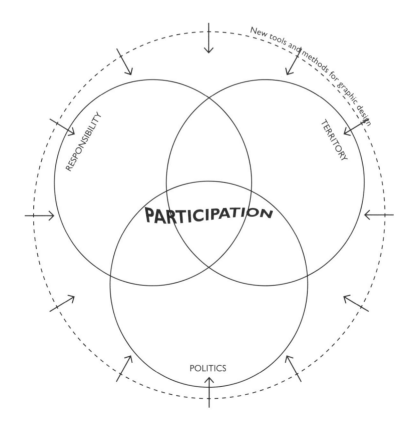

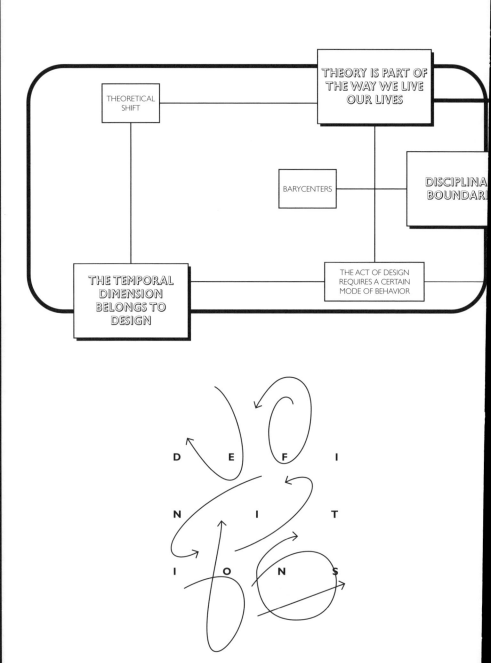

THEORETICAL SHIFT

THEORY IS PART OF THE WAY WE LIVE OUR LIVES

BARYCENTERS

DISCIPLINA BOUNDARI

THE TEMPORAL DIMENSION BELONGS TO DESIGN

THE ACT OF DESIGN REQUIRES A CERTAIN MODE OF BEHAVIOR

D E F I
N I T
I O N S

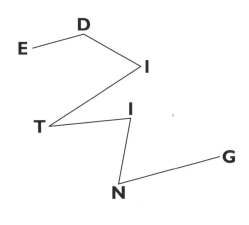

RECTION

N PRODUCES
S AND EVENTS

Theoretical Shift

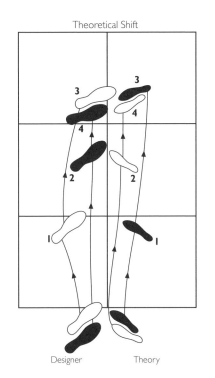

Designer   Theory

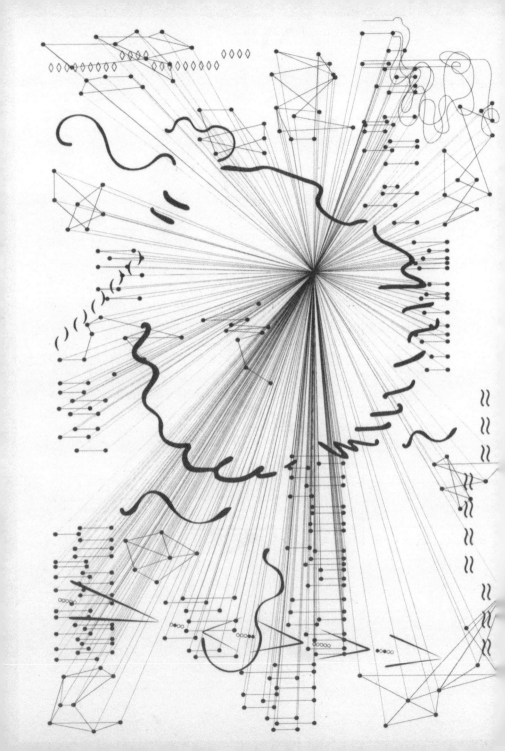

BENEDETTA CRIPPA

Over the past few months I have had the chance to take part in putting together *Graphic Design Worlds*, following the event as it gradually took form. Involving engagement with and exploration of a variety of different "worlds," this is an exhibition which has cast light on a number of important aspects of the Italian landscape.

Telling, revealing, interpreting stories

In 1968, when the youth protest movement was at its height, the poet Muriel Rukeyser wrote: "The world is made of stories, not atoms."[1] For me, this phrase encapsulates perfectly one of the peculiarities of graphic design, a discipline which has always been closely bound up with the world and its stories; which is still in a very privileged position when it comes to the development, interpretation and narration of the stories and imaginations that now seem to spread through the world at the speed of light.

It is no coincidence that in the last few years the practice of graphic design has often been associated with terms that relate specifically to the action of story-telling. Nowadays, designers like to see themselves as "mediators," "translators," who act upon reality in order to establish connections between different systems and contexts. It is only apparently contradictory that the explicit taking up of such roles goes together with an ever increasing reluctance to be confined within clear-cut definitions. This phenomenon has existed for some time abroad and is now beginning to make itself felt in Italy, taking on characteristic forms and opening up specific directions.

---

1. M. Rukeyser, *The Speed of Darkness*, Random House, New York 1968.

If every design project is a story—that is, the visible part of "another" story—it is also made up of a variety of stories and paths, which mould it and determine the direction in which it unfolds. It is interesting to note how—undoubtedly encouraged by the idea of "worlds" that is at the core of *Graphic Design Worlds*—various designers have chosen for the exhibition to focus upon that kind of stories, each in his/her own specific way: experiences and encounters, work processes and courses of developments, as well as personal vocation, cultural background and the influence upon the imagination of individual experience. So, for example, Joseph Miceli chooses to share his passion for hip-hop music, FF3300 take the spectator "behind the scenes" and describe their own work methods, while Tommaso Garner "un-veils" a range of images put together over years of research. Each of these examples reveals how individual stories not only have a professional influence within the discipline itself but also take on new value as revealing that point where an initial spark can generate a flame.

Networks and Movements

Growing interest in the processes of design is undoubtedly encouraged by the technological evolutions which are such a feature of the world we live in—a world which one of the greatest of contemporary sociologists has defined as "the network society."[2] The web has made it possible to establish networks of relations which would have been unthinkable twenty years ago: it has never been so easy to ask the opinion of someone who may be thousands of miles away, to send and receive data, ideas, suggestions. Furthermore, travel itself is becoming ever easier and taking ever less time—and this is a condition which young designers have learnt to turn into opportunity. As emerged from the meeting at the Triennale Design Museum, designers themselves see part of the fundamental importance of the contemporary design as lying in the relations established during its construction, the energies it draws upon; think, for example, of Invernomuto, who see graphic design as an opportunity to establish connections. In effect, what designers see in design is a means of creating worlds. Thus the exhibition itself focuses primarily upon the relations that the basic process of design can generate and consolidate; an eloquent example of this is Studio Temp's decision to recount the tiny universe generated by their various years of collaboration with a single printer.

2. M. Castells, *The Network Society*, Blackwell 2000.

(Let yourself get) "Contaminated"
Relations change, (the sense of) time moves on, and one's very relation to space itself also appears to be changing. As it facilitates connections with others, the web generates a sort of virtual ubiquity; one is always available, always able to intervene—even if in a partial manner—in contexts that can be very different to one's own in both geographical and cultural terms. Hence one no longer has to remain within what have always been recognized as the "centers" of Italian design and creativity if one wants to remain connected to the main sources of energy, if one wants to exist in a network of stimulating relationships. It is interesting to note the number of Italian designers in this exhibition who have chosen to live and work in the places where they grew up. Such places are thus re-read and re-interpreted by these very figures, becoming the object of an approach to design that draws upon the designer's surroundings and also intervenes upon them. This leads to design projects that are focused upon a specific territory, and are intimately bound upon with the multiple layers and stories that make up the weave of everyday life. Angelika Burtscher and Daniele Lupo, for example, have chosen to open a gallery—a sort of cultural center—in Bolzano, in a courageous attempt to invert the mechanism of osmosis which would instead generate a flow of talent and energy away from such settings. Similarly, the designers at Tankboys grew up and studied in Venice and have now chosen to live and work in this city, motivated to do so by a firm desire to play an active role within their own environment. As for Bianca Elzenbaumer and Fabio Franz—whose very choice of the name Brave New Alps underlines their place in a specific cultural and geographical setting—they intervene upon a variety of contexts and yet have brought to this exhibition a reflection upon the social and historical world to which they belong.

All of these aspects—and the various complexities they raise—are still translated into the kind of objects that are specific to graphic design. They are to be understood by leafing through books, unfolding posters, seeing how different materials and multi-dimensional spaces are interpreted. However, above all, what one must bring to bear here is the ability to read the stories which enable design to exploit the full potential of the processes it involves. Today, graphic design is the most sensitive interpreter of its own—and other—stories, opening up approaches towards a point of arrival which is itself an opportunity for new forms of interaction.

THE WORLDS OF GRAPHIC DESIGNERS

Achille Castiglioni demonstrating to students
of IUAV Architecture Institute University of Venice,
with Sergio Polano (video image still), 1997

Åbäke met Sergio Polano on
the steps of Venice railway station
on a mid-September morning for a
day trip to the museum of Type.

Benjamin: Recording...

Sergio: ...There is something that I have to tell you... I'm doubtful about what we should do, because words turn into speeches but writing only generates text: two intimately different matters. What you will get at the end of our talk for the exhibition will be a translation: a text instead of a talk; and you know how much is lost in translation... It's like, you know...

Benjamin: But maybe we should have directions, like in a theatre script

Sergio: ... It's happening! [Laughs]

Benjamin & Patrick: [Laughs]

Benjamin: So, maybe we should start describing the space then? We are in a workshop... which is very quiet. It's a letterpress workshop in Cornuda called Tipoteca. an archive of type, which has been collected by a printing press! (Grafiche Antiga) As a "working museum"... So it's not only a museum but also a workshop.

Patrick: And at the same moment Fabio and Bianca (Brave New Alps) are making posters... to emphasize that point.

Benjamin: Let's begin at the beginning... I mean, our introduction to this particular place was part of the workshop we did last year at IUAV. And that's the first print we've made here together with students

Daniela Venturini and Irene Bacchi. It's all the marks that have been collected by the museum from printing presses that closed down—of the Venetian lion.

Sergio: Yes... It was also on the IUAV seal once.

Benjamin: The police, everybody's there. And something we were drawn to is the lion holding a book in its paw; if the Republic of Venice was at peace, the book was shown open, if at war, the book was closed. And we thought that was an amazing kind of sign for a state to use.

Sergio: The symbolism of the lion of Saint Mark with the sword and the book comes from an ancient Venetian tradition, according to which an angel, in the form of a winged lion, would have said to the Saint, shipwrecked in the lagoons, "Pax tibi Marce, evangelista meus. Hic requiescat corpus tuum,

Detail from Tipoteca Italiana's cliche collection of the Saint Mark's Lion

announcing that in those lands he would one day find rest and worship for his body. The book, often mistakenly associated with the Gospel, repeats these words of welcome and, in most representations, is usually open bearing the Latin words "pax tibi marco evangelista mevs." The sword, in addition to the meaning of strength, is also a symbol of justice. Therefore all of the characters with which Venice likes to think and to describe herself are symbolically shown: majesty, power, wisdom, justice, peace, military power and religious piety. There are many symbolic interpretations about any combination of sword and book: the open book a symbol of state sovereignty; the closed book, however, a symbol of delegated sovereignty; the open book (the sword on the ground is not visible) is popularly considered as a symbol of peace for the State of Venice, but this is not corroborated by any historical source; closed book and sword erroneously seen as a symbol of the state of war. However, these interpretations are not universally accepted, as the Serenissima never codified its symbols. But, uh, those lions... There is... You know the trademark of Venice?

Benjamin: The Venetian identity?

Sergio: Well, a marketing identity. The City of Venice has created the trademark of Venice—designed by Thibaut Mathieu, art direction by Philippe Starck—, "an identifying symbol whose use is granted to its partners and whose proceeds are earmarked to improving the quality

of life of Venetian citizens and protecting the city heritage." ... Yes, so it has been said and what has been done—a disaster, in my opinion—you may find easily online... There is a kind of bold V for Venice and the lion on it came from Place de la Concorde, and it is...

Benjamin: What's the difference? It's much more muscular, no? The Concorde lion... Has the identity been implemented?

Sergio: Have a look... It's a masterwork

Trademark for Venice by Thibaut Mathieu / Cake Design, art direction by Philippe Starck, 2003, and "Angels in America" logo by Milton Glaser

Patrick: You know the story about Saint Theodore? Or... You know, the opposite column. Where you have... Saint Mark's Lion... and then you have the guy who's kind of... Standing on a crocodile.

Sergio: Yeah.

Patrick: And that was apparently the original identity for Venice, wasn't it? He was the original saint before Saint Mark was stolen from Constantinople...

Sergio: On the column on the side of the Palazzo Ducale stands the winged lion of Saint Mark's. This is a very old bronze statue, probably originally a chimera, to which wings were subsequently added. On the side of the Library, however, stands San Teodoro, a Byzantine saint and warrior, the first patron of the city, killing the dragon. ... The lion has been used for... As a silhouette for the Biennale... The trademark of tthe Biennale.

Patrick: That was Enrico Camplani?

Sergio: Camplani and his partner Pescolderung, Tapiro design office, yes.

Benjamin: That is an homage to that lion.

Everyone: [Laughs]

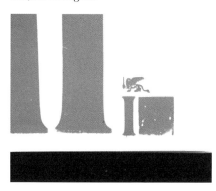

Detail from cover of CATALOGHI

Benjamin: That is the cover of a catalogue for a project we set up together with the students of IUAV, a comprehensive catalogue of the Biennale... The Art Biennale.

Sergio: A-ha.

Benjamin: So, a small group of students attempted to visit all the pavilions

of the Biennale on Wednesday (their day off) and collected all the free material, which has been reproduced in this catalogue alphabetically.

Sergio: Hm! [Laughs]

Patrick: It was an attempt to see all of the shows in the Biennale, something that would ordinarily be impossible. So this is a souvenir and also the motivation to gather these materials which... In the end they represent the countries participating. Some of them are really well done, there's a lot of care taken over the typography or... those things. And others are just very bureaucratic, or maybe a little bit unloved.

Collected and designed with Irene Bacchi, Riccardo Berrone, Luca Coppola, Irina Righes, Daniela Venturini & Alex Rich. With thanks to Sandro and Daniele at Tipoteca

Sergio: I did a video about that last Biennale... Ten minutes in the Biennale—I think in ten minutes you will receive everything. But once, online, I collected all identities of Italian state ministries and public institutions.

Patrick: Really?

Sergio: Mm... Have a look online.

Patrick: Can't wait to see that...

Everyone: [Laughs]

Benjamin: There is also a story that italic got invented in Venice...

Sergio: Italy?

Benjamin: Italic...

Sergio: Ah!

Benjamin: ...The character

Sergio: It's true... Well, in typography, by Aldo Manuzio, in 1500, and cut by Francesco Griffo aka Francesco da Bologna (a dangerous guy, since in 1516, after he returned to Bologna, he was charged with the murder of his son-in-law, who had been beaten to death with an iron rod).

Benjamin: Sì.

Sergio: It was the cursive handwriting, translated into the lead by the punch. For economy in the beginning, to print little books and with less paper, less ink. They were printed all in italic; the mixing of roman and italic happened later. And as far as I remember, he cut only the lowercase letters, using roman for the uppercase.

Benjamin: Are there some specimens in this museum? The originals?

Valerius Maximus, 1514. Printed by Aldus Manutius.
Courtesy Saint Martin's Archive

Sergio: There are no surviving Griffo punches. Novarese, for one of his typefaces, cut the letters in the same way: lowercase italic... uppercase roman.

Benjamin: So it was an economical decision?

Sergio: Yes, it was economical; it enabled Manuzio to print smaller books. In the same way as for Gill Joanna type. If you use the italic, it's so narrow.

Patrick: But earlier on you were talking about the choice of a typeface being political or having social implications. Like the distinction between Bodoni and Didot. Didot is affiliated with the revolution... And Bodoni has aristocratic associations?

Sergio: An ideological choice. But I think one should care more about whether it fits or not, but what does "fitting" mean? You have to decide.

Benjamin: Maybe that's an example.

This poster is related to that workshop we did with the IUAV students. It was designed with Irene Bacchi and Murano Tipografi, one of the last letterpress printers in Venice...

Sergio: Once upon a time, all posters were like this, in the streets... [Laughs]

Benjamin: Exactly. But they're still producing those posters for the church and so on. The basis of the workshop was that every student had to find a master for the duration of the project (two and a half months). They had to work with this master and to learn his skills. For the duration of that project they would devise their own project together with that master. So it was based on apprenticeship and a multitude of different specialists.
There were bicycle companies, boat makers, chefs, vaporetto drivers, glassblowers and so on. One of those specialists was the printer; when we asked him to print the poster what came out quite quickly was that... Because it was a different language; then they didn't have the right amount of letters. And obviously in the Italian alphabet the "k" is missing. So when typesetting the poster he suddenly realized "No! I'm not gonna have enough 'k's'"...

Sergio: [Laughs]

Benjamin: Because, of course,

Poster advertising one day exhibition at Querini Stampalia Foundation in Venice. Printed by Irene Bacchi and Tipografia Murano

on this poster there are a lot of "makers" and so on... So, in a way, the missing letters became a typographical choice. We had to just do the letter count... And whichever letter we had enough of would be the choice of typography.

Sergio: To have briefs and limits, that's a good starting point to design. If someone asks you "I would like you to design my house." Then you say "Where?...," [Shrugs], "How big?," [Shrugs], "How much money?"... "Dunno."...

Everyone: [Laughs]

Sergio: "Do what you want, you're free!" The best condition for design is to struggle against and within limits: this is freedom.

...

Sergio: You have a collective name (Åbäke), and your strategy is interesting, because with such an uncommon, even graphically, name, you slow down the reading, and so you require more attention. In Roman public epigraphs, wide spacing and no punctuation compels a kind of deciphering ... in a different way, you are slowing down the act of reading, no? And how to pronounce it? ... A way to become me-mo-ra-ble... You know?

Benjamin: ...I always have the feeling that I pronounce some English words wrong... So you always repeat it three times, you know, like, till someone corrects you. It's not a question of memory it's more like... Already before saying the word you know you're wrong— you don't trust yourself.

Sergio: [Laughs] In the tube, asking for a destination, I always get "What?"...

Everyone: [Laughs]

Sergio: [Laughs]... Never... "Ah, you mean Covent Garden!"... "Yes, going there"...

Patrick: Loughborough

Sergio: Maybe...

Benjamin: Leicester Square is the hardest one...

Sergio: Perhaps they know the slang of London better ...

Patrick: Cockney?

Sergio: Cockney! Yes, you know... They speak cockney... And I don't speak cockney... I'm from Italy... I'm a foreigner—plz, speak English for foreigners.

Benjamin: Accents, we were talking

earlier about accents—how they're part of your identity, in a way...

Sergio: Stronger in the countries where vowels often have accents, and have a meaning. Say "è or é" —it's different. Open or closed, you know. Are there such problems in English?

Benjamin: It absorbs, English is a language which absorbs very well.

Sergio: No, I mean, if you say "Pèsca or Pésca"—in Italy it means different things because of the accent. In English does this problem exist? No! It doesn't... There is no problem with accents...

Benjamin: Not for me... [Laughs]

Everyone: [Laughs]

Benjamin: You'll have to ask Patrick...

Patrick: Anthony Burgess talks about how English should be written in phonetics—because there are so many possible interpretations. I'm from the north and we say "Bath" but in the south of England they say "Barth"... So you extend the "a." But, there are no rules. These kind of things are quite permissive... As a language I think. Which is probably why it's successful, that it will absorb anything and change and mutate...

Sergio: Yes, but... There's no problem with the accent on the vowels. I know that there have been arguments about phonetic transcription of English and not only Burgess. But the problem, we were talking before with the accent is that you change the meaning of words in Italian. You have the perception of sound. It is true that Italy is the "opera country" but somewhere people are more sensitive to it, and in other places not at all—in Veneto it's difficult to find people who will hear the difference between "Pèsca/Pésca"—no... problem in accent. the form of the letters is connected on one side with our kind of alphabet it is more or less related to the sound. The other parts of world where is not connected with sound, I think. Maybe there's... China. There's no connection with... Is more connected with the form... Meaning of the form.

Patrick: We were talking earlier about how, in a way, you could look at Novarese and say he provides a visual accent for Italy, and then the same for Eric Gill.

Sergio: It's very British...

Patrick: You wonder which one comes first. We did a project in Milan with the British Council producing a daily pamphlet on the design fair. We wanted to introduce the idea of nationality in quite a benign way, so, the first day we made this publication using Gill. The next day we made a mix of Gill and Novarese... "Stopped" Gill Ultra Bold, a transitional typeface as we were becoming more Italian.

The Incidental. four issues designed, edited and produced over five days of the Milan Furniture Fair 2009

You were saying that you digitized a Novarese typeface?

Sergio: Yes, we digitized (Michela Scibilia, my partner in our Lapiswerk office then, and I), under his supervision and with his approval, a Novarese type— that we presented as a teamwork for an international competition ... lost! Our desire was to help him in the digital realm, and share a type design with him [Laughs]

Benjamin: What was it called? The typeface...

Sergio: It was one of the typefaces he was developing at that time, the beginning of the 1990s. He decided to give it a name just for the competition: "Regista", that means Director.

Patrick: Do you think we could use it for the publication?

Sergio: Oh, yes... It happened many years ago. As far as I remember, another of his fonts is similar.

But Regista has never been used for print, and we never gave it to anyone—Novarese died shortly after, and since then Regista has been kept safe, and concealed, in memory of a friend, let's say.

Now it's time to disclose it, to honor Novarese. It's only in the list that I published in emigre magazine in 1993: 7 letters, Regista.

Regista's first and only appearance in "Emigre" magazine, 1993, no. 26 accompanying the article "Aldo Novarese: Letters Are Things" by Sergio Polano, with the help of Pierpaolo Vetta

[Dog Barking]

Patrick: We like the idea of you turning up on Novarese's doorstep in the late 1980s, an architect-teacher-writer teaching himself, fontographer, to realize the final masterpiece! We were talking earlier about the limitations of graphic design now, and how with a show about graphic design the inherent problems of representing representation, that maybe graphic design wasn't meant to be in a gallery, and... we're trying to find ways in which to generate content (which is really what the workshop was about). And which I suppose we're doing now.

Benjamin: But it's also... It's also generating content and new relationships, I mean, exactly as you were describing just knocking on the door.

Sergio: Mm... Just knocking on the door! About the exhibition... I refused to know anything about you to have, you know, a starting point completely... clean, in a way. But Giorgio [Camuffo] urged me to see some images of the exhibition... We had a discussion about that. And what I saw were kind of installations: they show themselves, not something else.

Benjamin: Mm?

Sergio: One point of advantage for the graphic designer, in that case, different from an architecture exhibition. The architect has to show something that is not there... No? The object is missing, because the building can't be there, it is somewhere far away. So he should have models, and drawings, photos, video or other media. Instead, the graphic designer (working with ink and paper—and monitor) has to do with a matter that's easier to show, that could be there.

Benjamin: But in the meantime it's the same! It is exactly the same problematic—that this event is long gone. It was last year and so what we're talking about is just a printed piece of paper, the content might have disappeared. And it's valid for quite a lot of graphic design material which is associated to remote content. In that sense it sort of relates to that kind of architecture. Architecture is now more into conversation, the content of an architecture exhibition is now more about dialogue than shape. This summer we started a project in Helsinki with the Museum of Finnish Architecture, which sounds like a big institution but they have very few visitors...

Sergio: Is Timo Keinanen still there?

Benjamin: No—there's a new director Juulia Kauste. We started researching their archives with artist Nene Tsuboi and proposed that they work on this idea of the missing element. We did research on all the lost competitions. The lost entries for competitions and talked about this painting by Sir John Soane, who is there, in the corner down here among all his unbuilt projects.

"Perspective of various designs for Soane's public and private buildings", watercolor by Joseph Michael Gandy, 1818

This is probably common to most architects—to not build rather than to actually build. We suggested the museum to use the models as

a discussion tool for the Finnish architects' community. That is, a version of Helsinki. There is all the existing infrastructure of the city but... alternative versions. Now the project is to have a room in their permanent installation which would be dedicated to...

"Unbuilt Helsinki", Åbäke & Nene Tsuboi. Courtesy Museum of Finnish Architecture

Sergio: Unbuilt...

Benjamin: Unbuilt Helsinki, yes...

Sergio: Designing an exhibition of architecture is always a drama for that reason, you know. But, let's say... If you have something to say, then you may talk or write. If you have nothing to say, silence is still the best solution. [Laughs]

Everyone: [Laughs]

Benjamin: You mentioned the Object Lessons—we visited Castiglioni's studio yesterday. There's a big vitrine of objects which he collected and they actually come to life when he talks about them with students...

Sergio: But also for himself! That

Reflection of the vitrine at Studio Museum Achille Castiglioni. Courtesy Triennale di Milano

collection arose from his love for objects, but it was also a research tool, as every work of design should require research, knowledge of the past, the history of objects.

Benjamin: What was noticeable with this collection of objects was that they were just piled up in a cabinet (ready to be activated?) like the props of a play...

Sergio: Yes.

Benjamin: ... or film than studied objects, I don't know how to say it but... There were like a lot of those really round glasses and... [Laughs]

Sergio: Ah... Yes! ... [Laughs]

Benjamin: ...Very exaggerated

Sergio: He was shy about speaking in public so he often began with something funny, making people laugh...

Patrick: Yes, props again.

Sergio: Yes...

Patrick: This idea of celebrating the banal ... yesterday we went to the Boschi di Stefano House, an art collection in Milan. It was the home of a couple who supported Italian artists of the early and mid 20th century. The walls are packed with paintings, but in one room there's a cabinet filled with small sculptures and ceramics; there's a Manzoni egg with a thumbprint next to a small painting, next to sculptures by Fontana. And then among these artworks there's a small, highly polished brass object. It's an award for Antonio Boschi, and it's the one thing that comes from him. It's a coupling for two train carriages... which is still in production today... and made him wealthy enough to acquire the works around it. You never see it because it's always hidden, working. But then it's a really lovely thing, and it fits in so well with all those other objects and I suppose it's not an accident that he put it next to the other art pieces ...

Giunto Boschi, Nineteen Sixties, gilt metal, 8x8x5 cm, Milan, Museum-Home Boschi Di Stefano

Sergio: Absolutely not! This is the "uncommon beauty of common things" as were saying the Eames... Useful things are so common we don't see them... No, you have to show, to exhibit them for them to be perceived, taking them out of their context. You may make them appear... and focus attention on them...

Castiglioni's talk to students at IUAV, 1997

Patrick: So is that why you invited Castiglioni to do a performance at the school?

Sergio: It was so funny, everybody would like to have him visit, and I also asked him to design two things for the school. One was an idea for an architectural museum, later aborted and also the furniture for the faculty Council room... [Laughs] The designs were rejected... The Castiglioni brothers always had a kind of irony mixed in with humour in their objects. There is no real need to design almost anything, because everything has already been designed. Are you able to do a new kind of hammer? Hm... Difficult. [Laughs] But materials change! That's true, new kinds of materials. And the Castiglioni were also part of the Italian tradition: our designers came from architectural faculties or were self-taught. Sometimes

invention is simply connecting seemingly unrelated things. There is also a component of joke in that...

Benjamin: But to go back to the Tojo lamp, making connections, which are seemingly unrelated...

Sergio: Same with Gutenberg...

Benjamin: Gutenberg was... Was he funny?

Daniele setting the cover of CATALOGHI at Tipoteca Italiana in Cornuda, Italy, June 2009

Sergio: I don't think he was so funny [Laughs] himself. But he put together completely different technologies. Very stable, no? We've been printing this way until yesterday and now it seems that memory is completely lost. Type is something heavy, you have to open the drawers...

Benjamin: It goes back to the idea of being a specialist.

Sergio: I fear the specialist... [Laughs] But not specificity of thinking...

Benjamin: But with a comprehensive vision, no? That's something we're quite interested in bringing here, a project we're hoping to follow up. It was a collaboration with a glassblower in Finland. We worked with a glassblower on an alphabet in one of iittala's factories. They produce very functional glassware but they also produce glass birds which are seemingly very ugly... a collection of...

Sergio: [Laughs]

Benjamin: ...Of strange glass. The origin of those glass birds was a hobby for the glassblowers, something on the side of this functional glassware. But for many years it's been part of the production line so they don't have a hobby anymore. We were trying to reintegrate a hobby in the work line... the alphabet came from the idea that everyone knows what letters should look like. So if a glassblower could get involved in the process of thinking how the glass letters should look, this could generate new forms. We were really more interested in the process than the product. The approach to typography, through the eye of a glassblower was a completely different process, which is made in one minute—because it's hot.

Rayograph of individual letters in the glass alphabet

Sergio: Yes

Benjamin: Then it has to cool down for five hours, so you can't really look at it even once it's done. It's a making process more than a designing process and we had to find a common language and that was really difficult. The first thing we said was how we would like it to be—to set boundaries and create rules. We said it had to be blown and not poured, it had to be a serif font, and it had to be self-standing. So her first reaction was to say "No!"...

Sergio: [Laughs]

Benjamin: And then we started talking. And eventually we came to an agreement, a kind of have common language. For example the serif became this sort of coin, which is attached to the stick. Which has to be broken when you get rid of the object. But once glued, or attached the coin, then, in a way the letter becomes... The object becomes self-finished—you don't need to

Rejected iittala Bird's. Nuutajärvi factory, 2008

polish or to grind it afterwards...
And that's something, which
glassblowers are really keen
on—to finish the object hot.
And the shapes, which are solely
glassblowing shapes... Which...
don't have any application... This
one is called the ring of Saturn,
which is a beautiful process. When
it's made, it really looks like, well,
Saturn but it makes a perfect "O"...
Or this was her inspiration, the "Q"
with the tail... It was a way to fill
the broken part of the object

Sergio: [Laughs]

Benjamin: That M was also another
impossible object to make because
it wouldn't fit back into the Kiln, so
she had to make it in two parts...
And they would embrace in the
middle, kind of... With little hooks.

Sergio: They don't look anything...
like letters.

Patrick: [Laughs]
Sergio: So, everything may look like
a letter at the end, no?

Benjamin: Of course

Sergio: So, you said you only use the
uppercase letters? Because the
lowercase are very difficult...

Benjamin: That's the next stage, we
wanted to bring this process to
Murano to see what it would be
like. They have fundamentally
different methods from the ones
used in Finland... we'll probably do
the lowercase in Murano.

View from window of Vetreria Artistica Galliano Ferro,
Murano, September 2010

Sergio: What I was trying to say is
that we inherited the uppercase
from the Romans and the
Romans were the first to make
letters walking on a line—Greek
letters don't walk like that.
And lowercase don't walk at all.
So, since you are doing 3D things
that should stand, the uppercase
fit better.
They are born self-standing.
But the... Q is always a problem,
it is born with a long queue...

Thanks to Daniela Venturini for assistance in this conversation, Daniel Flodin for transcription

They say an image is worth 1000 words.
How many words does a magazine page hold?
How many letters compose them?
How many magazines are there in the world?
How much information do they convey? Every week, every month etc.?
Do you think it is going too fast?
    SLOW-Alphabet started when we were given the opportunity
by a magazine to fill a page with our content. It became an attempt
to design a typeface with a slow pace. A professional typographer told us
once he needs 50 hours to design an entire alphabet. According to some
specialized books, 256 signs are "needed" for a font to be "decent".
In five years, we negotiated 30 letters. At this pace, we'd need more
than 37 years to complete the set. Usually when we design a typeface
for a project, we generally try to keep some kind of visual likeness
throughout but with SLOW, the design of the signs are evolving
according to our aging, knowledge, taste of the day, new discoveries,
change(s) of mind(s) and format of the magazine.

SLOW ALPHABET BY ÅBÄKE
Thank you to "Graphic Design Worlds" for hosting.
Other letters can be seen:
'B' in Sugo #0, Ma Edizioni, p. 19, 2003 (IT)
'W' in ldn: three: volume 10: #3: flight of fancy ii,
      last page special insert, 2003 (HK)
'C' in Sugo #1, Ma Edizioni, p. 112, 2004 (IT)
'A' in Ryuko Tsushin #498, p. 86, 2004 (JP)
'a' in IDEA #309, last page of special insert, 2005 (JP)
'R' in Graphic magazine #7, p. 156, 2005 (UK)
'H' in Lodown #45, p. 138, 2005 (DE)
'K' in Cream, Summer edition #01, p. 12, 2005 (HK)
'L', in Math #2, p. 16, 2005 (UK)
'Ä' in Tecknaren #2, p. 17, 2005 (SE)
'X' in [kAk], p. 21, 2005 (RU)
'E' in Esquire #19, no 7, p. 80, 2005 (JP)
'Q' in Composite, 2005 (JP)
'M' in Grafik #129, p. 68, 2005 (UK)
'N' in Art4d, #116, p. 88, 2005 (HK)
'3' in Axis #116, p. 112, 2005 (JP)
'G' in Groove #96, p. 51, 2005 (DE)
'¶' in Metropolis M #6, p. 13, 2005 (NL)
'm' in Muoto, p. 39, June 2005 (FI)
'F' in SP06, August 2006 (NZ)
'ST' in Cream #05 of the summer edition, 2006 (HK)
'ÿ' in Periodiek #3, p. 6, 2006 (BE)
'9' in LUX, p. 52, September 2007 (PT)
'U' Ultrabold, p. 35, 2007 (UK)
'P' in Useless #6, p. 39, 2007 (UK, USA)
'G' in Slimvolume Poster Publication, 2006/2007 (UK)
'g' in Arnolfini bulletin, September 2008 (UK)
'S' in Slanted #6 Herbst, p. 17, 2008 (DE)
'I' in Quotation #1, p. 18, Autumn 2008 (JP)
'=' in Concept Store magazine #01, p. 51, 2009 (UK)
'O' in iconographicmagazine, p. 12, 2009 (ES)
'j' in Laser, p. 91, 2009 (DE)
'Z' in ME Magazine, p. 47, 2009 (USA)
'ö' in design?design!design..., p. 34, 2009 (SE)
''' in Wallpaper, 2009 (UK)
'T' in Iaspis Forum on Design and Critical Practice:
      The Reader, p. 119, 2009 (SE)
'V' in Mousse #23, p. 59, 2010 (IT)
'D' in ARC RCA magazine, p. 35, 2010 (UK)
's' in Book catalogue, chapter 13, 2010 (UK)
'n' NICO magazine #5, p. 217, 2010 (UK)
'Â' The Sound Graphics Catalogue, p. 1, 2010 (JP)
'r' in Vom #6, 2010 (DE)
'B' in Some Magazine #0 Autumn, p. 30, 2010 (DE)

WORK HARD & BE NICE TO PEOPLE

Anthony Burrill

ANTHONY BURRILL

What is graphic design for you, and how do you use it in relation to the world? **Anthony Burrill** I think graphic design is a good training for life. It offers an approach to being inquisitive and interested in lots of different things and because graphic design is involved in a variety of areas, you can become involved in many different disciplines and projects. There are various levels of graphic design. There is the regular everyday, necessary work. The end that I operate in is more experimental, I like pushing forward the language and practice of graphic design. That is the kind of area that I am in, really. I have been doing it for a long time.

You have been working on your own since the very beginning? **AB** I graduated from the Royal College of Art in 1991 and I have worked independently ever since, I have always had a studio at home, just myself and a computer, and that is it really. I have built up a network of relationships with other designers and clients, the Royal College provided a good beginning for that. I developed the network in London, then it spread, and now through the Internet and e-mail it is easier to connect with like-minded people and work internationally. Using the Internet, we can work anywhere. Since I built that network in London, I felt I could happily leave the city with my family—we have children, and I wanted them to grow up in the countryside. I still travel to London every few weeks, so I am still physically connected to it.

Usually designers we have met in the end say they feel there is not a separation between life and work, really: is it the same for you? **AB** Yes. From the moment I wake up. I think that every aspect of my life is intertwined. If I am

working on something and I am not happy about the way it is going, I feel physically anxious. And when a job is finished, I feel so happy; it changes physically as well. The work is really an extension of me as a person.

How important is collaboration with other people for you? **AB** I like to explore different things; by putting pure work out there, people respond to it and I think that you meet like-minded people through the work that you do. I enjoy meeting people and collaborating. I think that nearly all the projects are collaborations. A good example is when I worked with Jenny Packham, the fashion designer. She saw my exhibition at Colette, e-mailed me and said she is a designer too, she would be interested to talk about possible collaborations. I didn't really know anything about her before I met her, she showed the work that she makes and there seemed to be a crossover between us. The fashion show is like a performance, it is very theatrical. Having my work in that kind of setting, it was fantastic. When I stood there, watching the models, listening to the music and the crowd, to see my work in that environment, it was really exciting. It was so different to how my work had been seen before.

In a way you could see your work from a different point of view, on a different dimension? **AB** Yes, I am used to seeing the work in a magazine or on a poster, but then taking it into three dimensions with that scale, it felt like a natural progression. In general, each thing I do, I build on my knowledge and experience, and try to take it further. It gives you confidence. You take the most successful aspects of what you have done with a project and try to develop it further. I am always aiming to get to the "next level." Also I think that you speak to different audiences in different ways. I naturally adopt a different voice for each project I am working on. There is an emotional and mental shift. There are different expectations from you in different contexts. If it is advertising, for example, you can do a very specific thing, and if it is film then it is something else, and then fashion, of course you have to make something beautiful.

As you said before graphic design is a key to explore different worlds, fields, disciplines; you also work on different dimensions—2D, 3D, motion. Still you say "I am a graphic designer"? **AB** I think so. I think there is a kind of graphic way of looking at the world; people who are interested in graphic design, their brains work in a similar way, respond to similar things. Probably it is just a human thing. It is still the same process, it is still communication: you are communicating an idea, a message, a thought, and I think that is the whole thing really.

How would you describe your approach, do you have a method or something? **AB** With some projects I just have an initial strong idea, it is a kind of reaction. I can work very quickly, and I try to keep the idea as simple and pure as possible. Other times I find it harder to develop my ideas for a project. Sometimes the idea develops subconsciously, I go to bed, thinking about it, and in the morning I wake up and an idea is there. I suppose subconsciously I do research all the time, I like looking at things, reading, and picking things up. I do not consciously sit down and think of an idea, it just happens.

Would you say that you design "worlds"? **AB** Yes. I have completely created my own bubble that I live and work in. Living outside London, also, I live in a very tranquil village, the studio is very quiet, I think everything there is quite finely tuned, so I feel comfortable, the studio is very simple and quite minimal. I definitely have created my own world and my visual language as well. I have created that language really, so it defines my world.

The idea of building your visual language is really interesting. What is it made of? **AB** I think it is made of things that I am interested in, a kind of simplicity and choice of typefaces, layers, materials, ideas, etc. There are things I feel naturally comfortable with. When I am working on a project there are some constant reference points. It is like with handwriting: if everybody in this room were given the same kind of shape to put on a piece of paper, they would all draw it in different ways. There can be so many factors: the things that you saw when you grew up and when you are young, and things that made you feel happy. Of course then you don't have to be a slave to history, you take the best that you want and play with it. But not just to make things look cool. My personality is naturally optimistic and happy, with a sense of humour. It is not just about making work that looks cool, it is about developing a depth of understanding underneath it. I think that in design education the last thing you want to make is a design that looks cool; it must have that understanding and depth.

What kind of relationship do you have with the past and with contemporary visual culture? **AB** I was born in the late 1960s and I grew in the 1970–80s, and I have taken things from every decade. Lots of my work has got the flavour of modernism, and of 1960s and 1970s, viewed through a modern filter. Through the Internet nowadays we have access to all kinds of visual reference, everything is everywhere. The culture that we are in now is everything, all at the same time.

You mean a "postmodernist" attitude in a way? **AB** Yes that is what it is. There is no one predominant fashion: in London people dress in so many different ways, they are interested in so many different things. It is all colliding together now.

In the recent years, you participated in different exhibitions and also did some installations. How do you deal with the exhibition context and the audience? **AB** I have been involved in the *European Championship of Graphic Design*, curated by Erik Kessels, at the Graphic Design Museum in Breda, and that really opened my mind to other possibilities. In 2009 I had a show with Michael Marriott in London—*The Right Kind of Wrong* at Mother advertising agency—where we built a large typographic tower; after that I had a show at Colette in Paris and then at the Kemistry Gallery, in London. So last year I had a lot of exhibitions. It seems to have taken me into a different area. It is quite a strange thing to exhibit graphic design, because graphic design is everywhere. When you put things in a gallery context, the work that you show has to be challenging for people: you don't want to show just magazines, you want to make work that people would normally not think about as graphic design.

What do you mean when you say that the exhibition in Breda "opened your mind"? **AB** I was doing lots of commercial projects and advertising, and I did not feel really satisfied doing that kind of work. Not everybody in advertising is like Erik Kessels, who is really the only person I have always been interested in working with. The industry has gone through so many changes, and I think that people are less willing to take a chance. They make work that everybody has to agree on, so you have twenty people who have an opinion about your piece of work, and this makes the whole thing really boring and lacking in originality. During that exhibition in Breda I met lots of interesting people, and I thought: "I want to do my own thing, I don't want to work commercially anymore." After that I did a lot more exhibitions and produced my own work. Also working in areas like fashion is quite different from advertising; it is more inspiring and interesting.

DE DESIGNPOLITIE

Can you tell us something about your world, starting from your background and the decision to work together? **Richard van der Laken** Pepjin and I met in art school and we decided to work together. I think we liked each other, maybe not exactly in our work but especially in our points of view. It has always been a sort of "anti" attitude: you want to do things slightly differently and you are always kicking a little bit against already existing patterns. It is a cliché, but clichés, most times, are true. This was the starting point of our professional career, De Designpolitie, and—in a much more professional and developed way—it is still our starting point.

Do all the people in your studio share the same attitude? **RvdL** No. The point is that people who work in our studio are assistants or they are project management people, and that is another cup of tea, that is more about the process. The interns who work with us need to share our point of view, or they have to commit to it. But they are also here to learn from the way we do things, and we also learn from them—and this is very inspiring. **Pepijn Zurburg** As regards project management, this is really hard for us. When we are trying to choose a difficult path, there can be tension between the client, the assignment and ourselves. On the one hand, you cannot say to everything, "I will not do that, because my standards are so high..." On the other, it can be somewhat adventurous for the commissioners; it takes a very brave client to say, "Well, just take a hike and we'll see where it ends." So the project manager can find himself torn between those things. **RvdL** This is, of course, something we really had to learn. Now we are able to move around the subject, or the client. When we started we had pretty high burning rates of clients; now we are much more able to keep people satisfied. When you want to do something, the context is always really important: you want to do something that is good for the client, for the project and for the audience, and for us as graphic designers. Now we are much more capable of handling that. **PZ** What I think we have also learned is why we have this attitude: it is because this is a way to make interesting things, things that are different from what already exists.

Can you explain this further, what do you mean by having an "attitude" in your work? **PZ** As a graphic designer you are always telling the story of the client, but you also have your own voice. So you have, in a way, to always relate the assignment to yourself: how much of your own voice you put in it. There are certain periods when we are, so to speak, into typography, and everything is black and white, and then there can be a lot of illustration, because it has also to do with our own voice.

Another point that we would like to shed light on is how important it is in the worlds of graphic designers to build connections with other people, who may share the same values or contribute in different ways to their work. Is this actually important for you as Designpolitie? **RvdL** From the beginning we have always worked with friends, or people we connect with. A funny example is an image we shot about thirteen years ago, and I think it is really an illustration of Designpolitie's world. It shows other designers and other people we worked with, but also clients: all kinds of people who are involved. We call this image the "Designpolitie Family." It is funny to see that right from the start we were aware of this aspect.

You do mean that you felt you are not "solo" artists or designers? **RvdL** Yes. Of course in a way we are very "solo," we want to do our things, but also always to work together with other people. I think a good example is the Gorilla project. We got an assignment a few years ago from *De Volkskrant*, a national Dutch newspaper, and it was very interesting but also weighty and too much for just the two of us to handle. That is why we called in another two guys we know—Herman van Bostelen and Lesley Moore—to work with us. And we networked up very well. I think this is also because of this network of people you have; you trust them and you know what they are able to do...

Why did you decide to stay in Amsterdam? Do you have a special relationship with this city? **RvdL** We studied in Utrecht, not very far away from Amsterdam. But we noticed that, as soon as we started as De Designpolitie, most of our clients were from Amsterdam. After a year we had the opportunity to move to this studio, where we have already been for about thirteen years. For me it is very important, but I do not think that the way we work is specifically related to Amsterdam. **PZ** And I still am living in Utrecht. I think that from Amsterdam it is more logical to work for everybody, not to be "stuck in the province" as they say.

How did you decide to become graphic designers and what does "graphic design" mean to you? **RvdL** In a way, you also become graphic designer by accident. It is not that when you are eighteen years old you say, "I am going to be a graphic designer," I do not really believe in that—you want to become an artist or a fireman or a doctor or whatever... **PZ** Or you like drawing. **RvdL** Yes, that is how it started with us. You like drawing and you add something, maybe typefaces or whatever, you do the newspaper of your school, and then suddenly it starts to roll. What I think is really interesting about graphic design is that it is very broad, it is one of the broadest disciplines you can imagine: you can be an illustrator, you can do typography, you can design books, websites, you can be an art director, you can think about strategy... For the future it is becoming even broader. I think that what is interesting about graphic design is also the problem with it, because sometimes it is hard to get a grip on it: what exactly do we do? There are these very famous words by Tibor Kalman that say that graphic design is not content, it is language. It is also very important to keep in mind that you always use it for something else, for stories, that you are in a way a kind of a storyteller.

But do you wish that people can also recognize you, your voice? **PZ** Nowadays you have all these websites where you can look at anything, and there are people out there who can do illustrations and typography a thousand times better than we do. But I think the important thing is the fact that "we" do it. So we are not an author but there is a sort of craft. **RvdL** One thing that we are very interested in is that as designers we have clients with their story, but also the audience, which is very important to us. Sometimes we go around to the client and talk to the audience directly, we ask questions... Sometimes the client does not have a clear idea of who the audience is and we as outsiders can see what they are trying to convey quite clearly.

Talking about method and process in your work, how important is research for you? **PZ** I think you have two different things: research in its broadest sense and then research that is really focused on a specific project. **RvdL** As far as projects are concerned, we do not research very deeply. I do not mean that it is shallow, but it is very important not to go too deeply into it, because otherwise the doors close and you are not able to be fresh any more. That is my opinion. We always keep a certain distance from the project, the client, the whole content... **PZ** If you research the target group, the audience, and all kinds of nuances, it would risk being an overly market-driven design. Design ideas can be immediately clear from the brief—one sentence that sounds very interesting—but can also be something that you already have in mind. **RvdL** It is not "think big and act small," it is "think small and act big!" We always try to search for small ideas: then it is something that you can translate into readable stories and that you can relate to as a viewer. And when you blow it up in a very monumental way, then you have many more opportunities.

Would you say that you are designing "worlds," in a way? **RvdL** I think that is a very spot on word. We always do focus on a certain context so we create a certain world and identity and an environment. **PZ** Generally speaking, there is so much communication out there—commercials, TV, and all this chaos—that it is important to make something which is clear and stands out from it. You might focus on the one or two strong things that you highlight, to set them apart from the other stuff. **RvdL** But then in a way, in our work there is always some kind of comment on the clients, the products, the environment, the audience, and also on our role in the whole process. We always try to find a certain moment when we can comment the whole thing.

Is this the "commitment" you are talking about in your ABC *book?[1]* **RvdL** We think that, as graphic designers, you always have big responsibility because you have access to all kinds of media, whether it is a website or a poster campaign, or magazines, with 100,000 copies—that means that hundreds of thousands of people read it. You have a responsibility, so you'd better be good, you had better tell a good story, otherwise when you deliver a bad story everybody reads a bad story. You always have a commitment to society, to the context in which you work.

More specifically, what is really urgent in your opinion, what is the real challenge for graphic designers? **RvdL** I think that for example privacy has come to be a very specific thing also in visual communication, so this is something we should relate to: where privacy stops or when you should keep a certain distance from it. **PZ** I think that the challenge now for graphic design is to stay on board with things that really matter. You always have this division between graphic design and art, or designers working only in the cultural world, making posters for museums or for themselves, and who, apart from the client, maybe only talk to each other, or are only about producing cool images. But the danger with that is that they are outside society. We think that real graphic designers should deal with real problems, on the street, for real clients, for society. It would be a shame if graphic designers think "we are so important" while they are only making posters for themselves. **RvdL** For example, in my opinion, it is something that happens at festivals like the one in Chaumont. That is a bit strange: they talk about engagement, and of course you can see this engagement in all those posters, but in the end they do not reach anyone at all, but fellow designers. And that is also the kind of disease that you have in the Netherlands; for example the Rietveld Academy or the Werkplaats Typografie have this tendency to focus on a very small world. In the end you have this: "I am a talented, culturally focused graphic designer and this low culture is not my culture, so I am not going to do it." Maybe this is something to discuss: what are we going to do now? How is society changing and what are the real questions? The nice thing about Gorilla, for instance, is that the stage was given to us,

---

1. *The ABC of De Designpolitie,* with contributions by L. Schouwenberg, E. King and D. Snellenberg, Valiz, Amsterdam 2008.

the newspaper gave us this platform. And this gets back to the responsibility that you take: we have this stage, we have to deliver something every day, then we had better be good.

So you think there is a problem with graphic design education? **PZ** I think that presently in Holland most graphic design courses are about training people to be designer-artists. The whole part of actually working on bigger questions is a kind of neglected. For instance it is really strange that the final exam in most art schools still asks the students to come up with something and do that. I mean, when you start working as a graphic designer a client never comes to you and says "please make me something and do it in the way you like, please write the text and make pictures yourself." **RvdL** And that is where you see lots of students struggling. So it could be an interesting question to change this. Also I think that in art schools it is important that you work together, that you discuss, the networking, the ability of using each other's skills. In Holland all the different disciplines are very much separated from one another—photography, graphic design, fashion, etc.—they do not really interact. Which is really stupid, because when you start to work you immediately need to co-operate with other people. **PZ** One thing I would like to add about education. I do not know how it is in Italy, but in the Netherlands there are always students who come out of the art schools who are really skillful, with the computer and software, but then they are struggling with the actual design process. So this is something we do in our studio with internships. **RvdL** Next to the "think small and act big" cliché, we also have another cliché that is: "It always starts and it always ends with typography." This is very banal to say, because every intern who comes in here thinks "I am going to make the Gorilla," but in the end the bulk of the work, in the long run, is to get one concept into a product that represents it. And to do that you need to do a lot of "stupid" things like layout and typefaces, or like "Is it going to be red or blue?" Our design process, I think, may be somewhat boring, it is not very intellectual.

A NOTE ON THE TYPE

PEN = 0, 1, 1, 0, WEIGHT = 100, SLANT = 0, SUPERNESS = 0.75, CURLYNESS = 0:

This is Meta-the-difference-between-the-two-Font, a typeface designed by Dexter Sinister in 2010 and derived using MetaFont, the now-thirty-year-old computer typography system programmed by Donald Knuth in 1979.

MetaFont is both a programming language and its own interpreter, a swift trick where it first provides a vocabulary and then decodes its syntax back to the native binary machine language of 1s and 0s. Knuth originally intended MetaFont as a helper application for TeX, the computer typesetting system he created to facilitate high-quality typography directly by authors. Donald Knuth, a Stanford professor and author of the multi-volume computer science "Bible" "The Art of Computer Programming" (1971), was dismayed on receiving galley proofs for the second edition of his book. The publisher had just switched from traditional hot metal typesetting to a digital system and the typographic quality was far worse than the original 1971 edition. Knuth figured that setting letters on a page was simply a matter of ink or no-ink, on or off, 1 or 0, and therefore a perfect problem for the computer. He planned on spending a six-month sabbatical writing a typesetting program and produced (almost ten years later) the near-ubiquitous (in mathematics and science publishing, anyway) computer typesetting program, TeX. MetaFont was designed from the start as TeX's manual assistant and faithful servant, producing as required the high-quality fonts at whatever size and shape on command.

MetaFont was also intended as a tool for designing new typefaces on its own. As MetaFont was programmed by Knuth, a mathematician, the resulting typographic design method relies on equations (multi-variable algebra and a bit of vector arithmetic) to specify letterforms and computer code to compile these instructions into a usable font—all of which is more the native province of mathematicians than type designers. In the American Mathematical Society's prestigious Josiah Willard Gibbs Lecture of July 4, 1978, Knuth gave a talk titled "Mathematical Typography," and suggested that, "we may conclude that a mathematical approach to the design of alphabets does not eliminate the artists who have been doing the job for so many years." True enough, but the relatively steep technical slope of using MetaFont for type designers combined with the limited interest in making typefaces by mathematicians has resulted in only several handfuls of MetaFonts being produced over the last thirty years. As such, scant documentation and support exist for someone trying to create a MetaFont today.

OK, let's change the parameters of what you have been reading by setting the following excerpt from "Design as Art" by Bruno Munari (1966) in Meta-the-difference-between-the-two-Font with PEN = 0, 10, 2, 22, WEIGHT = 140, SLANT = 0, SUPERNESS = 0.72, CURLYNESS = 0. Like so:

Culture today is becoming a mass affair, and the artist must step down from his pedestal and be prepared to make a sign for a butcher's shop (if he knows how to do it). The artist must cast off the last rags of romanticism and become active as a man among men, well up in present-day techniques, materials, and working methods. Without losing his innate aesthetic sense he must be able to respond with humility and competence to the demands his neighbours may make of him.

The designer of today re-establishes the long-lost contact between art and the pubic, between living people and art as a living thing. Instead of pictures for the drawing-room, electric gadgets for the kitchen. There should be no such thing as art divorced from life—with beautiful things to look at and hideous things to use. If what we use every day is made with art, and not thrown together by chance of caprice, then we shall have nothing to hide.

Anyone working in the field of design has a hard task ahead of him—to clear his neighbour's mind of all preconceived notions of art and artists, notions picked up at schools where they condition you to think one way for the whole of your life, without stopping to think that life changes—and today more rapidly than ever. It is therefore up to us designers to make known our working methods in clear and simple terms, the methods we think are the truest, the most up-to-date, the most likely to resolve our common aesthetic problems. Anyone who uses a properly designed object feels the presence of an artist who has worked for him, bettering his living conditions and encouraging him to develop his taste and sense of beauty.

When we give a place of honor in the drawing-room to an ancient Etruscan vase which we consider beautiful—well proportioned and made with precision and economy, we must also remember that the vase once had an extremely common use. Most probably it was used for cooking-oil. It was made by a designer of those times, when art and life went hand in hand and there was no such thing as a work of art to look at and just any old thing to use.

Unlike more common computer outline font formats such as TrueType or Postscript Type 1, a MetaFont font is constructed of strokes drawn with set-width pens. Instead of describing the outline of the character directly by drawing each letter shape inside and outside, counter and letterform, a MetaFont file describes only the basic pen path or skeleton letter. Perhaps better imagined as the ghost that comes in advance of a particular lettershape, a MetaFont character is defined only by a set of equations rather than hard-coded coordinates and outline shapes. So it is then possible to treat parameters such as aspect ratio, slant, stroke width, serif size, (curlyness!?) and so on as abstracted input values that can change in each glyph definition, creating not a set of set letters, but instead a set of set parameters, any of which can be changed each time the font is rendered. By changing the value at one location in the MetaFont file, a consistent change is produced throughout the entire font. The resulting collection of glyph definitions and input parameters is not then a single font but, instead, a meta-font.

Let's try that again... You may recall from earlier that MetaFont is both a language and its own interpreter. (What does that mean?) Taking a clue from that riddle, we could turn MetaFont's name back on itself, by taking it apart, beginning with the end—"font."

"Font" is a word whose current common usage (particularly in the context of personal computers) has twisted its exact definition. Returning to its roots, a "font" is simply a collection of characters of one particular design, or precisely, typeface. More specifically a "font" is the particular realization of a certain typeface in a certain medium, according to certain parameters such as size, width, weight, style, contrast and shape—for example, a font of William Caslon's letters cast in hot lead at 14 points or a font of Standard Grotesque at 96 points carved from oak or even a full font of 12 pixel letters stretched 150% and rendered on a 72-dpi screen from the Arial typeface. However, this collection of parameters (size, width, weight, etc.) according to which a font is rendered from a particular typeface are not fixed. New parameters can be added at will and this is where the "Meta" of MetaFont begins.

"Meta-" is a prefix of Greek origin that originally simply meant "after," but due to a strange turn of events* came to mean "of a higher order, beyond" in Latin and later modern languages (excluding Greek where it retains its original meaning).

* Yes, its current use as "of a higher order" is due to Aristotle's book on Metaphysics, but he would never have called it that. Aristotle would refer to the subject of that book as "First Philosophy" or "Theology." The title "Metaphysics" comes from Andronicus of Rhodes (1st century BC), who was the first editor of Aristotle and placed the book on Metaphysics after the book on Physics in his compilation (so, it was quite literally "after" Physics). Best regards, Derek

So then you have metalanguages (languages used to describe languages), metahistory (the study of how people view and study history), metatheorems (theorems about theorems), metarules (rules about rules), etc. Indeed you can "meta-" just about anything.**

** Wait, are you guys really calling it "Meta-the-difference-between-the-two-Font"? Sorry man… it's a bad name, but you'll soon realize that yourselves. I won't press you. I'll just wait around till you see it.

Let's try another version, demonstrated by typesetting this list from "Famous Last Words" by Michelangelo Pistoletto (1967) with PEN = 0, 1, 1, 0, WEIGHT = 25, SLANT = 0, SUPERNESS = 0.71, CURLYNESS = 0:

When a person realizes he has two lives—an abstract one for his mind and a concrete one, also for his mind—he ends up either as a madman, who, out of fear, hides one of his lives and plays the other as a role, or as an artist, who has no fear and who is willing to risk both lives.
Man has always attempted to double himself as a means of attaining self-knowledge. The recognition of one's own image in a pool of water—like recognizing oneself in a mirror—was perhaps one of the first real hallucinations that man experienced. Part of man's mind has always remained attached to that reproduction of himself. With the passage of time, this doubling, this process of duplication, came to be used in ways that were ever more systematic and convincing. The mind

created representation on the basis of the reflection of the self; and art has become one form of this representation.

Man began to use reflection as a strategic point for measuring of the universe. No longer content with the first hallucination of himself, he convinced himself that he could double the whole universe. This was his way of trying to understand it. Mathematics was constructed out of the realization that oneself plus another could make two and that oneself minus another was one. In the beginning the lesson was rather brutal. It wasn't simply a matter of what happens today when we hide one of two apples behind our backs to show baby that there is only one. At the beginning "minus one" meant that one of the two was dead—that the beloved mother or father or brother, who when added to the self had made two, was no longer among the living.

Man began to measure the universe in terms of his own direct experience of life and death, then went on to the great task of creating good and evil. In the light of the day he said "white" and in the darkness of the night he said "black." And always remaining at the center of things he created perspective. The world was seen in terms of vanishing points and points of view with respect to the position of man's eye at about five feet above ground level, and from that point he created high and low.

Past and future, near and distant, profound and superficial, true and false, single and multiple, subjective and objective, static and dynamic. These are a few examples of the complex of antinomies that has grown up around the human being as the fruit of his mind. In constant expansion, the process began with the first man who walked the earth, and it has continued until today. The world that we daily inhabit both physically and mentally is made up of the conflict between the two extreme halves of every proposition and every judgment.

In 2009, "The New Yorker" ran "The Unfinished," a piece about American writer David Foster Wallace following his death six months earlier. Midway through the tribute, D.T. Max quotes from an early letter that Wallace sent to Gerald Howard of Penguin Books, in which he explains that his work is neither primarily "realism" nor "metafiction," but rather, "if it's anything, it's meta-the-difference-between-the-two." Typically, it's a throwaway line that returns, then stays with you. Does the "difference" here refer to a mathematical distinction in quantity, or to a more common sense of distinction or dissimilarity (or even disagreement?) Or both? Wallace's chain-of-words is as slippery as the logically-recursive sentence "The first rule is: there are no rules," but with a difference. Instead of simply setting up an endless loop between two poles, it observes that loop from a higher point of concentrated disinterest. There's no simple way out of this one, and yet there seems to be just enough there to keep trying.***

*** Zadie Smith makes a case for this in an essay on Foster Wallace, using his short story "The Depressed Person" from "Brief Interviews with Hideous Men" as an arch example: "The effect on the reader is powerful, unpleasant. Quite apart from being forced to share one's own mental space with the depressed person's infinitely dismal consciousness, to read those spiral sentences is to experience that dread of circularity embedded in the old joke about recursion (to understand recursion you must first understand recursion)."

Exporting Wallace's chain from literature to a more general use, we could plug other values into the equation. For "realism" we could insert "practice" and for "metafiction" perhaps "theory." (These poles can be endlessly swapped with similarly productive confusion —try "concrete"/"abstract" or "modernism"/"postmodernism.") And yet the "meta-the-difference-between-the-two" between any of these two isn't simply resolved by some alchemical fusion, as in "practice"+"theory"="praxis," practice informed by theory and vice versa. Less of a compound than an extraction, more a subtraction than an addition, m-t-d-b-t-2 is then actually a skeleton, a script, or a good idea in advance of its realization.

Donald Knuth began his Josiah Gibbs lecture, "Mathematical Typography," with an apology of sorts, saying: "I will be speaking today about work in progress, instead of completed research; this was not my original intention when I chose the subject of this lecture, but the fact is I couldn't get my computer programs working in time." He continues, "Fortunately it is just as well that I don't have a finished product to describe to you today, because research in mathematics is generally much more interesting while you're doing it than after it's all done."

Meta-the-difference-between-the-two-Font has a similarly incomplete character. As a set of simple letterforms and a collection of meta-design parameters, M-t-d-b-t-2-F will create unending numbers of different fonts from now onward, always only moving forward and compiling a collection of surface effects onto its essential skeleton to produce a growing family of "hollow" fonts whose forms have more in common with handwriting than they do with hot metal counterpunches (not to mention modern digital fonts).

The clumsy result, with its chewy name Meta-the-difference-between-the-two-Font, arrives before the effect that is applied to it, returning to a moment before fonts, just before Gutenberg's first black-letter Gothic types attempted to match the scribe's penmanship. At this point, to computer-automate the production of handwritten calligraphy, and to more or less ignore four hundred years of typographic tradition, is essentially absurd.

It seemed like a good idea at the time.

One final trial, this time used to set an excerpt from "The Open Work" by Umberto Eco (1962) with PEN = 0, 1, 1, 0, WEIGHT = 25, SLANT = 0, SUPERNESS = 0.6, CURLYNESS = 10:

At this point, however, the critic of contemporary poetics might suspect that such undue attention to formal structures of contemporary art is much more interested in abstractions and abstract speculations than in man. This misunderstanding would be merely another expression of the belief that art can speak of man only in a traditional form—which essentially means that art can speak only of yesterday's man. To speak of today's man, however, art has no choice but to break away from all the established formal systems, since its main way of speaking is as FORM. In other words—and this amounts to an aesthetic principle—the only meaningful way in which art can speak of man and his world is by organizing its forms in a particular way and not by making pronouncements with them. Form must not be a vehicle for thought; it must be a way of thinking.

A few years ago, Sidney Finkelstein, a British music critic, published a little book in which he set out to tell the public at large "how music expresses ideas." Most of the book dealt with the possibility that Brahms, because of his interest in the seventeenth century, was a "reactionary" musician, and that Tchaikovsky, because of his interest in popular issues, was a "progressive" musician. No need to resort to aesthetics to discuss such a point. Suffice it to say that, despite Tschaikovsky's popular concerns, highly melodic compositions have never been able to change the viewpoint of the bourgeoisie who favored them, whereas Brahms's "return" to the seventeenth century may have been crucial in giving music the direction it took at the end of the century. (But Brahms notwithstanding, a musician can be considered "progressive" to the extent he manages to translate a new vision of the world into new musical forms. Schoenberg, in his "Warsaw Survivor," is able to express an entire culture's outrage at Nazi brutality: having worked on farms for a very long time, he was able to find a way to look at the world musically. Had Schoenberg used the tonal system he would have composed not this "Warsaw Survivor" but the "Warsaw Concerto," which develops the same subject according to the most rigorous laws of tonality. Of course, Addinsel was not a Schoenberg, nor would all the twelve-tone series of this world suffice to turn him into one. On the other hand, we cannot attribute all the merit of a composition to the genius of its creator. The formal starting point of a work often determines what follows: a tonal discourse dealing with the bombing of Warsaw could not but lapse into sugary pathos and evolve along the paths of bad faith.)

This brings us closer to the heart of the matter: it is impossible to describe a situation by means of a language that is not itself expressed by that situation. All language reflects a system of cultural relationships with its own particular implications. I cannot, for instance, translate the French word ESPRIT from a positivist text as the English word "spirit," whose implications are profoundly idealistic. The moment an artist realizes that the system of communication at his disposal is extraneous to the historical situation he wants to depict, he must also understand that the only way he will be able to solve his problem is through the invention of new formal structures that will embody that situation and become its MODEL.

(The excerpts used to demonstrate the font have been slightly edited to facilitate easier reading in this context.)

PLATO
  Republic II, III, X
  Ion
  Symposium

ARISTOTLE
  Poetics
  Nicomachean Ethics

David Hume
  Of the Standard of Taste

Immanuel Kant
  Critique of Judgement

G.W.F Hegel
  Philosophy of Fine Art

Friedrich Nietzsche
  The Birth of Tragedy
  Attempt at a self-Criticism

Leo Tolstoy
  What is Art?

E.D. Hirsch, Jr.
  Validity in Interpretation

Hans-Georg Gadamer
  Truth and Method

Paul Ricoeur

Jacques Derrida
  The Truth in Painting
  Letter to Peter Eisenman

Michel Foucault
  The Order of Things

Edward Bullough
  'Physical Distance' as a factor in
  Art and as an Aesthetic Principle

Arthur Danto
  The Artworld

Mikhail Bakhtin
  Discourse in the Novel

Clive Bell
  Art

R.G. Collingwood
  Principles of Art

John Dewey
  Art as Experience

Susanne Langer
  Feeling and Form

Nelson Goodman
  When is Art?
  Languages of Art

Martin Heidegger
  The Origin of the Work of Art

Maurice Merleau-Ponty
  Eye and Mind

Stephen David Ross
  A Theory of Art: Inexhaustibility by...

Stephen Pepper
  The work of Art

V.Y. Mudimbe
  The Invention of Africa

Trinh T. Minh-ha
  Woman, Native, Other

James Clifford
  On Collecting Art and Culture

Tony Fry and Anne-Marie Willis
  Aboriginal Art: Symptom or
  Success?

F.T Marinetti
  Futurist Painting: Technical Ma...

Umberto Boccioni
  Technical Manifesto of Futurist
  Sculpture

Kasimir Malevich
  Suprematism

Wassily Kandinsky
  Concrete Art

The Importance of the Dutch Football Club Ajax
and Total Football (Totaalvoetbal) to the Sport of Graphic Design

ELLIOTT EARLS

Give me your tired, your poor
Your huddled masses yearning to breathe free

Precariously situated between commerce, art and communication technology, graphic design[1] as a practice has the potential to be one of the most commanding forms of cultural engagement. Graphic design as a practice should be refocused to serve as a powerful form of Nietzschean Hammer, testing our culture for the hollow ring of false idols.[2] And yet like a methane-bloated raccoon corpse precariously buoyant in the summer sun, the culture of graphic design needs to be poked with a stick so that from its fecund corpse a thousand flowers may bloom. Sixty some odd years of formalized graphic design education has produced a highly commercialized field with deep links into the flaming soul of capitalism, but has failed to yield a substantive critical culture, nor yield a significant body of work outside of overt commercial concerns.

In Ovid's *Metamorphoses*, Daedalus the father of Icarus was a cunning craftsman and artisan who designed the labyrinth which was used to

---

1. The discipline to which I refer is variously called graphic design, visual communication or communication design. For the sake of simplicity hereafter it will simply be called "graphic design."

2. "Refocused?" In 1935 the German proto-graphic designer John Heartfield produced *Hurrah, die Butter ist Alle!* (Hurray, the Butter is Gone!) which directly challenged Adolph Hitler and the unchecked rise of German nationalism. It is perhaps a specious claim to suggest that the cycloptical eye of graphic design was ever truly focused on John Heartfield. But the "refocusing" also implies a turning away from its current focus.

imprison the gruesome Minotaur. And because Daedalus constructed the labyrinth so cunningly that none but he could escape, Daedalus and his son Icarus were locked in a tower in order to prevent this knowledge from spreading. Daedalus, the cunning craftsman, fashions two pairs of wings in order to escape their tower prison. In preparation for flight Daedalus warns Icarus to fly neither too high near the sun, nor too low near the sea because of the attendant dangers.

As we know, Icarus did not heed his father's warning, flew too high and drowned in the sea. Often this allegory focuses on Icarus and is used to illustrate the dangers of overreaching, as in the nature of this essay. But more importantly and often overlooked in this story is the simple fact that unlike Icarus, a grieving and overwrought Daedalus gained his freedom by arriving safely at his destination. One of the many allegorical points of this story being that Daedalus, through the strength of his will, depth of his intellect and dedication to craft (techne), achieved freedom from his prison. Like the mythical Daedalus, graphic design as a field has become a prisoner as a result of its cunning. Even though Daedalus' knowledge of the secret of the labyrinth held the beastly Minotaur at bay, it was also ironically the basis for his own imprisonment. So too graphic design's cunning understanding of the relationship between communication and commerce has helped the culture industry fashion a labyrinthine system of desire which holds both the designer and the consumer hostage. The only way for graphic design as a field to finally fashion wings, take flight and successfully produce both a substantive critical culture and a powerful body of work outside of overt commercial concerns, is for it to completely re-imagine the systematic education of the designer. The field must finally challenge the fundamental assumptions upon which graphic design education is based. And just as Dadelus achieved freedom from his tower prison, graphic design must seek freedom from the shackles imposed by corporate culture, commerce and capitalism.

The Issue Is Not Money

For the past forty years graphic design as a practice has peddled the shrunken head of modern "transparency," "form" and "appropriateness" to corporate culture while leaving the modernist body (i.e. truly radical idealism) writhing in a pool of its own blood. Graphic design as a discipline and educational system for far too long has hidden behind the modernist principle of transparency in order to sublimate its own agency. This sublimation has been in deference to corporate and consumerist agendas. In spite of the idea that postmodernist thinking has permeated every aspect of contemporary life, and despite the considerable impact of post-structuralism on design thinking, graphic design as a mainstream professional practice remains irreparably fused to the conception of the designer as a transparent vehicle for the transmission of "corporate" communication.

Regardless of hipster notions of culture jamming, shopdropping, parafiction, postmodern aesthetics, social practices in design, appropriation and "the designer as author," the simple truth of the matter is that the education of the contemporary graphic designer is still largely about aiding corporate entities of all sizes in their commercial goals. And this in a nutshell is the problem. Unlike music, film, dance, poetry, painting, sculpture, theater, writing, mime, magic, weaving, knitting, quilting, ceramics or photography, graphic designers are simply not taught that the discipline can engage the humanities in profoundly meaningful ways. Graphic design process, methodology, craft and theories can be marshaled in service of those things that are most pressing in the human condition. These skills can be focused to speak to the soul of man, not the wallet. The issue is all about coming to an understanding on the most fundamental level of the *raison d'être* of graphic design in contrast to other arts. Mainstream graphic design in its current form is specifically different from most other artistic practice in that its *raison d'être* is tied to selling shit. It is important to note that the use of "selling" in this case refers both to crass commercialization as well as the "selling" of a message for any corporate entity regardless of their commercial goals. The use of "selling" in this sense includes formatting a third parties' information in a persuasive form, be it for Mother Teresa or for Girls Gone Wild.

Graphic design as a practice can be understood as situated at the intersection of three larger sociological processes: capitalism, the societal role of information/communication technology and art (the practice of embedding ideas in visual form). Graphic design education can be seen as a response to these factors. The education of the graphic designer can serve as ground zero in a fight to fundamentally alter the *raison d'être* of graphic design.

What's the Problem? I Thought Things Were Going Swimmingly?
Graphic design as a field, with a very few notable exceptions, has failed to produce a substantive body of criticism that contributes positively to design or artistic practice. It has failed to nurture a culture of criticism capable of

dealing with the most advanced forms of its output. This disconcertingly weak critical discourse regarding the content and character of the field is absolutely linked to the simple fact that a large percentage of its cultural output simply cannot withstand nor sustain serious criticism. When the lion's share of work being produced in the field cannot sustain an interpretive form of criticism, then a viscous cycle of vacuous discourse is established. It is nearly impossible for the would be serious critics and theorists within the field to sustain a meaningful public critical discourse when the brand implications of a logo redesign are typical fare. Graphic design as a practice should go beyond the successful transubstantiation of corporate values into the form of a logo (à la Paul Rand's logo for IBM, or UPS). Graphic design criticism focused on the brand implications of a new logo helps to render graphic design as a discipline powerless. This condition can and should be changed through the education of the graphic designer.

All criticism, from the written form to critique in design school, begins with the fundamental principle that all work can be called into crisis. Critical thinking forms the basis for the establishment of a feedback loop. Work is made. Work is shown. Work is discussed. Work is thought about. And then work is made again incorporating the raised awareness that results from this process into the new working methodology. A thriving and substantive culture of graphic design criticism is an essential component to push the field forward.

Morris Weitz has posited that any form of criticism necessarily deals with four broad categories; description, interpretation, theorization and assessment.[3] To these four I would also add contextualization. So in a fecund form of criticism, the critic essentially describes the work which he then attempts to make sense of by stating what he believes the work to be "about." At which point he theorizes the work. He attempts to tie his interpretation to a larger body of theoretical knowledge. Through this process the critic is situating the work within a historical context. Finally the critic levies an assessment of the work. Historically the problem with graphic design criticism revolves around the fact that in most cases the critic never needs posit an interpretation. A vicious circle of vacuousness has been established by positioning the graphic designer almost exclusively as a communication

3.   M. Weitz, *Hamlet and the Philosophy of Literary Criticism*, University of Chicago Press, Chicago 1964.

conduit.[4] By contrast, work that is repositioned by giving primacy to the humanities and simultaneously devalues the role of transparency and commerce, demands a rich interpretive process.

In order to fully understand the problems and promise of graphic design it is important to try to situate graphic design in a historical philosophical conversation concerning Aesthetics. Traditionally Aesthetics is the branch of philosophy concerned with the nature of beauty and art. Obviously categorization of nearly any variety can pose problems usually involving definition. By attempting to see graphic design in its most powerful and ideal light we can begin to understand it as a form of Instrumentalism. In the Instrumentalist view Art has a function, it does something. It aims to be "instrumental" in the life of its viewers. It is meant to goad or inspire the viewer to a kind of action. To the extent to which the work moves the viewer, to that degree the work could be considered "good."

While postmodern linguistics and institutional critique are seemingly set up at odds with the traditional realm of Aesthetics, understanding these issues as part of a continuum of thought regarding Truth, Beauty and Goodness (even if they constitute an attack on these concepts) is far more productive and accurate. Situated on this continuum, graphic design as a mainstream

---

4.   The dangerous naiveté of this argument is not what it may seem. The various histories of graphic design are replete with examples of designers, educators and design writers being very much aware of the most sophisticated linguistic and communication theories. And not only being aware, but monkeying with the notion of the designers' agency within this equation. Historically schools like Cranbrook Academy of Art and Cal Arts, and magazines like *Emigre* have all played important roles in foregrounding these issues. Further, they have played a critical role in de-educating and re-educating the designer with regard to these issues. And that may be the point. When we essentialize, when we attempt to understand what lies at the core of graphic design by examining the structural relationships within our culture, what are we left with? In other words by getting "real" for a moment and taking a hard look at what the vast majority of graphic designers do on a day to day basis, we can finally glimpse behind the veil and understand its *raison d'être*. In this light we can see that the postmodern agency of the designer within the communication equation is not so much a sham but rather a simple fact that has been thoroughly co-opted by corporate consumerist agendas. As a simple example I refer you to Sony's botched 2005 guerilla marketing campaign for the PSP game system where Sony hired graffiti artists in major cities to spray paint totemic images of kids playing with the unit. This campaign was widely derided as an attempt to buy the street credibility. Further we can understand the historical role of Cranbrook Academy of Art, Cal Arts, *Emigre* magazine, and a number of the writers and educators associated with these institutions as renegade de-educators and de-programmers. By their very existence they in fact "prove" (test) the rule.

practice is inextricably bound to the philosophy of Instrumentalism within Aesthetics. In a Platonic view, Art is meant to serve society by promoting moral and responsible citizenship. In Plato's view, art should move people "properly." Leo Tolstoy by contrast substituted a moral theory for an aesthetic one. In the simplest terms, both Plato and Tolstoy demand the instrumentalist artist and artwork to "move" the viewer to the betterment of self and society. As with graphic design's exclusion of radical idealism and the utopian impulse from the modern program, here again graphic design half-asses it. Graphic design as it has been practiced in the mainstream for at least the past sixty years has concerned itself with "moving" the viewer, but largely in service of a corporate agenda.

The problem is materialist. Instrumentalism as an aesthetic practice fails when it flies in the face of positioning the artwork as an agent of *positive* social change. It is not enough to simply move the audience. It is far more important to determine whether the work moves the viewer to the betterment of himself and society as a whole.[5] The solution to this problem is to reestablish exuberant idealism and meaningful engagement with the humanities within the field. The solution to the problem involves training the young designer to engage culture in ways that take on the full program of Instrumentalism as a philosophical practice.

More importantly graphic design as a field has also failed to produce a substantive body of work that has at its core those things that fall outside the realm of overt commercial concerns. In the interest of fairness it is important to point out that there are a few notable exceptions to both the idea that graphic design is sub-critical and the idea that it has failed to produce work that has at its core those things that fall outside the realm of overt commercial concern. But these exceptions prove the rule. Of course in any of the many plausible histories of graphic design it is also possible to expand the set under consideration to include examples that, although ridiculous, undermine the central thrust of this essay.[6]

---

5.   Determining causality within any complex system is extremely difficult if not practically impossible, but this does not mean that one should not try. In fact attempting to come to a deeper understanding of the possible ramifications of one's actions is nearly a pre-requisite for self-actualization.

6.   The most direct way to attempt to destroy the merits of this entire argument is to simply perform a kind of regression analysis. Regression analysis in philosophy "is understood

As further examples we could discuss the importance of Noam Chomsky's or Ferdinand de Saussure's work in the field of graphic design. Or we could speak of the importance of the work of Barbara Kruger, the Guerrilla Girls or Gran Fury. However in each of these cases we would be venturing into the realm of the ridiculous to suggest that their important contributions were as self-professed graphic designers. They are outsiders whose work has been incorporated into the field. By contrast, nearly every other artistic discipline has produced substantive contributions to aesthetics (Clement Greenberg, Sol LeWitt), philosophy (Leo Tolstoy), literary criticism (Umberto Eco) as well as to their own chosen form of expression.

Concerning the Importance of Total Football to the Sport of Graphic Design
In a June 2010 article in *The New York Times*, Joachim Ladefoged discusses "How a Soccer Star is Made." In the article he goes to great length to contrast the American approach to athlete development with the method pioneered by the famed Dutch soccer club Ajax.

In the article Ladefoged discusses the importance of the Dutch Academies' influential tactical theory of "Totaalvoetbal" (Total Football): "The Dutch national team plays in the Total Football tradition that relies on players who know what they want to do with the ball before it reaches them and can move it on without stopping it. The British author David Winner, in his book *Brilliant Orange: The Neurotic Genius of Dutch Soccer*, calls this approach 'physical chess,' and the Dutch can be quite haughty about it. They abhor the cloying defensive tactics associated with the Italians and the boot-and-chase way the English played for years, and it has been observed that they sometimes appear more intensely interested in the artfulness of a match than in the result."[7] Total Football is largely based upon a dynamic system

---

by the critical realist explication as a *post hoc* attempt to identify a restricted closed system." In other words, the merit of this entire essay swings on an attempt to delineate the field of graphic design in a certain way, to essentialize it. So an opponent to this essay would simply say: "You have defined a closed system. Your definition is too narrow. Your argument fails because you have excluded the diversity of approaches to graphic design education and you have excluded the infinite professional possibilities for the practicing designer." But what I am really doing here is asking, "What kind of concept is graphic design?" and this essay attempts to characterize that concepts' problems, promise and remedies.

7.　J. Ladefoged, "How a Soccer Star is Made," in *The New York Times*, June 6, 2010, http://www.nytimes.com/201%6/06/magazine/06Soccer-t.html?pagewanted=all.

where each player must be able to fluidly assume any role on the field. The goal keeper is the only player in this system in a fixed role. As the game unfolds, each player will at times assume the role of a defender, midfielder or attacker depending upon the tactical situation on the field. In this system it is extremely important for each player to possess the necessary technical and physical skill to play many positions. This approach to football places high technical demands on its players, and its success as a tactical system depends on fundamental training. According to Ladefoged, the ability to execute Total Football is the result of a relentless and extreme focus on fundamentals. This approach contrasts with a more prevalent focus on team dynamics and team development. The field of graphic design needs to adapt its systemic approach to undergraduate education by placing a fanatical Ajax-like emphasis on fundamentals.

In some very substantive ways training the young designer in the tactical strategy of Total Football should be the goal. A relentless pursuit of formal fundamentals at the expense of less focused esoteric practices is necessary. Just as Ajax sacrifices development of team dynamics and actual game play in lieu of tangible skill development, tempo work and conditioning, so undergraduate education needs to sacrifice "real world" projects, designer-client interaction and professional practices in lieu of a monomaniacal focus on formal fundamentals. Traditional foundation studies should be expanded to two full years. While the last two years should put an emphasis on typographic and letter form design, page layout and composition. This training should be craft-based and should almost exclusively emphasize the development of formal "chops." In the traditional system of education in America as an example, undergraduate education (BFA) typically lasts four years while graduate education (MFA) takes an additional two. In the most traditional sense non-major based "foundation studies" last one year, while major based skill training lasts three. This should be rebalanced to place far greater emphasis on absolute fundamentals at the expense of more "esoteric" professional development.

The second primary component of the education should be an equal focus on the philosophical category of Aesthetics. From the first moment a student arrives in a design school, he should receive a rigorous education regarding Aesthetics. This training should begin with discussions of Platonic aesthetics and by the end of the education expand to include both the writings of artists who were important theorists as well as semiotics, linguistics and postmodern theorists. This is completely achievable: *Art and Its Significance: An Anthology of Aesthetic Theory* edited by Stephen David Ross is a collection of writings dealing with aesthetic theory from Plato through Sol LeWitt.[8] Clearly if it is possible to excerpt and provide an overview of this discourse in a 500-page book, it is more than possible to deal with this subject matter in a comprehensive and rigorous manner over a four-year period.

The third primary component of this undergraduate education would be discussion groups to make tangible the connection between the philosophical component and the formal component of the education. These loosely structured discussions would track the development in the studio and in the reading, and would attempt to drive home the correlation between form and content, between Aesthetics and form. This would be set up in order to mercilessly ensure that intellectual connections are drawn between the current material under discussion in the Aesthetics component and the work being done in the Form component. Undergraduate education should be a studio-based experience broken into three core elements: the Fundamentals of Form, the Fundamentals of Aesthetics, and the connection between the two. On a more detailed level, the Fundamentals of Form and Aesthetics should be focused as follows:

1. The Fundamentals of Form:
    i.   Drawing
    ii.   2D design
    iii. 3D design
    iv.   4D design (motion)
    v.   Photography
    vi.   Software instruction
    vii. Typography and layout

2. The Fundamentals of Aesthetics:
    i.   A historical survey of Aesthetics and the tangible relationship to Form
    ii.   Art history
    iii. Design history

---

8. State University of New York Press, Binghamton (NY) 1984.

The goal behind undergraduate education in graphic design should be to produce a Total Footballer. In order to achieve this, a student absolutely must posses the ability to produce compelling form nearly at will. The "formal monster" quickly becomes the sophisticated designer once that ability to make form is brought under the control of the intellect. This is the job behind the philosophical component to the education.

With this as a foundation, graduate education in graphic design would then be free of remedial bullshit. Foundation studies are so named because one is laying the foundation for future work. All too often post-graduate education cannot contend with the real issues that it should be contending with because it is forced to deal with remedial issues. In far too many instances re-training the graphic designer supplants the heavy lifting that should be taking place. De-training, un-training and counter-training should be the real goal of graduate school, but this is only possible if the necessary groundwork has been laid. One cannot forget what one never knew.[9]

The single most important activity in graduate school should be critique. Unfortunately the manner in which critique is practiced in the vast majority of design schools does little to actually aid the student. As a matter of fact the "defensive model" of design school critique represents the single biggest impediment to the effective education of the designer.

As a kind of schematic,[10] the typical design school critique is based upon the primacy of the thesis. In other words nearly all design critiques involve placing a student in a defensive posture in relationship to the work shown and to their "idea." Typically a student will present his/her work and then be asked a series of questions by the instructor and by their fellow students. The unstated goal (the a priori) of the critique is to suss out logical inconsistencies

---

9. Forgetting is quite possibly one of the most important skills that an artist, designer or craftsman must learn. Knowledge, craft and technique once fully assimilated must become automatic and must be forgotten.

10. This entire essay is an attempt to create a kind of conceptual map. This map is a schematic representation of an actual territory: design and art school. Out of necessity in this process of mapping certain details and territories are left out. The goal is not to faithfully recreate the actual terrain, but to simplify and produce a productive schema. This again speaks to both the nature of maps, and regression analysis. I am not suggesting that there are not a number of different critique methodologies in place in design school. I am suggesting that there are certain commonalities that permeate design (and art school education), and the goal is to think critically about them.

between what the student says is his "idea" and the work presented. Both the instructor and the students' peers are looking for logical inconsistencies in the "idea" (as communicated by the one showing work) and between the idea and the actual work. Like this, "could you discuss this red horse that I see here in your design?" The student then responds with something like this: "As you know my piece deals with domestic violence, and the red horse here is meant to represent man's Id, his basic desires and drives." In this scenario if the instructor finds that the student's answer makes sense, based upon what the instructor knows about Freud, the Id and horses then the item can "stay" in the design. If on the other hand the instructor thinks the answer makes no sense, then the student must remove the item from the composition in order for conceptual harmony to be restored. Critique needs to be refocused around an interpretative critique methodology that focuses on close reading the object. Critique within design school should be focused on the power trio of interpretation, theorization and assessment.

In brief, the problems with this begin with the simple fact that in this method the actual work as an object is sublimated in deference to the work maker's language. In this form of critique, the critique is actually dealing with what is being communicated verbally. It is not primarily looking at the work, and attempting to understand it as a discreet object. Further, in this form of critique the logical consistency of the "idea" becomes the litmus test for the work, not the logical consistency of the object (the work). Often powerful work establishes an internal logic structure that may not conform to linguistic logic. The illogical possibilities of the visual realm are its own form of logic. The third major problem in this form of critique is the simple fact that it forces a kind of reductionist simplicity as a conceptual through line for the work. Because the student is always forced to defend the work, the work out of necessity becomes simplistic, logically bound and linguistically driven.

A simple prescription for the restructuring of critique around an interpretative methodology:

1. The goal of critique is to call the work into crisis, and is based upon the principle that all work can be called into crisis.
2. The maker of the work does not speak about the work.
   a. The work speaks for itself.
   b. Questions are not directed at the maker.
3. Work must be completed at least 48 hours prior to critique.

4. A peer is required to write a comprehensive criticism of the work focused on Morris Weitz categories prior to critique.
5. The written critique must attempt to call the work into crisis from multiple theoretical vantage points.
6. The written criticism is read to begin the critique.
7. A free ranging conversation follows which attempts to understand what the work is actually "about," following from the principle that all work has an "aboutness," it is the residue of human labor and unlike a rock or tree, it is "about" something.
8. The internal fault lines of any given work are exposed and broken apart.
9. The work maker reads a prepared statement at the end of critique addressing salient issues.

Graphic design as a practice will finally be invested with its full measure of power when its culture is able to incorporate and sustain a number of characteristics. It must be able to sustain and nurture a rich critical discourse focused on the products of graphic design. The criticism produced concerning these products must be interpretative in nature, not simply limited to description, and evaluation. Those products as a whole must transcend the simple transubstantiation of corporate values into visual form. Its practitioners must come to an understanding that instrumentalist work decoupled from positive social ramifications is nothing more than base consumerism. Further the field must be flexible enough to incorporate hybrid forms of work that are largely based upon graphic design principles, history and methodology but eschew traditional designer-client relationships.

Without the institutional incorporation of these forms, graphic design ends up marginalizing its most powerful form of cultural output. Hybrid forms of work which rely heavily on graphic design methodology, history and training need to be fully embraced by the field. The many possible histories of graphic design include powerful figures like John Heartfield, El Lissitzky and Kurt Schwitters. And while the field as a whole during the education of the graphic designer, seems to acknowledge a deep debt to this kind of work, contemporary examples are not simply missing but almost tacitly forbidden. (Evidence for this supposition resides in the ridiculously vacuous nature of the fields' professional awards.) And here in a nutshell is both the problem and the promise of graphic design as a contemporary practice.

Historically the most powerful articulations of graphic design as a cultural practice have been pushed to the margins or assimilated by other disciplines. John Heartfield, possibly the single most important graphic designer in history, is a marginal figure at best within graphic design and is a far more important figure within the "Art" world. Contrast Heartfield's cultural profile and "importance" within contemporary graphic design with that of Paul Rand and it becomes clear that commerce trumps humanities.

There is no immutable law that states that in the great panoply of important dead men, Paul Rand must be lionized before John Heartfield. Maybe if we specifically did the opposite—that is if we recognized and embraced the contribution of designers like Heartfield—the field would strive to cultivate this kind of work.

DANIEL EATOCK

Let's start from your story, from you as an independent graphic designer, in London... **Daniel Eatock** Well it is funny, you call me an "independent graphic designer," but I am not a graphic designer. And then also I am not really living and working in London. I mean it is not a mistake, I can see how you made your conclusions, but there is a conflict: because I studied graphic design and I used to have a quasi graphic design practice, but I never considered myself a true graphic designer. I always felt like a rogue, someone who is playing at being a graphic designer. A casual graphic designer ad libbing, doing things on my own terms, finding an alternative way around doing things the proper way. I also have a difficult relationship with the term "graphic," it suggests a style and the way something looks—like a "surface" designer, or a "visual" designer. I was never really interested in visual things, I am more interested in ideas, in concepts that lead to visual results or objects.

Yes, we should have known that, especially after you published your book, Imprint.[1] *Then you mean that you are not interested in graphic design, but you are in art or in design?* **DE** Nothing is fixed, everything is evolving, my practice has always been like that. I have made many graphic design projects, my book *Imprint*, published in 2008, gathers together a combination of works: there are design projects, art projects, and projects that are neither design or art, like my plywood bed, something made out of necessity, approached with the same reductive logic. Subsequently the book has

---

1.   Princeton Architectural Press, New York 2008.

become a kind of interlude, a reflective in-between space that gathers and presents many types of works together in a non-hierarchical way avoiding easy categorisation. It feels disingenuous now more so than ever, to refer to my work as "graphic design," the things I am making and exploring fall a long way outside. I am an artist, but my work does reference design, and I am interested in teaching and exhibiting in the context of graphic design, my work can fit in those spaces really well because it uses a lot of methodology and languages that are connected with graphic design. So when I got your invitation, to think about the show, I didn't want to say "I am not a graphic designer, I can't do this," because I think I can question my own practice and make something that is relevant to the exhibition, even though I am outside of what traditionally graphic design is.

When you say that you would define yourself as an artist rather than a designer, is it because other people ask you to do so or because you feel the need to trace a border, if there is any really? **DE** Categories exist for everything. For the longest time I did not declare myself. I just made work and allowed the audience or viewers to determine for themselves what this work was. But then I found myself in a no-man's land, in this in-between position, outside of any critical discourse of design as well as outside of any discourse on art. That gave some freedom, but I don't think this freedom is so good. I don't know how to describe it, but I want to be engaged, I want to feel that my work is making a contribution, that it is not just introducing things without a position. For me to call myself an artist, that was an easy decision... my work was already there, but it is just more about the way I see my own practice, and refer to it. It is a natural progression and a step to enter a more critical discourse around the work I am making.

How would you describe this process, and what is the role of the book by Lucy Lippard, Six Years: The Dematerialization of the Art Object, *which you often mention as a significant reading for you?* **DE** My dad is a graphic designer and my mum a typographer, when I grew up I knew I wanted to be a designer. But when I went to college at eighteen, I found it difficult to deal with the subjectivity of choosing a colour, a typeface, or making a drawing. Then exploring the college library I discovered a book called *Six Years*. In this book Lucy Lippard was writing about artists in the late 1960s and early 1970s when art became dematerialised, less about aesthetics and more about ideas. At that time—it was in the early 1990s—graphic design was ultra-visual, super graphic: you know, Neville Brody and David Carson, Cranbrook, CalArts... the aesthetics was so layered and visually rich that I felt sick; it was too much. Then I looked to theories originating from an arts context, and in a way I could make a direct comparison. People making conceptual art work were responding to many things—the market, the political situation—, art shifted from being concerned with form and aesthetics to being more about concepts and ideas. So rather than the eye and being based on the look, it was about the mind and the brain, and the way you can think about something. Then I applied these principles to graphic design, trying to strip away everything, in a way to "dematerialise graphic design," allowing the idea to be at the front. Since then all the work I have made has followed that path.

Would you say that you are trying to design or build the world or the environment you live in, from your bed to your book, etc.? **DE** For me there is too much substandard, ill-considered graphic design in the world, and I saw my role as a way of stripping away all the shit to get back to the essence, to the minimum that we can have to make something function. Once you get back to that, then you can create a space for meaning or concepts. I think that graphic design is so much about hiding things, it has become so decorative, that the first thing I felt the need to do is just get back to some kind of basics. Like an archetypal functional thing, that can also have a conceptual twist, so that it makes it more rewarding for the reader/user.

So you feel that you have a responsibility not only for yourself, also towards other people? **DE** When you make anything I think you have to consider the user or the viewer or the audience. The joy of making things is that you can share them. Every time you make a work, you want to see a kind of benefit in making somebody think or question. Ultimately I think it is very sharing.

Then building relationships and collaborating with other people is important for you... **DE** I have always found it difficult to work with other people, almost impossible; I am not good at that. I am usually so sure of what I want to achieve, that there is very little room for other people to add things. The way I have found to work with others is to make works that are open invitations for people to participate. It is not like a collaboration, I do my part of the project, which identifies what the work is, and then I make it public

and I relinquish control. It is like making a frame/template, the content is added/completed by somebody else. Most of my relationships connected with my practice are with people whose work I find interesting: artists, designers, writers, curators, etc. and students.

What kind of student do you want to have a relationship with? **DE** Just committed students. 100% commitment: that is the only thing I ask really. It is not about a quality or a past experience. Teaching already suggests that you have more knowledge than other people, but I am trying not to make that kind of presumption. I prefer to begin equal; it becomes more like a conversation, so I can share things I know. But I only want to share with people who are really committed. Teaching demands so much energy, time, and patience, that the minute I feel that the people I am working with are not committed then I get so irritated, it quickly feels like a waste of time when I could be making my own work.

Being here in your home and studio, observing you preparing lunch for us, cutting the bread you have made yourself, making coffee, one can get a sense of the quality of life you have. It is also clear that this concerns the very space you live and work in, your home and studio. Can you tell us something about this? **DE** Yes. When I left college, I realised that to rent a studio and to rent an apartment costs twice as much. So as a young person, being twenty-two and not having any money, you realise that this is the only option. But it became a pleasure, it is amazing. I can live in my studio. And that means that I do not need to travel, to spend money to get on a bus. I can wake up and, just after breakfast, I can begin making. And then I can do my washing at the same time, I can have a shower, and continue making. I can speak to whoever is on the phone, and continue making. There is no separation. Friends will come by to visit, and then they become part of the work. So it has become a life which is very fluid, with no boundaries. I do not have a routine: I might not work for a week, and then work every day. Some days I check e-mails late in the evening, but with a sense of awareness that maybe I should be reading a book, having a dinner or relaxing. I think I am always trying to challenge my own expectation of what should be done.

You said that you decided to "live in the studio," not "to work at home." Is this deliberate? **DE** I chose to live in the studio. Some people choose to work from home. I think there is a big difference. A home environment or domestic environment in a way is a place to switch off, and I choose to live in a workspace because it is about being active.

Just one last question. For Imprint *you decided to interview yourself. Which question should designers really ask themselves?* **DE** ?

A3

A4

Cola

EXPERIMENTAL JETSET

How would you describe the Experimental Jetset world, and your environment? **Experimental Jetset** When we think about our "world," the first thing that springs to mind is our studio as a physical space. It functions as an atelier, a working place, as an archive of our own work, as a library. It feels like a shelter, as a hiding place. The villain's headquarters. We are quite attached to physical spaces. We know that there are artists and designers who can work from any place in the world, people operating from "virtual studios," but we are not like that at all. To function, we really need to encapsulate ourselves in our own physical environment.

Besides the three of you, how important is it in your life and work to build connections with other people? Would you describe these relationships as a network, or are there better terms to describe them? **EJ** As a graphic designer, it is inevitable that you are part of a network of clients, artists, printers; in the same way, it is inevitable that, as a human being, you are part of a network of friends, partners, family, etc. We only exist in relationship to the other, that's a basic condition of existence. However, we have to admit that we are not very interested in the concept of networks per se. We find it much more interesting and challenging to find, within the networks we are part of, some sort of isolation, some sort of separation. We don't want to dissolve completely in a world of networks; we also need the possibility of disconnection. It is important to be connected, to try to establish meaningful relationships with people and institutes, but at the same time we believe that there should also be some space for isolation. Because we are convinced that isolation and separation are important conditions to come to singular, idiosyncratic ideas, new insights, original ways of thinking, progress. Connections are only meaningful when there is something to connect to, something to connect from. So, for now, we try to focus on that "something."

As far as concerns connections with other graphic designers or professionals in related fields, is this something that happens, or something that you look for? **EJ** Well, as we already described above, we think that disconnecting is as important as connecting. We don't want to lose ourselves in some sort of virtual network culture. Having said that, we do believe in the concept of solidarity. We think small design studios and individual designers should care for each other, defend each other. This whole subculture of "micro-studios" is something really special; we think we should protect it as much as possible. More and more, culture is taken over by slick, large "communication" studios, advertising agencies, marketing people. In the middle of this madness, we should try to keep the idea of the small, independent studio alive. So, wherever we can, we try to support our scene. Whenever we talk to clients, we always try to convince them to work with small graphic design studios instead of large agencies. When clients contact us with an assignment, but we are too busy, we always send them a list of small design studios. Because we really believe in this whole tradition of the small independent design studio.

We have read in an interview with you—in Studio Culture[1] *—that you see the music band model as more inspiring for you than the traditional studio model. You also said that life in the studio "is a way of living, a specific way of looking at the world." Would you consider your way of living and working as a potential "model" for other people?* **EJ** Before we answer this question, we want to clarify something. When we said that we consider the rock band a very interesting model for a design studio, we were certainly not talking about the concept of "the designer as a rock star." We just meant that we really like the rock band as an example of a small unit of people, with a very concentrated, singular vision. What we don't like is the concept of the glamorous, superstar designer; we have always rejected this idea. We hope this is clear! Now, to answer your actual question: indeed, we do consider the rock band to be an interesting model. A rock band is a very tight socio-economic

---

1. Edited by T. Brook, A. Shaughnessy, Unit Editions, London 2009.

unit: just two, three or four people, sharing one collective artistic language. For us, this is a much more interesting model than the mainstream design studio, which has a very typical boss/workers hierarchy: "junior" and "senior" designers, interns and directors, "creative" and "administrative" people. We really dislike these traditional separations; we think they create alienation from the end-product. What we like about the band model is the fact that a band is small enough for every member to feel involved and responsible, but large enough to have the benefits of a collective way of working. Do we consider the "band model" as a potential model for other people? Well, on the one hand, we have a (perhaps silly) utopian belief that society would be better if it would be divided into smaller economic units. That way, workers would be less alienated from their end-products, and we would all enjoy the fruits of our labor in a more meaningful way. But then again, we would never want to pretend this model would work for all people. Maybe there are people who actually enjoy working in large structures, completely losing themselves in anonymity, feeling alienated from their labor; who are we to force our model on them?

Is there a special link with the city in which you decided to settle your studio? Why Amsterdam? Do you think that Europe today can offer a fruitful milieu? **EJ** Amsterdam is important to us. As a city, it represents some of the values that we also try to reflect in our own work. On the one hand, Amsterdam is a very neat, organized city; a traditional stronghold of Social-Democracy, a typical Dutch grid-like environment. On the other hand, Amsterdam has strong subversive undercurrents, a history of anarchists, squatters, provos, poets, artists, hippies. So there is always this very interesting tension between culture and counter-culture. And when we look at our own work, we see that tension as well. As for Europe, to quote Jonathan Richman [American singer and songwriter], "the old world might be dead," but we "still love the old world." We know that a lot of designers and architects are really interested in the new, upcoming economies: China, India, the Middle East. These designers are probably right: these new booming economies will undoubtedly be the future, and Europe will turn into one big open-air museum. But still, we'd rather be in an open-air museum than in one of these hyper-hyper-capitalist mega-cities. So let the more entrepreneurial types travel East; we will remain here, to watch over the ruins of the Old World. Someone has to do it.

How do you read graphic design, how would you describe graphic design for you? EJ "Turning language into objects," that is exactly how we would define graphic design. And that is also why we find the subject of your exhibition, the theme of "worlds," so interesting. The word "world" is very close to the word "word." Building worlds with words; this is very similar to the idea of "turning language into objects." There is a very clear link between using language and creating worlds. In a biblical sense as well: "In the beginning was the word." We are total atheists, but we have to admit that this whole "word/world" concept is quite interesting to us. We think the act of turning language into objects (and thus building worlds with words), is based on a very primal human urge. Language lives inside us; so, as an act of reversal, humans will try to achieve the opposite: to live inside language. To try to turn ideas into a physical environment: that is basically the story of culture, isn't it? For us, this whole idea of "turning language into objects" is also very much linked to the Marxist concept of dialectical materialism. In the words of Marx, "If humans are shaped by their environment, this environment must be made human." So that is pretty much our conviction: the idea that we are shaped by our surroundings, and that we have to shape our surroundings in return. A very modernist view on culture, actually.

Do you, as designers, feel you have a responsibility towards society or the world around you? EJ We absolutely feel a responsibility, and a strong commitment. What we always try to do in our work is to emphasize the fact that we are living in a constructed, designed environment: a world that has been shaped by people, and thus also can be changed by people. We try very hard not to create images that will imprison people in some kind of illusion, or magic spell: instead, we want to produce artifacts that will keep people constantly aware that they are looking at a constructed object. So, by using subtle-yet-stubborn technical devices (folds, cuts, perforations, empty space, etc.), and by trying to let the designed object refer to the medium of graphic design itself, we try to "break the spell," to make clear to people that a poster is not some sort of magical, god-given image, but that it is a constructed, human-made object: a piece of paper with ink on it. We once read that Brecht, in his early plays, used to have a banner on stage that proclaimed "DON'T STARE SO ROMANTICALLY." So that is basically what we try to do in our work: to try to disrupt the romantic gaze. So we feel we have a responsibility. But it is first of all an aesthetic responsibility; a set of beliefs that manifests itself in the designed object. Do we think graphic designers should have a commitment? We don't know. There are designers out there who seem to function without any social commitment, and they make work that we feel is really important. And then there are designers who are totally driven by social commitment, and they make work that we feel is less interesting. Some designers are socially important, without knowing it, without even wanting it. You cannot force social commitment onto people, we think.

In 2008, opening the Networks of Design *annual conference of the Design History Society, the French sociologist Bruno Latour argued that the on-going extension of the word "design" can offer an index of the change in the ways we deal with objects. According to him, "design" is one of the terms that has replaced the word "revolution": not in the sense that design is revolutionary but meaning that design is a substitute for revolution and modernization, meaning that, today, designing—that, in Latour's view, is always re-designing and implies a certain degree of humility—is an "antidote to hubris and to the search for absolute certainty, absolute beginnings, and radical departures."[2] Would you agree with this view?* **EJ** To be honest, we do not know enough about Latour to react properly on his lecture. Totally unrelated to Latour, we have indeed noticed that the meaning of the word "design" has shifted a bit, lately. In popular media, the word suddenly has a certain gloss. More and more, it seems to represent the shiny world of iPhones, iPods, iPads, TED speakers, a friendly-green sustainability, a bright sort of pragmatism, "innovation," "added business value," "social design," "network economies," etc. The people behind this newer, sexier brand of design seem to radiate a glamorous sort of optimism. We are certain that these new design leaders have the best intentions, and in fact, we have no doubt that these brilliant minds will probably deliver us to a better future. But still, it is a world we personally don't feel attached to. When we look at our personal interests, it is exactly the "hubris" we are interested in. In our own way, we try to explore those obsolete formats, dead languages, forlorn utopias, forgotten subcultures, lost worlds. We still believe there is something to be

---

2.   B. Latour, *A Cautious Prometheus? A Few Steps Toward a Philosophy of Design (with Special Attention to Peter Sloterdijk)*, keynote lecture, "Networks of Design," Falmouth, Cornwall, September 3, 2008, http://www.bruno.latour.fr/articles/article/112-DESIGN-CORN-WALL.pdf.

said for "absolute certainty, absolute beginnings, and radical departures," if only for the tragic beauty that can be found in those failed attempts. We are fascinated by the margins of design, radical gestures, isolated ideas. We believe there are still interesting things to find in the ruins of modernist movements, in the hubris of the Old World: plans, scenarios, or, in the words of the English writer Owen Hatherley, "spectral blueprints."[3]

Graphic design and designers of course are not in a vacuum, and there are other figures and worlds that revolve around them. As far as foundations and museums are concerned, how important are they, in your opinion, in discussing and supporting the culture of graphic design? **EJ** Foundations, museums and other government-funded institutes are important, because government funding is basically the only alternative there is right now for the dominant ideology of the so-called "free market." Whereas "free market" thinking is motivated mainly by maximizing profit (by giving the consumer what they want, and thus what they already know), government funding has the potential to enable artists and designers to explore "unpopular" concepts. And we are convinced that it is exactly in this sphere of "unpopularity" where the real innovation and progress take place. This is the concept of the "cultural vanguard," and we very much believe in this. We are not saying that we are against the "free market" per se. But we do think that there should be some space left for alternative systems, zones ungoverned by dominant market thinking. And government-funding is a very concrete way to create these alternative spheres, to explore other ways of thinking, making and seeing. Unfortunately, as more and more European countries are transforming themselves from Social-Democracies into Neo-Liberal economies, and as more and more museums and foundations are dependent on private sponsors, we see that "free market" thinking is increasingly infiltrating culture. This has a very concrete effect on the practice of graphic design: more and more cultural institutes shed their ideological feathers, and choose to work with advertising agencies rather than with small, independent graphic design studios. It is a sad state of affairs, but for now, there's not much we can do about it. We should just keep on going, against the grain.

---

3. *Militant Modernism*, Zero Books, Ropley 2009.

May 14, 2010 / London

FUEL

[Giorgio Camuffo] *I can still remember one lecture you gave at a conference in Italy—the theme was art and design. You sat down and said: "We are graphic designers, take a look at the yellow pages, and you will find us under 'graphic design.'" Do you remember that?* **Stephen Sorrell** Because, few years ago lots of people were pretending they were more than graphic designers, trying to "elevate" themselves, and we were not ashamed to be called "graphic designers," even if we feel that what we did and do is quite broad.

Since then, in fifteen years, have things changed? You have become publishers as well with Fuel Publishing; has this new path changed your approach or how you see yourselves? **Damon Murray** We are still independent and do graphic design. I don't think that our approach has changed, we still produce stuff that we are interested in producing. At this stage we are really interested in making and publishing our own books; but we still see ourselves as graphic designers, that is just what we are doing. When we are making films and we are doing film titles and things like that, we do not necessarily see ourselves as directors, we still are graphic designers but we are making films. So the whole kind of graphic authorship argument, the fact that we are generating our own content, etc., we see this as being part of graphic design, not separate from it. Our definition of graphic design is broad rather than narrow. This perception has not changed over the twenty years we have been working together. **ss** We have always felt that with graphic design you can be a photographer, you can art direct, you can draw the typography... And in our books we also edit the text and the writing, and it is not just a visual thing. So although the design is very important, the content and the subject matter is what drives them. We are not just designing books that look nice. The content is like a starting point.

Could you tell us something about your background? **ss** We both went to college at Central St Martins in 1987. Then we both went to the Royal College of Art in 1990, which is where we started working together as Fuel, that was originally four of us. We published our magazines, which were also called *Fuel*, and that is really when we started generating works and publishing our own works. And again we were doing the photography, commissioning writing, editing, etc. **dm** Everything. From this work some of the subjects we covered then found their way into films, experimental digital film, and then we pushed that further and made books of our own work, and that has progressed into this. The whole thing is quite a natural progression; we have always done work that is our own, that is not commissioned work, so we have always been able to work for ourselves. **ss** We have always had our own ideas that we want to communicate.

Your website features a painting that portrays you two shaking hands and looking into each other's eyes. Does this have a particular meaning for you? **ss** Well, Damon's dad does the paintings, and he has probably painted one every five years. The one online was the third, and it was painted when

we became just two of us. I suppose the handshake is like a partnership agreement. There is a new one, actually: this is a kind of development of the handshake! [The new painting portrays the two sitting in a library, engaged in an arm wrestling match.] It is a library somewhere in Italy, we got it from the Internet. We wanted it to represent our books.

Besides the painting, what are the bases of your partnership? **dm** The thing is we share interests outside graphic design. We are not really up on the latest graphic design trends;

we are more interested in... all things outside graphic design, because they are things that we potentially bring into our world of graphic design, by publishing or film, or in whatever medium that we can make them work. And that is what keeps our relationship going, and what makes us turn up for work every morning. **SS** I think it is also because we did go to college together and we have learned

how to be designers together. At college we were working as a group, and it felt easier to work ideas out of each other rather than working on your own: you learn from each other.

What about relationships with other people or professionals? **SS** Particularly with the books we have made, it is definitely a collaboration with the authors, because we are editors as well as designers, and we work very closely with the authors on the contents and how the book should look. For a number of our books we have worked with the same author again, and so that kind of relationship is important. We don't have so many relationships with other graphic designers, this doesn't work for us really. We know a few other designers but we do not collaborate with them.

You mean it is a choice in a way? **DM** Yes it is deliberate. **SS** Not to be horrible, but we are making our own mark, trying to be distinctive. **DM** You have to follow your own path. If everyone around you is a graphic designer you think, "What am I going to learn from these people?" because they are all trying to follow the same path. I think for us it is a natural thing, going in a different direction, saying "I am interested in these artists, in these authors, in these films," and thinking how we can bring elements of those to graphic design, rather than focusing on typefaces all day, because this is not going to get you anywhere, it is not going to progress you...

As far as concerns publishing, how do you choose the authors, the texts, the subject? **DM** I think there are no rules about how that system works. I think there almost could be a Fuel book on any subject, but our involvement has

a large part of it. When we are publishing, if we do not feel fully engaged in the project, then it doesn't really feel like it is worth for us putting the effort into it. So, we need to know that we feel part of that process as well.

Many graphic designers nowadays are trying to produce books on their own, and this appears to be an expanding phenomenon. Do you have any opinion on that? **ss** It is nearly all publishing, and we are still designing books for other publishers as well. But I suppose that other graphic designers and teams publish generally about graphic design. I do not think there are really other graphic designers publishing books with the same broad subject matter that we produce. **dm** I think it is true, it is like an underground phenomenon, and those type of publishers have an interest in graphic design. Our interest is in crime; is in archival images and in Russian tattoos; it is not necessarily in graphic design. Although we obviously do have some interest in that area, it is not something that we will necessarily publish a book on. So from that perspective I think that is why we are slightly different as publishers, because—this is a little bit presumptuous—we feel our books have to work in a real environment, which is the publishing environment, which is the bookshop environment, where on a Saturday afternoon someone might pick one of our books off the shelf. I think that a lot of books that are published by other designers work in a graphic design environment. We want to reach people outside, through our design but outside of the graphic design world. Generally speaking, we produce five thousand copies of every book, and you need to make some money back to make the whole process viable. Other stuff is produced more underground. I am not saying that scene isn't viable; it has its own kind of hierarchy, I am sure, but it is not necessarily the one that we are interested in, because it appears to be quite narrow, as long as it is only talking to other graphic designers.

Did you have any reference or inspiration when you started, and when you decided to start a publishing company? **dm** When we were at college there was really no one doing anything that interested us; there was a standard path that people followed from college to the BA and then the MA, and then they went to work for big design companies. We were a little bit different: after we left college, we just set up on our own. We didn't know how anything happened, so we made it up as we went along. And it is the same with the publishing company. There isn't any model we could follow, especially with these books, because... I don't think that many publishers would publish these books necessarily, because they are quite odd quirky things, and they might not have seen a market. So there is no kind of formula.

When you say that you did not know how things happened, do you mean you had not had proper training to start working? **DM** If there is anything I recommend to kids at college, is to learn something about business. We came out of college and we didn't know anything about business. **SS** And also about handling getting things printed. Students need to know certain things when they talk to printers, and we were never told that. **DM** Maybe that is because we went to very creative colleges, like St Martins and Royal College of Art, and we were taught more how to think conceptually. It is a massive thing, because at the end of the day graphic design is an industry and people may build careers to make money out of it; but no one seems to teach the economic part of it. However small, no one speaks about it. It is assumed that you can pick it up from someone or somewhere else.

What percentage of your work takes the publishing company? **SS** I think 50 percent.

All your books are your production, from an economical point of view? **DM** Yes. **SS** Thames and Hudson do the distribution, but that is when the book is finished, so they sell it. But in the act of creating the book we do everything.

Has your relationship with commissioners changed since you invested so much on your own projects? **SS** I do not think so. **DM** The people we work with they know our work, and they know us; and generally they are people we met and we get along with, so they know what they are getting.**SS** I think there is a sort of natural selection. We don't get offered the type of work that isn't suitable for us.

You mentioned that you want to reach a broad audience, and not just the graphic design community. So how do you imagine your public and readers? **DM** I think our audience is ourselves. I think it is almost a waste of energy trying to think whom your book is going to appeal to. If you can make it the most interesting thing you can, so that it appeals to you, then hopefully by default it should appeal to other people. If you are thinking "ok, my audience is graphic designers, so they're going to be twenty to thirty-five years old, they are going to be in this bracket of income"... that is when you start to lose touch with what interested you in the subject of the book in the first place. It is holding on to the moment of interest that is important, making sure that spark finds its way into the final form of the book.

... else it would be kind of producing a fake, in a sense? **DM** Yes, it is like you try to rationalize the whole process too much, and there is no life left in it after that. You need to feel a bit more rather than narrow it down. We are not calculating.

One last question. Do you feel that the notion of world and worlds can be a good access point for discussing or presenting graphic design, and specifically your work? **ss** I think that our books are like little worlds. **DM** I think that is why we try to do all our books. The nice element with reading a book is that you become immersed in it: you are in a place that is in your head but it is also in the paper. That is the place that we are always trying to get to in our books. So people can come and find it out for themselves. Yes, it is a world.

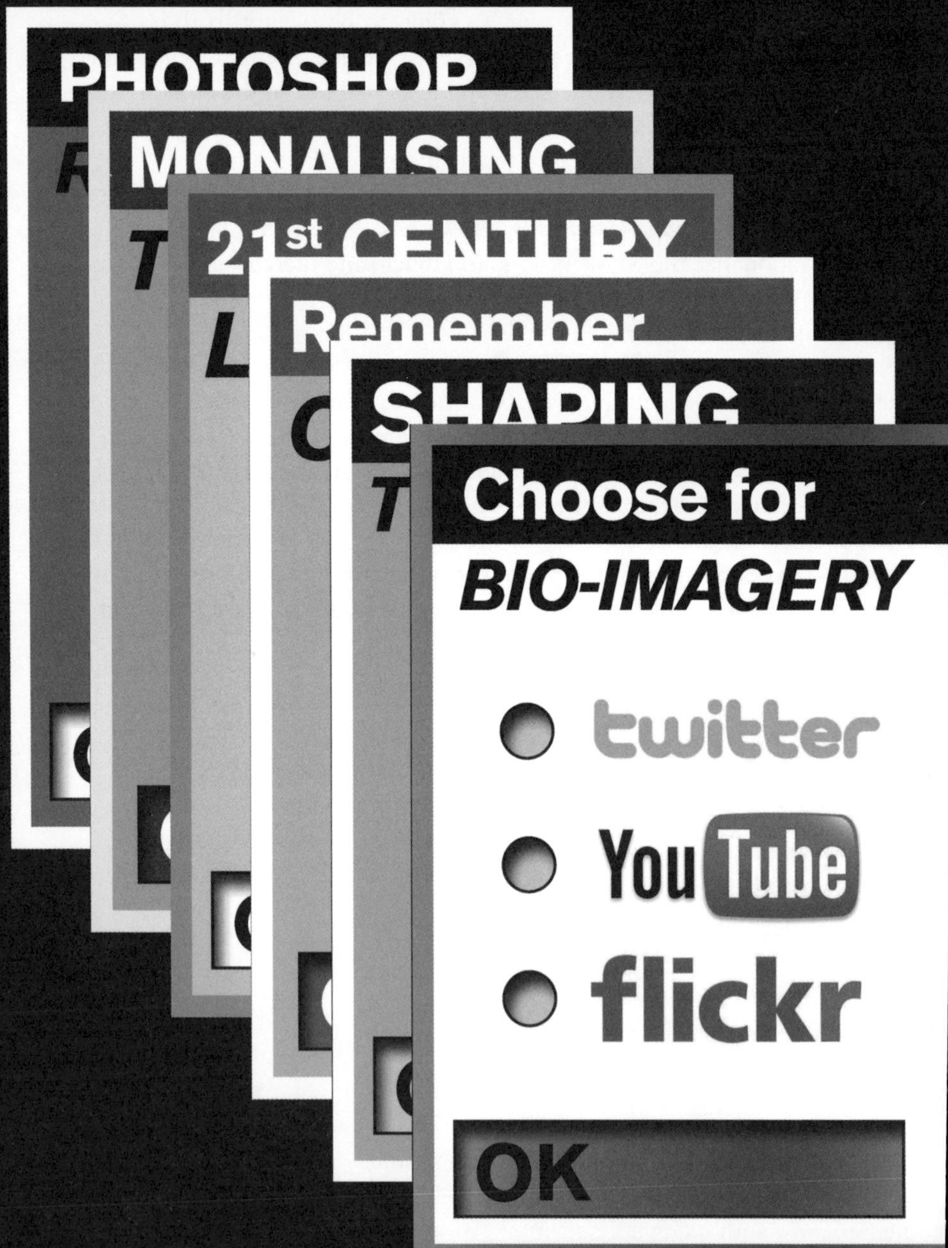
PHOTOSHOP
MONALISING
21st CENTURY
Remember
SHAPING
Choose for
BIO-IMAGERY
twitter
YouTube
flickr
OK

MIEKE GERRITZEN

From Dada to Data

The profession of graphic design, which until the 1990s appeared to be small, craft-based and highly cultural, has in the 21st century expanded into a popular, democratized discipline at the center of the arts and the modern media. Graphic design is a profession in a permanent state of change, influenced by technological advancements. The printing tradition has made way for a world of transitory media.

Graphic design is a young profession, around a century old. This interesting cultural discipline arose during the same era when movements like Dada, De Stijl and the Bauhaus were taking shape. These developments had an important impact on the design profession's freedom and versatility. During this period, beauty, social consciousness, opposition and criticism came together, but so did commerce, art and a cross-disciplinary mentality. It was a time when art had not yet been definitively divided into different disciplines. William Addison Dwiggins first used the term "graphic design" in 1922.

If we look at how the profession developed so quickly, we see that technology was the driving factor. Along with technical advancements, it was the first generation of graphic designers who set the parameters of the profession. The first standard paper sizes and typesetting fonts date from this era.

Only after World War II did the profession acquire more depth. Graphic design developed as a sociocultural area. The limits of the profession were defined between the 1950s and the 1980s. Graphic design courses were established at the art academies. Graphic design became a profession in the Netherlands, with its own association. An interesting debate got under way around socially engaged design and the aesthetics of the field. Morality was a key point for discussion; many considered it highly important for designers to hold political opinions and be able to air them through the visual language of their work. On the other side, some designers believed that it was more important to focus on an accelerated state of evolution thanks to technological progress. The two ideas were at odds at the time, but the debate kept things lively.

Graphic design heritage did not become important until the 21st century. The field took forty or fifty years to become a profession with clear parameters. Since the 1990s, the state of the field of graphic design has begun to look more like it did in the 1930s, when art, design, other cultural disciplines, commerce, and technology overlapped.

The arrival of the Internet in the early 1990s brought about a great shift in the graphic profession. Today, everyone busies themselves with graphic design every day. In the age of the Internet, mobile phones, billboards, printed clothing, and so on, everyone communicates through images. Interactive images, legible images, moving images, dynamic images, all influence our thinking and call forth emotions. This change has affected the role of the graphic profession. Professional designers must redefine their position, as a metaposition, now that graphic design has been democratized.

Everyone Is a Designer

With the rise of new media in the 1990s, there was an explosive increase in the use of images for communication. The Internet is the basis for this relatively new form of communication, to which everyone is now contributing; people interact largely via screens, which transmit input from more and more people, in forms such as photos on Flickr ("Share your photos. Watch the world.") and videos on YouTube ("Broadcast Yourself").

The media are becoming increasingly image-heavy, and the objects around us are becoming media—it is not only shop advertising, traffic signs and billboards that function as informative objects but buildings, cars, high-speed trains, airports and clothing as well. Our environment used to be made up of things; nowadays it consists of information. We have developed a jumpy, nonlinear thinking style that allows us to comprehend complex information through images.

Hordes of people post images online; these amateurs now receive graphic software packages and simple image-processing programs free with their new computers and cameras, and sometimes even directly installed on their mobile phones. Today, the young and old process their own holiday snapshots, place them online, even design their own visual identities.

For decades, graphic designers have taken inspiration from the possibilities afforded by printing and craft techniques. The qualities particular to visual reproduction, the various styles and methods of presenting different kinds of information, laid the foundations for today's visual communication. Lots of images are often automatically generated and constructed on computers; an object or style can be determined, rendered and visualized with a single keystroke.

After the mid-1990s, when the first image appeared on the World Wide Web, attention began to be paid to digital environments, such as browsers, and the first web designers appeared. Yet despite growing interest in network environment design, online aesthetics are still poorly developed compared to those in the physical realm. Facebook and Twitter are the most popular forms of communication today. Huge numbers of people spend time every day in the extremely unattractive environments of these social networking programs. This form of communication recalls the early days of the Internet, when technology was the main driver of aesthetics.

Developers have incorporated the basic elements of form, layout and style in design software packages. Most of the filters in these programs are based on techniques, effects and visual styles that were invented for older media. The famous designers of the past developed these characteristic styles and visual languages in their work and created authorship and fame in this way.

The new generation of designers is less concerned with developing individual visual languages but instead sees designing mainly as a matter of choosing from among the range of styles and movements offered in software packages. They combine and manipulate existing styles, often unaware of the fact that the visual languages they use were even created by designers. They lack knowledge and cannot refer to their predecessors. Meanwhile, amateur image producers have no idea whatsoever that their work could be contributing to the world of culture.

The threat of visual inflation is mainly caused by the image-producing masses, who lack basic knowledge of visual culture. More and more products that deliver custom-tailored information are coming on the market. Consumers now serve themselves instead of being served. The Internet and network technology have utterly changed the way we communicate, campaign and publish. The flood of new images is unstoppable, and the tools and gadgets for making and consuming them have become heavily marketed everyday products.

Design schools keep proliferating. The technological possibilities for image-making are becoming more advanced all the time; every month a new product with higher image resolution comes on the market. We are zooming in closer and closer on the image and losing our distance from the act of image-making. We are adrift in a visual culture. Creativity is the driving force behind the Western economy; design schools are multiplying like mushrooms. But are we in any state to adequately educate the thousands of design students?

It is an evolutionary fact: human beings find moderation difficult and wage a constant battle with self-control in consumer society. After food, traffic and the environment, it is time to take a critical look at visual culture. Is there such a thing as an organic image? A free-range image? An image that has been allowed time to grow, to develop a relationship with the world around it? An image that has been handled by skilled image processors?

The Art of Graphic Design

Graphic design, the visual communication profession, is part of a global network and is a sanctuary for text and image, dynamism and change. With styles, ideas, views and methods proliferating, design is part of the bombardment of images that surrounds us. The media are increasingly made up of images, and our environment is becoming media. And graphic design is all about the image.

Forget the rules and received wisdom about legible text. Text is image: all images that have become iconic through fame, repetition and recognizability are perceived and used as typography. This expansion of the meaning of typography adds value to the language we use to communicate. An icon such as a portrait of Barack Obama, an Apple logo or the sound of an incoming e-mail message is a legible sign, as much as a word that is made up of letters and literally readable is. The language of identity is what determines our visual culture of reading images and looking at language.

Images are often associated with "low culture" and words with "high culture." But this narrow way of thinking is disappearing. Graphic design has dispensed with categories. The morality of the 1970s and 1980s has made way for a broad view of the world, globalized and meditated. Contrasts go together effortlessly; commerce and culture, scholarship and glamour, subcultures and obscure worldviews have a dynamic effect on the economy, and socially engaged designers find inspiration in populism. Cultural niches have a powerful economic influence.

Buildings, cars, fashion, products and art communicate. The explosive growth in artistic production over the past decade has had an enormous influence on the traditional world of art and design. A new generation of professional artists and designers is appearing on the scene. They have grown up with the Internet, mobile phones and virtual worlds. For them, technology is a fundamental part of culture and identity. The new professionals create their own context and do not necessarily seek a connection with the established cultural elite, e.g., museums.

A new world is taking shape around graphic design, because this is a profession that immediately feels the effects of the digital revolution. Graphic design has an influence on the aestheticization of society, the creative industry, and how people interact and communicate through media. The profession continues to develop and respond to technological developments, and everyone is taking part. There is no need for a new definition of the dynamic profession of graphic design. It is in constant motion.

Here, in Graphic Design Wonderland, designers are completely free to pursue personal fascinations; raise social questions, large and small, for discussion; and convert society's changes and new insights into powerful and striking images. Sometimes these take the form of products you can buy online or at the supermarket. Sometimes you can only look at them, on the Internet or at a museum. Designers are creating a new market of cultural products with its own ideas, sense of engagement, characteristic visual language, and views on how the media influence and guide our lives. Designers are the ones who look at the world of culture and see how vast it has become.

Graphic design is developing an interesting autonomous side that provides today's world with reflection and depth. It is a form of cultural contemplation that in the past century we often encountered in fine art.

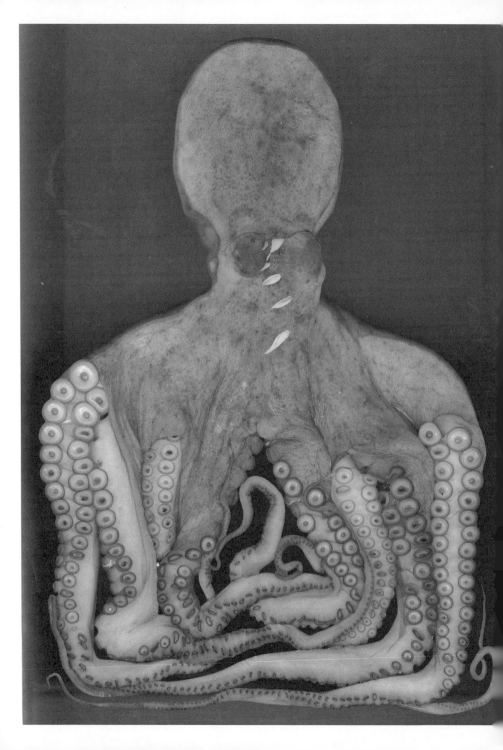

< Par défaut >
Christophe Jacquet (Toffe)
Manuel Joseph[1]

CHRISTOPHE JACQUET
TOFFE

Pig Cupid, His Rosy Snout Rooting Erotic Garbage
Mina Loy, poet, wife of Arthur Cravan[2]

Here, it is scanning that goes on, true; but just over there is matter. It is al-most matter, the poor matter that is, almost, the best shared between human-ity: grub. Or rather, it is the stuff that one generally doesn't stuff one's face with: heart, tripe, liver. These are the basic ingredients of a meal that makes no attempt to be a celebration—a frugal "digital" repast (to be eaten with the fingers); the crumbs of a New Year's Eve in a hovel. Born out of an experience of plastic form and graphics that has developed since 1984 under the influ-ence of a "Mac® environment," design as developed by Toffe is the "fragile" constitution of a food chain about which there is little that is Darwinian; that challenges an ethics which is supposedly related to the development of new technologies. Rather than information highways, complete with reserved lanes and toll booths; rather than traffic-jammed Internet(s), it would seem more suitable here to talk about two-lane local roads, with their lines of plane trees, their bumps and jolts, their Cronenberg-style accidents: a mêlée of human flesh.
OCDE and CD-Rom are the two mainstays of the Communication Internationale. Rather than taking apart, here one dismembers. The sacrifi-cial rite based upon the use of a decomposing machine (the scanner) evokes

---

1.   Extracts from *Signes*, double issue 13/14, 1995.

2.   A. Cravan, *Oeuvres*, Champs libres. A rare case of a publishing house where the director ends up in car park, guts and head in fresh air.

the foundation of world. The cosmogony, however, is that of the bazaar, because the decomposition deliberately omits anything putrid—which is nevertheless necessarily reintroduced in the form of the finished work. The exhaustion of virtual communities is put to the test by the de-communion of organs, scanned in low resolution within an apartment on which the property market has fixed its eye.

A body in parts is little different to body parts—that is, the social body; one might as well get political when the hypallage (a figure of speech in which there is a transfer of epithet to a noun head that is its—technical—grammatical "support" without being semantically related) promised by Toffe opens up a "third" way, from which rises up a "third" term: "organic." The "revolutionary" dichotomy between analogical /digital has been glossed so many times that the organic has fallen away into a trap set by the single-media Internationale, which stands hieratic and obscene in its commitment to a total network that serves its own ends.

"Cattle" is almost a d-formed anagram of "tackled" (finished off)
The spleen thus becomes transformed into an object-delator of the districts of social and spiritual demolition; districts of high-security meat—a digital soup inaccessible to what (for want of something better but, even so, with defiant intent) one might call "the people." Toffe's work is popular. It is not the sort of soup tarted up by the prophets of a two-speed society (without ABS); where the giblets—measured by the scale of the displaced—are giblets for the dejected and displaced, for those who feel useless and lost when faced with the "technicists" who have taken over from the "technocrats." Lycurgus, king of the Edones, cuts off his son's hands and feet, thinking he is trimming a vine. Dionysus gives him back his sight, and thereafter the mad king rules over a sterile world. Dismemberment, dissociation, foundation: when the limbs of a child can easily be mistaken for the limp oaths of those occupying the media-world. In Colombia, certain street kids are actually known as desechables—the "throwaways," disposable sacks of human organs. Toffe's images are not subject to intuition; they are actively disobedient towards the drawn line of an informatics horizon within which the human body is held square by pixels of misery. To denounce this misery, developed by development, means to exploit it—aesthetically speaking. If graphics is a "process creating order," Toffe is not the developer thereof; dismemberment is the basis, and the reduction to its basis, of a process.

"Wherever there is a cadaver, vultures gather" (Matthew 24,28). Deleuze claims: "The first organ to be privatized, to be pushed out off social space, was the anus. It is the anus that provides the model for privatization, at the same time as it is money that embodies the new abstraction of flux."[3]

"Chops" is an incomplete anagram of "chaps"

Illusory digital food chains are formed *via* the programming of a derisory system, which embodies the electronic media. They set as their goal the fabrication of images based on living components.

Obsessed by the idiosyncrasy of cheap cuts (tripe, or what in butcher-speak are "innards"), work is the relentless metonymic working-through of social ruptures and fractures. The dirty organic worlds thus constituted are off-key with respect to the a-political digital ergonomics of neutrality and fatalism. Technological *bricolage* (*bricolage* in Barthes' sense of the term) is a struggle, becoming a stinging critique of all the defeatist aporie resulting from the "media whole." *Via* a decoder, "flux" against "in-nards" to indicate there is "no exit."[4]

The apostles of cognitive psychology, of the treatment of signals, of the famous "ia" and "diktato1," seem unaware that "geography serves primarily to wage war." The new technologies themselves serve primarily the interests of economic groups. Hence, the humanity that is cut into pieces by interests ends up sidelined, reduced to cheap cuts.

"Leader" is an anagram of "dealer"

---

3. G. Deleuze, F. Guattari, *Capitalisme et Schizophrénie, L'anti-Oedipe*, Minuit, Collection "Critiques."
4. Last words of Bret Easton Ellis's *American Psycho*.

ERIK KESSELS
KesselsKramer

When considering the notion of "worlds," it was quite natural to think about you, especially for the relational quality of your work. How did KesselsKramer start? **Erik Kessels** I started out more as an illustrator, but it was quite a lonely profession. Then I worked for an advertising agency, and what I liked there was that you worked with a lot of people from a lot of different disciplines together in one place—you have writers, business people, designers. But in a lot of advertising agencies the work is quite corporate, so after about eight years, Johan [Kramer] and I decided to start our own place. We condensed the agency model, leaving out account people and keeping producers, strategists and creative people—designers, writers, art directors. When necessary, we also hired in outside talent, for instance particular designers who can add something extra to a job.

This attitude and approach also seems to be reflected in the environment you have decided to work in—the church, with over thirty people in it. How would you describe it? **EK** We see both the church and the company as organized chaos. Everybody works in whatever way suits them but we try to underpin this with a little bit of order. There isn't a lot of hierarchy, so when a new person arrives, it is good if that person has some idea of what they want to get out of the company, of what ideas they would like to contribute. From the very beginning, we give young people quite a lot of responsibility. Some people don't like working in such a system, so they leave in a few months, but others stay ten or more years.

So KesselsKramer is like a world that is open to exchange with people, with different disciplines and cultures? **EK** I think it is very important for creative people to be interested in the world outside their discipline. In my experience, people that only work within their field dry up pretty quickly. You need to look beyond your front door, especially nowadays, because the creative fields aren't so defined anymore. Graphic design is not purely graphic design anymore. I think anyone who wants to be a professional graphic designer nowadays needs to be more flexible, have bigger ambitions and, above all else, start with an idea. From one point of view, graphic design is now completely democratic. Everybody can be a graphic designer. Everyone has a computer with the relevant programs. Everyone has an opinion about what works and what doesn't. All of this means that the people designing professionally really have to focus on their one remaining point of differentiation, and that means starting with an interesting idea. It is not like the old days, when graphic design meant learning certain craft skills. At KesselsKramer, we are definitely not only about graphic design, totally not. We are also not purely about advertising either. We are not purely about anything. Our biggest challenge is to come up with the best idea.

Then you mean that it is important to be highly motivated? **EK** The only one who can push you is you. Also within the agency I encourage this kind of behavior, but not everybody is up to it. In the end, it is also about your personal passion. I think that if you are "creative" then you can use that for purposes other than only making advertising or only making graphic design. It is good to step beyond those borders. It is something I wanted to do ten years ago, but at that time it was not possible to cross the borders of your own discipline: people would say, "Listen, you do this and that is what you do, nothing else." But nowadays the field has opened up much more. The thing I like the most is to make an idea and use it to tell a certain story. You can tell stories for a client, you can also do it in a book, in a film... that is what I like. The most interesting campaigns I have made for clients are campaigns with a certain story in them, a narrative running throughout.

But is it your story or the client's? **EK** It is both. A story can be personal, but needs to contain universal elements that people generally can relate to.

Oliviero Toscani used to say, "It is not Benetton who uses me, but it is me who uses Benetton" to tell certain stories... **EK** Well in our case it is a little bit different. When you work for clients you have a responsibility to make the work as good as possible, and also ensure that your work is not full of lies. You also need to have a personal connection with clients: you can have all the good ideas you like, but if the person on the other side of the table doesn't agree, doesn't understand what you are doing, then it is useless. Toscani and Benetton had a great connection. Great advertising work needs the cooperation of two parties: client and agency. The same goes for books. A book needs a public. So if you only do it because you like it or the client likes it, then it makes no sense. What I really like, also with KesselsKramer Publishing, is that sometimes you see a group of people who are touched and enjoy what you do, and that is a nice thing. At the same time, it is important that you find new ways to do your work, that you find a new way to tell stories. With every job, you always have a big highway, the place lots of people go looking for answers, but you need to find the side roads because those are the most interesting.

Is this like "lateral thinking"? **EK** Yes, in a way, but it should never be about being tricksy. Sometimes what we do is very easy. For instance, if you see a

poster of a dance show on the street—in Amsterdam they are everywhere—
the typography is always dancing as well. And if you have a film poster
you always have pictures of the actors and then a lot of small type at the
bottom. It is always the same. So if you just do this differently, the results
are already surprising. But you also need to support your choices: why do
I do this? Does this work? You should not do it only to be different, it
should also have a function. Another thing I found about graphic design is
that a lot of people are very good in making it but then they are not very
good in promoting it themselves. It is always good when a graphic designer
can also talk about his or her work, because that is almost more important
than making something.

*This is a relevant topic: young designers should be aware of that, else the
very same images and posters would have it all.* **EK** In the future as I also
said, the opportunities will be limitless, but that is a handicap as well. I think
that every day new opportunities appear, but every day also people are getting more confused. Nowadays if you look at the work of young people, it
is brilliant; they are almost totally developed when they are twenty-three,
but you also see that a lot of young people have a sort of quarter-life crisis.
When they are twenty-five they have a total burn-out because they get too
much information and because their career develops so quickly. In ten-years
time technology will be so far that everybody can do everything, or can do a
little bit of everything. If you look now at somebody making a birthday announcement or a birthday card, they can make it look fantastic, something
that fifteen years ago wouldn't have been possible. But in the future I think
it is even more important that you focus on the main idea. I think it does not
happen every week or every month, but what I enjoy the most is that I make
something or come up with an idea that scares me. Maybe that happens once
or twice a year... that you are afraid of your own ideas. That is quite nice.
I hope to have that experience more often.

*How do you read your responsibility in your work, and in front of the public
or the world out there?* **EK** People have great responsibility in whatever
field they are in, but perhaps especially in advertising. For me, it is important
not to lie in commercials, not even by telling half-truths. It is funny, because
advertising is full of lies and compromises. So sometimes you should be ironic, funny or emotional and I think it is good to be entertaining, but I think

it is also good to be authentic. Also, to go back to Toscani and Benetton, I think that at a certain moment people started criticizing his work a lot. But I think that people forget that in the 1980s Benetton was the first company to show all those different "coloured" models on a billboard: that is how they started, and then they went further and deeper. Some people only judge it from the last

work, while there was also a certain story. I also think that the work of Toscani did a lot for advertising in general. Similarly, I believe that some of the work we did at that time had an impact because it was authentic. From the beginning in 1995 or 1996 we started to take photographs of ordinary people in the street and to use them in advertising. We thought that was just normal: why not use these people? They are like a mirror for consumers, helping us to see that not everybody is perfect. That was quite a shock at that time. But then suddenly agencies started to use only real people and that moment passed. You definitely have a responsibility, but I never had the feeling that we crossed the line. The funny thing in advertising is that the people who really cross the line never get criticized: if you look at television—and in Italy I think it is even worse—a woman is still in the kitchen and when she has trouble with the washing machine there is always a guy who comes in from the back garden to help. It is a stereotype. In a way those are the things people should really criticize.

In Italy advertising is very boring, many opportunities are wasted. **EK** Yes, it could be used as a way to build relationships and interaction.

NA KIM

Can you tell us something about yourself, your education in graphic design, andhow did you become interested in this discipline and practice? **Na Kim** The starting point for my interest in graphic design was more simple than premeditated. I studied industrial design at an engineering college in South Korea. Yet during the years there, printed materials always fascinated me as a communication object: the visual languages made of typography and images, the printing process and its outputs, everything in graphic design thrilled me. Books especially appeal me a lot, as objects that exist in space and time—and I guess this comes also from my education as an industrial designer. Moreover, while studying industrial design, I often found myself questioning the position of the designer as a passive figure in a process that responds to the client's needs according to well-analyzed statistics. In a way graphic design allowed me to distance myself from the capitalist drifts of the industrial system. I was more interested in exploring the possibility of self-determination as a maker or, as an author, than in designing as a service-provider. Of course, the idea that all graphic designers are free from the capitalist economic system is totally wrong, but I believe there is much more freedom for them. As I started my career as a graphic designer in Korea, I was interested in collaboration with other people from different backgrounds, including product designers, architects and artists, especially from different cultures. In many cases I found that collaboration allows me to widen my viewpoint on the situation. It was then that, by chance, I found out about the Werkplaats Typografie in the Netherlands. To me the Netherlands' cultural system seemed ideal, allowing more independent forms of collaboration. Werkplaats Typografie is renowned for its practical education system. There

I could have many possibilities to collaborate and experiment, taking multifarious positions, and that provided me many opportunities to widen my own world as a graphic designer. After graduation, I could combine all these different cultural issues—Korea and the Netherlands—by organizing some projects, like *Starting from Zero*, the ten years exhibition of the Werkplaats Typografie in Seoul, and the magazines *Graphic* and *umool umool*. Actually, it was not my plan to set a studio in the Netherlands, yet with these chances to produce some kind of cultural chemistry, I finally decided to join a shared studio with my friends in Amsterdam.

Meeting you in Amsterdam, in spring 2010, we got the impression that you have built—or joined—a small world: the space you work in, where other designers and creative people also work, which is also a gallery with a network of people around it. How did this studio sharing start? **NK** Amsterdam is such a small city and it is full of designers. This means that it is quite easy to meet people and to build a network here; but, on the other hand, this also means that relationships become easily fragmented. In my case, being a designer coming from abroad, I have been lucky as long as I have studied in the Netherlands. Many relationships are based on schools and institutions. Then, once you start to build your own world, after graduation, in Amsterdam you have plenty of opportunities to meet other designers, at many cultural events throughout the year. Two years ago, P/////AKT, a gallery space in East Amsterdam, offered part of its space as a studio. One of my friends asked me to join and now I am sharing the studio with six other graphic designers. In general we do not work together, but share the space and facilities. However sharing the same atmosphere also means that we influence each other, in a way. Also, since the gallery has a large exhibition space, sometimes we use it for self-initiated activities. For instance, in spring 2010 the curator of the gallery suggested that our studio could organize an exhibition about our work. So we decided to build "A situation room"—which is also the title of the show. For this exhibition we reproduced our studio right within the gallery space, bringing real objects, printed materials, one by one every day for a month; so on the very last day of the show, the "mirroring" process was complete. This is an interesting example of how we collaborate in the studio. Actually, the gallery is the main space in this building; the rest of it is divided into small working spaces, rented by people who are involved in the cultural field: a musician, an artist, a filmmaker, etc., all independent. I think that many small studios and teams are taking this kind of sharing model to start their careers here; and many designers often use their own studio space for exhibiting their works, as well as they do in some public spaces. Amsterdam is one of the most troubled cities in regard to housing and housing problems. Recently the squatting system has also been threatened by the political situation. Independent workers have to face a difficult context, but people seem to find a way to deal with this problem, and sharing the space, as we do, seems to be a good option. Moreover, compared to other countries, the Netherlands still offers government support for culture—and this also helps.

You are in charge of the layout and design of Graphic *magazine—which has grown into a significant voice, reporting on interesting topics concerning the worlds of graphic design. How did you start to collaborate on this project? To what degree are you engaged in building the contents of the magazine?* **NK** After graduating from the Werkplaats Typografie, I wanted to introduce its outstanding archive of works to Korea. On the occasion of the 10th anniversary of this institution, in 2008, I organized an exhibition in Seoul. Then many people in Korea were interested in Dutch graphic design and eager to get more information about it. The exhibition was very successful, drawing lots of attention. The editor of a Korean magazine, *Graphic*, wanted to release an issue devoted to the Werkplaats Typografie and to the exhibition, so he asked me to collaborate with him on it. Issue number 9 of *Graphic* was noted for its distinctive contents and design, and that is when my collaboration with the magazine started, in 2009. In fact *Graphic* was launched in 2007, and before I joined eight issues had been produced, focusing on the Korean graphic design scene and consequently being distributed only in Korea. But after issue 9, the magazine became bilingual and started to focus on the international landscape of graphic design and the distribution expanded overseas. Following issues addressed topics such as self-publishing, design exhibitions, young studios, printing journals, etc. More than anything, the unique character of *Graphic* lays in its one-theme-one-issue structure, and this makes it very effective for me to work independently as a designer. Basically only three people are involved in making this magazine, so most of the decisions are open to all of us. That means that I can suggest any idea from the very start of each issue and deal with many editorial activities, including the choice of topic, contacting contributors, distribution, not just making the layout of the magazine. For instance, with issue number 11, *Ideas*

of Design Exhibition, we wanted to show different approaches to exhibiting contemporary design. I suggested that it could be interesting to also present a sort of imaginary exhibition of the selected exhibitions featured in the issue. I invited an illustrator to represent each exhibition with his drawings. In the end, we displayed this imaginary exhibition in a real gallery, presenting the illustrator's drawings, and we photographed them for the publication. So in that case, the initial art-directing plan led to develop contents as well. Moreover, as I stay in Europe, it is easier for me to collect information for the magazine, via research I can make, connections I have in the Netherlands, suggestions from other people etc. In many respects, *Graphic* is an ideal project for a designer, because the designer can produce contents directly, participating the whole design and production process. In addition, getting to know more people and sharing ideas on what you are interested in are greatly attractive elements as well.

Considering the recent issues of Graphic *one may get an idea of what is going on in the field, especially among young designers. If it were up to you, how would you describe the "world/worlds" of contemporary graphic design?* NK "The autonomy of designers," I would say. *Graphic* issue number 14, *Work & Run: Young Studios*, partly deals with this attitude in contemporary graphic design. If you read the interviews with designers that are featured there and follow their ideas on how they work and communicate with society, I think you get a look into a lot of situations in the contemporary world. More and more designers reject working only as components of a capitalist chain, and would like to state something about themselves, the society and the world instead. These intentions can be read through many initiatives such as starting small studios, self-publishing, organizing exhibitions, suggesting alternative educational systems and so on. In fact, this kind of independent activity is not only to be found in graphic design, but is also valid for most of what happens in the contemporary cultural system. Consequently, the collaboration with the autonomous is inevitable and it fosters, as well as enriches, the "world" and the "worlds."

You have studied in different countries and at diverse institutions. What is your opinion on the issues of graphic design education? What are the problems, the differences, the main challenges that education is facing today? **NK** The most impressive educational aspect in the Netherlands is that practical training is fundamental. For instance, indisputably the Werkplaats Typografie is famous for its educational system with commissioned assignments, and most of the tutors in art schools in the Netherlands keep their careers as designers. Naturally students have more chances to use their skills and experiment different solutions sharing the ideas from practical experiences of the tutors. On the other hand, this situation also creates some problems: the tutors are not able to fully devote their time to teaching, and this means there is a lack of apprenticeship attitude in the relationship of tutors and students. Most tutors are young designers, so students could easily fail to encounter the experienced wisdom of the old masters. Many art schools in Korea have the opposite problem of the Netherlands. Teachers are old and experienced but they are distant from practical ideas on the field. I believe that to make a balance between these two perspectives would be a significant issue today.

<u>You can take the Slav out of</u>
Bulgaria, Poland, Slovenia,
Slovakia, Russia, Serbia,
Montenegro, Belarus, Croatia,
Bosnia and Herzegovina,
Macedonia, Ukraine,
and the Czech Republic
<u>but you can't take</u>
Bulgaria, Poland, Slovenia,
Slovakia, Russia, Serbia,
Montenegro, Belarus, Croatia,
Bosnia and Herzegovina,
Macedonia, Ukraine,
and the Czech Republic
<u>out of the Slav.</u>

KASIA KORCZAK

This past, moreover, reaching all the way back into the origin,
does not pull back, but presses forward, and it is,
contrary to what one would expect,
the future which drives us back into the past.
Hannah Arendt

As a foreigner living in foreign lands—in England, France, the Netherlands and Belgium—I am often asked to choose between identities, despite the terminology itself being skewed if not altogether faulty. On one hand, the very contemporary term *immigrant*: implying, almost *de facto*, a desire for integration, as a key factor for success in the host country. On the other, the romanticized if passé term *émigré*: an evocation of whitened knuckles, gripping an increasingly fossilized sense of *home*. Either way, I lose.

I am very much in the West but from—what used to be called—the East. As a child, I could never have known that the East would one day move west. What a strange idea. Who would have ever thought a direction could move in another direction? While Parisians, Londoners, and New Yorkers move east within their respective cities, to escape the ghost of gentrification and real-estate prices, the geopolitical establishment presents the shift west as manifest destiny. Today, a Pole sees himself first as a Pole, second as a European and third, if pushed, as a Slav. In an attempt at semantic seduction, Eastern Europe now calls itself "Central Europe." A new Atlanticism pulses between Poland and the Ukraine. But such manoeuvres often hide an unforgiving past. For too long now the Slavs have faced the sunset, and too often forget to bask in the morning sun.

Slavs are the largest ethnic and linguistic group in Europe, but is there really a common heritage to be found among such a thoroughly diverse group of nations? What does socialite Slovenia have to do with a slower, more diligent Slovakia? As is often the case, the problem lies with aspirations: between what we want to be and what we will always be. Slavs know to wish for the former without curling our lips at the latter.

Slavs come from far away but are no closer to understanding where "here" begins and "there" ends. The Slavic penchant for the absurd stems from a glut of being dislodged, often from within, as if from one's own present. Displacement happens long before the search for work or studies, it happens *in utero*.

Slavs at home are no less displaced than Slavs abroad. We are not nomads. We are rooted to one too many places. What's more: the places in our heads and hearts sometimes fail to recognize the ones on the maps and vice versa. We are the hair on a mother's head, pulled in different directions by her numerous children. It hurts but, as John Cougar Mellencamp once sang, it hurts so good. The country we call home, the country we used to call home and the country we dream to call home are all very distinct and disparate places. It is the result of a productive schizophrenia: we are in all of them at once, a ravishing sensation but one tempered by the slow, sobering devastation of never being in any one entirely.

Slavs do not mince words. Nor are we consensual. Criticism by its very nature must sting. But that is no excuse to turn to a qualifier for an antidote. "Constructive" criticism is simply a less frontal and partially handicapped term. Fat-free butter has no place in Slavs' critical vocabulary.

Slavs do not *spend* time. In the Slavic thesaurus, under duration there is no dollar sign. Time is not money because there always was plenty of the former but never much of the latter. For half a century, the two did not even occupy the same latitude and longitude. Now, though money is bountiful for the select few in certain Slavic countries, time remains somewhat antipodean to late capitalism. We do not measure time with colleagues, friends or family in barter-like terms of dinner, a coffee, or a drink. Slavs might stop by your home not for half an hour but half a month, not leave the house, not do much of significance, in the sense of being productive, but simply be present and *pass* the time with you.

Slavs daydream. Picking up the pieces from an oft-shattered vase, we glue them back together defiantly, knowing full well the vase will be tipped over once again by a clumsy history. When Slavs dream, it is a heavy, almost cata-tonic dream. One so removed from reality that it redeems the very radicality of what a dream originally suggested: another world, not this one, one where things were not possible but impossibly possible. The French architect and designer Yona Friedman once said, "Everything is not possible, but there is more possible than you can possibly imagine." In the West, we are told our dreams can come true, if only we apply ourselves. There is a rank positivism that breeds amnesia. It originated in Calvinist America, only to cross-over first via Blair and then via Berlusconi with differing degrees of success. Slavs are interested in failure, what it exposes, the pressure and accountability that it breeds. Dreaming is about process more than result. It is the path of thought turned into a line of flight, an escape *from* something more than the procurement *of* something, the fantasy more than the speculation of a job, the reverie of a pay-raise, or the hope of a score.

Slavs either drink to get absolutely hammered or do not drink at all. It is an honest restitution of alcohol to its proper place, as a vehicle for intoxica-tion. If the West sips, the East absorbs. Where the West consumes, keeping the alcohol at a safe distance, the East devours and has trouble keeping it at arm's length. Slavs look dumbfounded at people imbibing at cocktail parties. The casualness is disheartening. Are the umbrellas, the straws, the mixers, the improbable names all a side show to distract from the main billing? Slavs sit around a table, tête-à-tête, and each shot is performed in a ritual of increased intimacy. We commemorate alcohol. In fact, we Slavs have a weakness for commemoration. We like to mark the passing of every tea, every meal, every letter, every conversation, every instant, as if it could be our last. In the telefilm *Abécédaire de Gilles Deleuze*, at some point the French philosopher asks: if food is such a wonderful thing, how come we find it unbearable to eat alone? How come we need a conversation or company to go with a meal? Deleuze, like the Slavs, did things excessively (alcohol being one of them) or did not do them at all.

In popular culture, much has been made of this all-or-nothing approach to life. It has been touted as a particularly facile genre of radicalism. Too often, it is an affectation, and one that trades on a destructive or unhealthy cachet. Let it be known that Slavs are not punks. Life is hard-edged enough not to resort to the donning of dark clothes, dark make-up, and dark hair all by light-skinned people. With no need for faux extreme genres or real extreme sports, Slavs live the wildly dizzying swings from one extreme to another as the natural course of events. The day before yesterday Nazism, yesterday Communism and today Capitalism. It is enough to make anyone's head spin. Some people have to blur, even betray, one identity to fight for another. In pop music, this person would perhaps be Bob Dylan or David Bowie. In Slavs and Tatars territory, it would be Jamal al-din Al-Afghani, Vladimir Nabokov, Attila the Hun or Aleksander (Eskander) Herzen, among others.

With friends I often sit around dinner tables and argue over which nations we like the best and which the least. The responses of dinner guests vary widely but never fail to reveal a person's politics and passions. A recurring trope—what has Australia really contributed to the world?—is often met by an equally clichéd turn to Anti-Americanism. Regardless, I continue to excavate the intuitive, instinctive likes and dislikes often found in children (but often smothered in adults), and pummel them with the very adulterated world of politics and culture. It is akin to putting Nature and Nurture in a blender and making a smoothie called "Know Thine Enemy, Really."

While we debate the relevance of one people over another, we would do well to think of Lev Gumilev, the ethnologist and historian whose theory of

'I AM THE LAST OF THE EURASIANISTS' — Lev Gumilev

ethnogenesis entailed a rather moving, poetic, if not very scientific, notion of "passionarity." According to Gumilev, passionarity represented each ethnicity's power source or vital energy. This energy would undergo an evolution through various stages: rise, development, climax, inertia, convolution and memorial. Russia's uniquely European and Asian position, not to mention its tumultuous history, was proof of its high passionarity. For Gumilev, Europe is in a state of inertia, or introduction to obscuration, and the Arab world is on the rise. The Iranians would perhaps recognize this trope under another name— *gharbzadeghi* (literally translated as westoxication)—perhaps one of the most important leitmotifs of the Iranian revolution and the creation of a theocracy in its wake. *Gharbzadeghi*—the state of being "struck by the west"—refers to what some believe is the corrosive effect Western culture has on the foundations of Iranian and Muslim culture.

Eurasia represents, to my eyes, a historic and no less radical attempt to bridge and blur the East and West. I would like to end with Rudolf Steiner's canniness that applies whether in life, politics or design: "It is certainly valuable if the person also has a heart and not just thoughts. But the most valuable thing is when thoughts have a heart."

United States of Heinrich
United States of Red
United States of Vespucci
United States of Waldseemüller
United States of Pizarro
United States of Emericus
United States of Cortes
United States of Terra Incognita
United States of Yupanqui
United States of Balboa
United States of Córdoba
United States of Aguirre
United States of Mendoza
United States of Soto
United States of Pinzón

ZAK KYES

Can you tell us something about your background, your education, and your journey to graphic design? **Zak Kyes** Through various activities beginning as early as high school I made small publications and posters and organized related events and exhibitions for and with friends. These small projects brought me into contact with people from different fields and eventually towards art and artists. This led to a degree in art history in New York which I dropped out of to pursue graphic design; I found that through graphic design I was able to establish a position that could unite heterogeneous activities. For a younger generation of graphic designers the practice of graphic design became a passport enabling one to enter into multiple disciplines.

You have lived in different countries—America, Switzerland, the United Kingdom—and work internationally. Why did you choose to set up a studio in London, does it offer a good cultural milieu for graphic design? **ZK** There are compelling reasons to live and work in London, but the reasons that brought me here have more to do with my personal history than a strategic plan. London is uniquely positioned between other realities—cities, cultures, languages—and this state of being in-between is something that I recognize in my own working method. Raised in Southern California by a Swiss mother and an American father, my view of the world was always a product of two very different cultures. Working in London brought me into close contact with other disciplines; namely architecture, art and literature, as well as other cities, including Berlin, Delhi, Dubai, Lausanne, Los Angeles, Stockholm, and Zurich. Working between practices and places has revealed the possibilities of an approach not simply delimited by boundaries and cultures.

You work across different disciplines, and often initiate collaborative projects, involving people who are active in different fields. How important is for you to build relationships and connections with other professionals and creative people? ZK As a graphic designer, I frequently find myself in a position where one must be knowledgeable about many different practices and agile enough to negotiate their boundaries. This position of constantly being "between" has necessitated new approaches and led to a collaborative methodology. Often the verb "design" encompasses various roles extending far beyond the production of objects, such as editor, printer, curator and organizer. I don't profess to be an expert in any of these fields and collaborations are a tempting way to both feed an intellectual curiosity, and expand the agency of graphic design.

What role does critical thinking and writing play in your work, and which role should it play, in your opinion, in the work of graphic designers today? ZK In my view the intelligence within the field of graphic design lies in its ability to make connections between different disciplines. Broadly speaking I see a critical practice as a productive tool to help in negotiating between different bodies of knowledge. Criticality is not a formula and for this reason I believe in engagement over the mission statements of "Critical Design."

When we met in London, in May 2010, you said that you read the idea of "worlds" in terms of identity, as in "different identities for graphic design"... ZK When we met your exhibition project was still taking shape and my initial reading was that the ambiguity of the term "worlds" could be a way to address the various roles that designers inhabit and the worlds they occupy. Given my specific interests and the context in which I practice graphic design, it became urgent to develop multiple identities encompassing publishing, editorial, curatorial roles.

This notion of identity was at the core of the exhibition Forms of Inquiry: The Architecture of Critical Graphic Design *that you curated. Can you tell us something more about this huge project and the idea of an "inquiry"?* ZK The value of a proposal, or an "inquiry," is precisely the degree to which it leads to unexpected outcomes. In *Forms of Inquiry,* an exhibition that presented a moment of critical practices in graphic design, we adopted the term "inquiry" to describe this work. As Mark Owens and I speculated in the catalogue, this choice was intended to distinguish the act of "inquiry" from the ubiquitous incentive to "research," which has long carried with it a variety of assumptions and interpretative baggage. The distinction is important; for unlike empirical research, with its appropriation of the paradigm of scientific data gathering and problem-solving, the term "inquiry" suggests an almost anti-methodological methodology—posing questions and pursuing paths without necessarily knowing where they will lead. *Forms of Inquiry* concluded after two years, expanding while it traveled to six different institutions across Europe. While the exhibition has concluded our initial inquiry into graphic design as a critical activity and its increasingly fertile relationship with architecture, it has revealed that an inquiry always conceals another inquiry.

In your work on graphic design, architecture seems to be a relevant reference point, and this is true for Forms of Inquiry *as well. Do you read relevant connections, similarities or specific links between graphic design and architecture, as forms of practice and of investigation, as means to design worlds?* ZK I joined the Architectural Association as Art Director of the AA Print Studio in September 2006. This position has been enormously conducive to inventing a hybrid role that has included teaching, directing the design of publications, organizing lectures and exhibitions, and various other projects produced through the Print Studio. This work is carried out with a talented team of editors and two excellent graphic designers, Wayne Daly and Claire McManus. The Print Studio was originally established in 1971–72 by Denis Crompton of Archigram to shape the school's architectural discourse through the production and distribution of publications. Books have been a key reason for the School's success at a time when the speculative nature of architectural proposals found their most logical expression in un-built forms. Presciently the book became an ideal site for discourse and exchange.

You are a graphic designer, who also works as a curator and a publisher (with Bedford Press, since 2008). One might say that you greatly exemplify some "trends" that characterize contemporary graphic design worlds; that is the interest and engagement of designers in curatorial, editorial and publishing activities as means to reflect on their theoretical and practical tools and to develop critical discourse. ZK My work and the work of Bedford Press at the AA is a direct response to local concerns and, with the AA in particular, an extension of historical activities. Bedford Press was initiated in 2008 out of a basic material imperative to find a quick, cheap and rudimentary means of producing the school's internal printed ephemera. The products of the press include publications as well as pamphlets, invitation cards, posters and prints. Over the course of the past two years it has grown into a publishing imprint that seeks to develop contemporary models of publication practice. Now established as an imprint of the longstanding AA Publications Ltd., Bedford Press is a private press with the dual purpose of establishing an on-site facility for the production of printed matter for the AA School and as well to create a new typology of publications that extend beyond the Architectural Association's existing program. This initiative builds upon the AA's renowned legacy of independent publishing. The mainspring of the project is to reconsider both what is understood as architecture and what others understand architecture to be. The press aims to establish a more responsive model of small-scale publishing, nimble enough to encompass the entire chain of production in a single fluid activity, from initial commission to the final printing.

Secret Societies Have Served America Well

As most everyone knows, "America" as a moniker comes from a merchant known as Amerigo Vespucci, whose visit to the newly discovered continent provided inspiration for the name at hand. More precisely, it was a famous penchant for candid correspondence that ensured his reputation, and therefore, his nominalist heritage. Four of Amerigo's letters have been in public circulation, at least two of which are now known to be forgeries. But even the certified documents leave little cause for pride. Amerigo brags about having sexual relations with ferrets, geese, and "large bears of the forest." He also proudly confesses to exposing birds and insects to "the blinding flame of the magnifying glass, merely so as to quench my curiosity," and to pillaging the leather satchels of "blind old women, knocking them over with my staff as I pass."

Of course, the letters also bespeak the virility and valor that intercontinental travel demanded at the time, and their publication and widespread circulation eventually led a German mapmaker by the name of Martin Waldseemüller, working on his 1507 edition of the world map, to dub the mysterious new continent "America." When an uproar ensued, Waldseemüller reconsidered, and remembered that "Amerigo" is an Italian derivation of the medieval Latin "Emericus," which is akin to the German "Heinrich." Thus Waldseemüller's second choice was to name the land mass

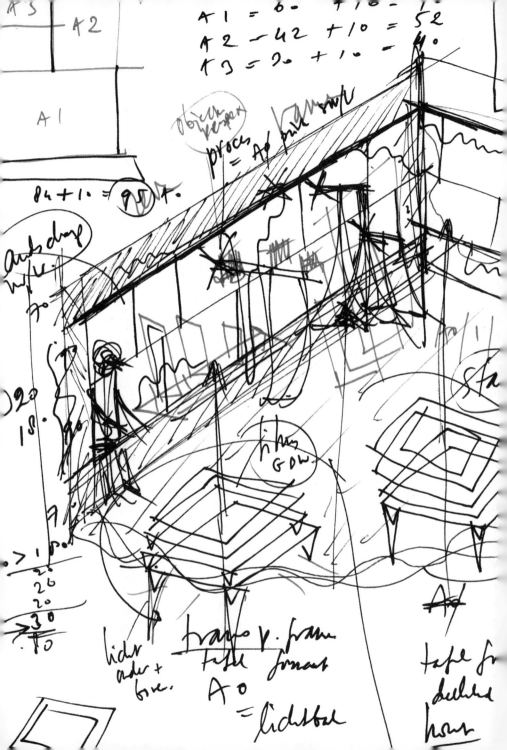

HARMEN LIEMBURG

How did you start to work as an independent graphic designer, running your own business? **Harmen Liemburg** Running a business is not just a goal in it-self, but a necessary means to function as an independent designer and work for various clients. I think I am quite active as a "cultural entrepreneur," but, as many other designers and artists, unfortunately I have little talent for the business part. In addition to that, I am a soloist by nature. Earlier I got a taste of what it would be like to be in an office situation. Instead of feeling obliged to show up at regular times because your colleagues or superiors expect it, I like to decide when and how I work myself. I have decided it is just not for me. On the other hand, when I collaborated with Richard Niessen, I experienced how much more energy can be created when you're part of a team.

Besides the fact that you feel like a soloist, is it important for you to have relationships with other people? **HL** It is almost impossible to work without being part of networks. When you start out, it is nice if you can to get advice from experienced colleagues. Later on, it is not enough to be talented, you need to connect to potential clients or find ways to get your own show on the road. In my experience, many jobs don't necessarily go to the best people, but to those who will "show their nose" at the right openings and parties. Being an idealist, I am interested in having relationships that are honest and heartfelt. Through working and traveling, I am lucky to meet great people that I have really something to share with, but I realize that you don't have to be friends with everybody you work with. I don't feel comfortable with this so-called "networking for networking's sake," but sometimes you just have to promote yourself too.

Besides other people's work, it seems that traveling and working abroad are also an important source to you. Is this correct? **HL** I am a curious person. I like to see new things, people, places. Traveling triggers new ideas and inevitably leads to a more nuanced perception of our complex world. So yeah, it is important. But I also enjoy to be home in my own environment, and travel in my mind through books and other sources. So far, I have had several opportunities to work abroad for a longer period of time, especially in the US where I have been many times. Wherever there is a computer, printer and internet, I can work, potentially. But it also takes energy to create a situation where I can really be productive. And besides that, there are few places where I can do my screen prints the way I am used to. Apart from my little community there, this is one of the reasons why Amsterdam is still important to me as a homebase.

Graphic Design Worlds aims at bringing into light how designers use their languages and media to comment on the world or to design worlds, in a way. Which one of these sides would you feel closer to? **HL** I guess both. My work is full of comments and observations about the world, but the tone usually is very lighthearted and ironic. I don't think I will ever do a hard core political poster though. The subtleties can be understood if people are willing to spend some time with the work and really dive into it. The work I am interested in myself, like Zeloot, Seripop or Mathias Schweizer, usually has an element of craziness or maniacism. This is also why I take an interest in amateur or outsider art. I guess since I got involved, I developed a deep obsession with printed matter, and looking at it in all its variety is a world that doesn't cease to excite me.

How would you describe graphic design in your own words, then? **HL** Over time, it turned out that I am less interested in graphic design as a problem-solving method for communication issues, and rather see the creation of printed objects as a goal in itself. But somehow, autonomous as the work may seem, there is always some kind of announcement or message involved. I never work because I feel the inner urge to do *something*—like the stereotypical artist—, there is always a reason, an event, and thus a message involved. I also need a certain pressure, a deadline, to direct my time and energy to transform all collected materials and "loose ends" into a specific design. I am using graphic design as a means of expression, and hope that the work will also keep its freshness after it has served its purpose.

Not only do you design your works but you actually produce them, especially using screen printing. Where does this involvement come from? **HL** When I was student at the Gerrit Rietveld Academy, I was eager to try out the screen printing workshop, but the guys in charge at the time were incredibly lazy and unwilling. This frustrating and disencouraging situation changed for the better when Kees Maas, graphic artist and printmaker, arrived at the school. Kees brought a completely different mentality. He always seemed to be willing to actively help and work with students, making things possible instead of throwing up barriers. I found this very stimulating. I quickly recognized the many qualities of the screen printing technique, and learned to get the most out of the tools and materials by trial and error. After graduation, Kees enabled me to continue working in his private screen printing shop, which enabled me to develop further as a designer making dirty hands. Screen printing has become my medium for expression and a major means to production and publishing my graphic work independently. What I like a lot about screen printing is its flexibility. Once the design is finished and the films are produced, you get out of the computer and literally enter the world of ink and paper, which has its own rules. You can change your mind about colors and printing order, remove, or add elements, so the work opens up again, and allows for changes that usually make the final result better. It is a very physical process too, standing up and running around sweating and dirty all day long, handling the screens and sheets of paper. After a full day of printing, I am usually pretty exhausted, and the only thing I want to do is to sit down and drink a couple of beers.

As far as we can infer, in your life there is no separation between work and private life, is this so? **HL** There is no distinction. Especially now that my studio is at home and I am not in a relationship, I am not exaggerating when I say that my life is pretty much dedicated to my work. The challenge is still to take a break from myself, get away from the computer and quit working once in a while. To a certain extent, this comes with being self-employed, it is no different than for a restaurant owner of a free-lance photographer. But I must say that my personal life has improved since I rediscovered sports.

Can you describe the process you follow in your work? HL It is a process of collecting, constructing, deconstructing, and then reconstructing everything again. I never start from an empty sheet. My inspiration comes from elements that are already there: usually commercial art, packaging design, traffic signs: common, vernacular graphics that anybody could see. I am constantly collecting "building blocks" for new work, but I need the right occasion to actually put them to use. I usually look for elements that somehow communicate with each other in such a way, that a storyline appears—often in a very open and associative way. By now, I have learned to trust my own working process. If the ingredients are good and if I spend enough time with the material then something good—whatever it is—should roll out... Through printing, I trained myself to take all the possibilities of the printing process into account while I am designing. Using the color of the surface, the layering of opaque and transparent inks, knockout, overprinting colors, etc. So, my working process usually comes down to collecting elements that are, but in a loose way, connected thematically to a topic. After that I am transforming those elements into vector drawings that enable to construct a composition. I learned to work with vector software as a cartography student at Utrecht University. At the time I had a job in lab producing diagrams and maps for scientific publications. We are talking about 1988, a few years after the first Mac was introduced, so I have witnessed the transfer from analog tools like photographic typesetting machines, technical pens and self-adhesive Halftone sheets to Aldus FreeHand, the first vector software, taken over by Adobe Illustrator. This first experience with graphics still defines my awareness of detail and technical quality. Anyway, when all elements are in place, and the design is finished, everything is deconstructed, and split up into black and white color separations. And then, after the films are made, everything is reconstructed again through printing, layer by layer. Up to film production, the computer is the most important tool, but I am not a slave to it. In the end it is a good marriage of digital and handcrafted tools.

Because of your approach, then, do you feel it is a problem when students immediately open the computer as they enter the classroom? HL Many people stay in the digital realm, working with pixels and low-res material; well, there is nothing wrong with it, but there is a whole world beyond that. Even if you don't want to become a printmaker yourself, as a designer you should at least have an understanding of physical qualities of reproduction processes and their distinct qualities. I like to bring these worlds together. As everybody else, I am working with digital tools every day, but I just can't help finding great satisfaction in physical results that you can actually smell, touch and feel.

So this is what you are trying to teach, to bring to students? HL I think it is important to stimulate students to look at other things than the computer screen. I love Google too, it is a fantastic tool and I use it a lot, but what pops up there is put there by human beings. It is not the world. The physical reality is endlessly richer and more diverse of course. Students shouldn't look for the solution inside the computer, but rather fill their brains with various types of information. Developing an attitude of curiosity is most essential.

You said that you have learned to "trust" your own process. You mean that there was a time when you felt unconfident with it? HL My teachers at art school said that my methods of working were too result driven. It took me a while to understand what they meant, but graduating with an experimental project finally opened my eyes. I have been through some maniacal periods when I was a student, during which I thought, "What's happening to me? Am I going crazy? I can't stop working." Now I realize that this is part of being immersed in the making process itself, and even enjoying it. But I am glad I am not in that maniacal state of mind all the time!

Being an independent designer, how important is the support from institutions, and how is it in the Netherlands, a country that is renowned abroad for having great design and for the public support in the arts and in the cultural field? HL Well, there's this sort of myth about why Dutch designers are so good, but I am not sure it is my job to explain this. The fact that we have the Foundation for Visual Arts, Architecture and Design has certainly made my life a bit easier. I am not saying that Holland is paradise in which the "manna" comes falling from the skies. There is a high standard. Unless your work is of good quality, you can just forget about getting access to that type of funds. But yes, the grants that I have received since graduation enabled me to travel, execute projects and installations, and thus were an important contribution to my development.

How do you feel about the public of your work, do you feel a kind of responsibility towards people out there? **HL** Since I am working to stimulate others to look beyond their computer screen and develop an interest in other sources, I feel I should be completely open and transparent about my own working methods and sources. Usually, talking about the working process is more interesting and inspiring than the final product, so for me this is a natural attitude. You will never find me theorizing about design, mystifying my personality, or talking about things that I cannot understand myself. My head may be in the clouds quite often, but I like to keep my feet on the ground.

door elhaa

citras wood = nijder blah
blem

van de tol

dichter

ullewan
naar

GEOFF McFETRIDGE GRAPHIC WORLD EXHIBIT

GEOFF McFETRIDGE

Would you describe your work as your "world"? Would you say that you design "worlds" in a way? **Geoff McFetridge** Inventing form out of the raw materials of my personal world is the root of what I do. Graphic design is preoccupied with speaking broadly to the world. Ideally, this is also part of my work. Yet, the experience of viewing my work should not feel broad. I would like it to feel like overhearing a personal conversation, offering something like an understanding of my outlook, world and interests. Working from within is central to my process and the easiest way for me to work. Being able to be as creative as possible, with as little wasted energy as possible is central to my decision-making. Like having a small studio so that I can adapt to my personal interests and changes in my work, or choosing to work in a variety of disciplines. For me to find balance in life, I think that you have to be quite mobile and flexible. For me balance comes from creating art, as well as commercial projects, non commercial projects, animation and film work; it comes from my family, as well as from bike riding, surfing and traveling. I view my studio as an ecosystem of sorts, a watershed. The rain up top fills the rivers below, and feeds the ocean far away. Everything should project the next thing forward. Dead ends are more than just dead ends, they are exponential in their effect, they can be unrealized opportunity, and also preclude other possible opportunities. An exponential bummer. So, to answer your question: yes, the world that I create is precisely the world I see and live in, it is not a distinct, separate, world. What I try to do is create things and represent ideas in the way I see them, without explanation. When working I recognize that my world and my perspective are unique, and it is this that I use to create unique work. And I hope that, through my view, the viewers can perceive the uniqueness of their own world. With graphics I feel that you can describe ideas that exist in the gaps left by language.

You were born and grew up in Canada, but then moved to California. Do you feel there is a special connection with the country you chose to live and work in? **GMcF** I think California is part of my work and to some degree Canada as well. I do love California, and California culture has always influenced me. Where we live is a very "un-urban urban" experience. Quiet and solitude are remarkably close-by in this city. As if culture is moving so fast that it creates pockets of calm. It is like when a giant truck drives by you and by breaking through the air a vacuum is created behind it, creating a pocket of calm air; I like to think I am operating in this vacuum. In cycling this is called drafting, letting another rider cut through the air for you so you expend less energy. So I am drafting Los Angeles. In California and the US a lot can still get done. Within any large city there is often a battle between distraction and opportunity. It takes some work to separate the two.

How would you describe graphic design and what are your main objectives as a graphic designer? **GMcF** When I think about graphic design I think about language, and that graphic design is interesting for people who like to mess with, use, or invent language. Looking at the world there is a part of me that is always searching for new language. Graphics made sense to me when I realized they were about communication, not necessarily being clear but definitely projecting ideas outwards. What is fun about making graphics is the feeling that you are creating something that will at some point be "read" by someone. It is a very powerful thing to engage someone in your own thought, and when you deepen the thought the experience is that much more powerful. When I listen to opera I do not cry, my wife grew up listening to opera and often listening to it she will cry. At this point most of the developed world has grown up with graphic design, we are all very versed in graphics as a language. That is why I believe it is possible to achieve my goal, which has been to create a logo that will make you cry.

We once read that you talked about "ultimate" graphics, in relation to poetry. Does this relate to your reading graphic design as a language? **GMcF** It is where language and imagery break down equally... I feel that the ultimate graphics are graphics that are built in your head. With graphics I am often trying to invent form, or finding form in the world and playing with it to convey an idea. You are always starting from scratch. So for me it was a revelation that what poets do with poetry is very similar; yet the big difference is that poets do not invent language when they start to create a poem, they do not start from scratch, they work with the language that exists. Poets gather the language and form specific and beautiful forms that must be created in the mind of the reader. This is quite an obvious concept. Of course language can be more specific and clear than graphics. It is interesting to me because of the roundabout way that I came to it. For many years I have used text in my work in conjunction with graphics to create work that I too feel is composed in the mind. Each piece independently means little, but in combination something is formed. The revelation is that as the work progresses, maybe it moves closer to poetry and away from graphics. This is the type of thing that is interesting to me. I want to explore the place between poetry and graphics, and find the place were language and imagery break down equally. At what point does an apple become a core? The sun does not know it is a star. What exists in the space between the word "yeah," and "yes." There are times when what I do as an artist and graphic designer starts to feel ridiculous to me. It is a game to find the limits of what can be conveyed with shapes and lines. So therefore, and ironically, it would seem that the "ultimate" graphics are not graphic at all. The form has completely been absorbed by the idea. When we read poetry we are not aware of the letters as specific shapes, we only feel the intentions of the poet.

In an interview by Steven Heller, talking about art and design, you say that much of what you do "plays with delivering art as design," and that you call yourself a "designer" but then call the things you make "art." [1] *Could you tell us more about this distinction, if there is any?* **GMcF** Calling myself a "designer" has offered me a great freedom to explore all sorts of projects that were only linked by my personal creativity or ideas. What I was trying to explain to Steven Heller was how I approach things creatively. For me, all the things I do seamlessly exist in one space, everything overlaps and mixes and exists simultaneously. Yet, when the work is shown in the world it will

---

1. http://championdontstop.com/site3/interviews/stevenheller.html.

THE WORLDS OF GRAPHIC DESIGNERS

be defined in different ways. Rightly so.

I could not do what I do if I were operating differently when doing art or design projects. I think it would make things very difficult, it is likely my head would become unscrewed from my shoulders. By working consistently I feel I can slowly evolve what I do in a fairly natural way. I have a sense that in the past designers used to retire to the country to paint watercolors, or contradict their own work with some sort of highbrow art practice. I want to do all these things simultaneously, because that is the way I see things. I admire Andy Warhol greatly. I would not compare myself to him, but I do wonder what would have happened if Andy Warhol continued to do commercial art throughout his life.

Your work encompasses filmmaking, art, music, fashion... Is there a sort of contamination, and how can you keep this going on? **GMcF** Yes there is a real contamination between the different media and fields I work in. There is also a certain amount of momentum that I feel I get out of working in different fields. And by varying what happens in my studio day to day I feel I am exposed to many different influences and challenges. I sometimes feel that I am building a house for myself. I think that building a house for myself would be amazing, but would also be challenging and I would make tons of mistakes. I would wonder if it would be better to hire a house builder, or an architect to do it. But, inside I would know that the experience of building the house, and living in a house of my own ideas is worth the trouble and mistakes that would be made.

As a designer and artist focusing on his own ideas and views, how do you read your relationship with clients? In a lecture you gave at DoLecture you referred to clients as "monsters without heads." [2] *What did you mean?* **GMcF** When I say they are monsters without heads it has to be understood in context. What I was describing was that corporations, or groups of people in business working in collaboration have an empty piece that is easily filled by an outside individual. When they put all their heads together there is a part in the middle where none of them touch, they really are just abutting the person next to them, and that person next to them. A person with a singular vision

---

2.   http://www.dolectures.com.

has the ability to unify their ideas. I think it is understood now that "brainstorming" and collaboration is a waste of time. I think that designers are better off thinking above and beyond the clients' concerns; "problem solving" is not enough. The designer should bring something more; a head possibly. This should not be confused with disrespecting clients. I do not think they are monsters, it is just a way to describe a sort of Frankenstein type phenomenon where when you sit down for a meeting with most clients it is very clear that they have intense and vital needs, even though their business may be thriving.

Considering your experience both as a student at the California Institute of Arts (CalArts) and as a teacher/lecturer, in your opinion, how relevant is the role of schools and universities for graphic designers? **GMcF** I always liked schools, although the relevancy seems to fluctuate. CalArts was very experimental and vital at the time I was there. It taught me a rigorous process of thinking and making that I use to this day. My learning there came out of a combination of the climate at the time, the people who I was there with, and of course the faculty. Just like the best books about design have nothing to do with design: CalArts is quite like that, you don't really feel like you are in a Design school. I think I was lucky I had taken my undergraduate degree from a very traditional school in Canada, at the Alberta College of Art. There I could learn all sorts of archaic techniques and professional practice stuff that also has really informed my work. It was like a program from previous decades: we actually had computers, but the computers were new and barely a part of the program. Everything focused on hand work and mechanical processes that are now completely lost in time. So I had two very different experiences at school. But in both programs my approach was the same. My view has always been that at school you should fail constantly and work hard, and push things so far that you actually make really terrible work. School is a chance to fail without consequence. School is not about building a portfolio, or a body of work. All you need is one great piece of design to get work, and you can make it the week after you graduate.

What is most important in design? **GMcF** The most important thing in design? To put work out into the world out of respect for the viewer and the world itself.

METAHAVEN

1. Definition
Speculative design is design that uses a variety of methods, from form making to writing, to formulate, illustrate, and embody a hypothesis.

2. Design's Recent Fear of Imagination
Speculative design is a playful antidote to contemporary design's anxious state of mind. The new global imperative to embrace austerity, reduce our climate footprint, safeguard our reputation, quit smoking, be obedient, invite only trusted friends and trust only those invited, gets its inspiration from a set of data from the past and present, and an anticipation of the near future. But that imperative often translates into design projects paralyzed by good intentions, and devoid of ideas. As opposed to the structural innovation of production processes and organizational forms,[1] many social design projects rebrand public life into some sort of participatory model—an "I'm good" sticker printed over the forehead. Yet under their attractive Anglo-Saxon veneer lurks a lack of imagination—or even, a fear of it. The current design climate, in spite of its favorite word, "change," is thoroughly conservative. Especially when and where it protests.

---

1.   A good example of this much more structural approach is Agata Jaworska's *Made In Transit*, a supply chain concept in which the production of fresh perishable food happens "on the way to the supermarket, shifting the paradigm of packaging from preserving freshness to enabling growth, a shift from 'best before' to 'ready by.'" It does not need the word "change" to make its point. See www.foodproductiondaily.com/Supply-Chain/Made-in-Transit-The-end-of-the-factory, retrieved November 29, 2010.

Besides bits and pieces of real change—which doesn't need that precise word in its banner to make itself known—the prevailing design ideology has strong elements of continuity with the neoliberal market regime that preceded it, and which it purportedly replaced. On Amazon, a book called *The New Capitalist Manifesto* is pre-ordered by the same people who read social media bibles like *Cognitive Surplus. Creativity and Generosity In A Connected Age* and *Here Comes Everybody. The Power of Organizing Without Organizations.* In both the neoliberal market ideology and sociopreneurialism, there is no space for opposition or even poking fun; both observe a natural dynamic—of markets (or of social relations)—which we shouldn't interfere with.

Early 2009, the *Huffington Post* published "The Architect's Dilemma: The Architecture of Excess vs. An Architecture of Relevance." Its author, Cameron Sinclair, took issue with the work of Pritzker Prize winning architect Zaha Hadid. He accused her of social irresponsibility: "While Ms. Hadid has certainly made a lasting impact in the architectural discourse, the physical structures created have been on occasion environmentally unsound, exclusive in nature and at times ethically dubious. They fight for attention, piercing the fabric of the city instead of weaving it into a stronger and more interconnected environment."[2] Sinclair's own NGO, Architecture for Humanity, has played a crucial part in "matching" architectural creativity to real needs, and of course we share his anger—but it is hard not to sympathize with Hadid as well with so much "do-good-in-your-face." It is on other points that we find conservatism hiding within Sinclair's progressivism. For example, what is fundamentally wrong with a building striving to be noticed? Having an article in the *Huffington Post* is nothing but striving to be noticed. Is that "ethically dubious"? In the comments section, the author lashes out at a critic, re-stating his purpose: "In a time when homes are being foreclosed, schools and health facilities and the number of natural and man made disasters are increasing we need to be training a profession that is relevant to the current state of the world not JUST for the few" (Sinclair's capitalization). Moralism can be debunked by a simple look at statistics. Cameron Sinclair, according to his Dopplr social networking profile for frequent flyers, has traveled 1,027,943 km between January 9, 2008, and November 15, 2010,

---

2. See C. Sinclair, "The Architect's Dilemma," April 13, 2009, at www.huffingtonpost.com/cameron-sinclair/the-architects-dilemma-th_b_185031.html, retrieved October 30, 2010.

and has visited ninety-three cities across the world in that two-year period.[3] This is good, for Sinclair will have enlightened each of those cities with his ideas for can-do sustainable architecture. But it is also a dash environmentally unsound considering airfuel exhaust's share in the onslaught of natural and man made disasters. Sinclair was recently selected as a Young Global Leader by the World Economic Forum, his website says.

Speculative design puts more emphasis on acquiring *advance knowledge* that homes are going to be foreclosed, than on providing shelter to the needy.

It aims to put such advance knowledge in the public domain. Indeed, analysts of all political signatures have been announcing the debt crisis, and usually, designers and architects haven't been listening. Dumbfounded at the economic crisis, the impulse response is that designers should now be fire-fighters not masterplanners. Speculative design proposes an alliance with forward thinking smart people rather than with saints of morality. It claims that there should be a space for making, informed by considered debate about society and politics, not emergency measures.

3. A Conversation Piece

This passage is to describe Metahaven's own experience with the conservatism of Change, as we took part in a heated debate in the city of Murcia in 2010 as part of Manifesta—the European Biennial of Contemporary Art. Every two years, Manifesta touches down in another European region to set up an exhibition; in Murcia, this had been at the cost of all kinds of local cultural resources. The setting of the discussion was a "gun metal gray" painted piece of furniture called the Backbench. Four design and art collectives held a discussion about art and politics: Red76, The Action Mill, Take to the Sea and Metahaven—while being filmed by artist Ergin Cavusoglu. One team in particular virtually, and probably unintentionally, colonized the exchange by assuming that everyone else were an activist NGO like them. "Change" was their masthead, written all over their website and business cards. The team had a repository of organizational methods to entice it; these seemed ready for implementation, if just everyone would listen carefully. It dawned that even in a "conversation," there is a speaker and a listener. Take to the

---

3.   See www.cameronsinclair.com/index.php?q=/events, retrieved November 15, 2010.

Sea[4] and Metahaven, claiming a space for disagreement, reservation or negotiation, brought about near-total mayhem. The event derailed into an art world version of the Jerry Springer show; bits and pieces of this can be viewed in Cavusoglu's careful editing in a five-channel video installation. In that piece, all artists in their voluntary exchange look vulnerable as they are, but scripted like actors. Our own role, other than being the diplomatic negotiators between opposing views, wasn't necessarily very coherent or heroic either. None of the collectives managed to fundamentally alter the condition of Biennials temporarily plundering local economies and all of them created a piece for the show which opened October, 2010.

Speculative design does not have an off the shelf recipe for change. It is based on curiosity. It does not quote from management bibles, and does not engage in group therapy.

4. Punk rock vs. prog rock

Imagination and foresight are useful things vis-à-vis compliance with standing rules. A comparison with music: when punk rock emerged in the 1970s it was a music genre, a counterculture, and a fashion culture at once. It blew away symphonic rock, prog rock and the likes—bands which took ten years to record a single album, not to mention their airbrush cover art. Punk offered a three chord way out of that deadlock. If we compare today's starchitecture to the symphonic rock of the 1970s, is design for social causes the new punk rock? Maybe not. Punk rock was aesthetically rich (Vivienne Westwood and Malcolm McLaren), it was aggressive, but also intensely humorous (Jello Biafra). The problem of social design is that it is counter-establishment, but not a counterculture. If architecture and design are to become "a profession that is relevant to the current state of the world"—Cameron Sinclair said it—imagination is as needed as social and environmental responsibility. Speculative design expressly allows for the counter-cultural, the absurdist, and the humorous. Science fiction writer China Miéville's recent *Letter to a Progressive Liberal Democrat*—an imaginative response to the British government's public sector cutbacks—stands as an example (in writ-

---

4. Take to the Sea is a collective of artists and writers operating from Sardinia, Cairo and Mumbai, consisting of Laura Cugusi, Lina Attalah, Nida Ghouse and others. They exhibited at Manifesta 8. See www.taketothesea.net for their takes on migration, identity and narrative.

ing) of the type of critical and political expressions we have in mind.[5] More about the UK government later.

5. Critical Design and Risk

The term "critical design" first occurred in Anthony Dunne's 1999 book, *Hertzian Tales*. A Wikipedia entry states that critical design deploys "designed artifacts as an embodied critique or commentary on consumer culture."[6] The article does not list any other sources than the writing of Anthony Dunne and his studio partner Fiona Raby. As of October 17, 2010, twenty users, most of them anonymous and some of them former students of the designer duo, contributed to the entry.

Critical design is skeptical of everything, but it holds its societal role dear. "Design for debate"[7]—consider that to momentarily be the same as critical design—uses speculative visual and conceptual projects to discuss technology and engineering not merely as post-hoc consumer choices, but as a vehicle for the free traffic of ideas and opinions on the pages and screens and platforms of the public media. To actually design for debate, Dunne and Raby, and their loyal band of students, rely on a hypothesis—a "space," they state, "between reality and the impossible, a space of dreams, hopes, and fears. Usually this space is occupied by future forecasts (commercial world), design scenarios (corporate world) and utopias and dystopias (literary and cinematic worlds)."[8] They are well aware of the dangers of irrational utopianism looming in their mission statement. Though design "could place new technological developments within imaginary but believable everyday situations that would allow us to debate the implications of different technological futures before they happen," they insert a warning: "'What if...' scenarios can be used—not to predict or anticipate the future—but as tools to help us understand and debate the kind of world we want to live in."[9] And though the team has designed such things as special

---

5.   See http://chinamieville.net/post/1361955242/letter-to-a-progressive-liberal-democrat.

6.   See "Critical Design" at Wikipedia: en.wikipedia.org/w/index.php?title=Critical_design &action=history, retrieved October 17, 2010.

7.   See Dunne & Raby, "Design for Debate," www.dunneandraby.co.uk/content/bydandr/36/0, retrieved October 17, 2010.

8.   See www.dunneandraby.co.uk/content/bydandr/496/0, retrieved October 17, 2010.

9.   Dunne & Raby, "Design for Debate," Ibid.

furniture for people who fear alien abduction, Dunne and Raby, at the same time, stand back from their dreams, realizing perhaps that they might incubate nightmares if someone does not read their manual.

Critical design did not come alone and isolated. It arrived into the world set against a particular socio-political background. The connection between critical design and its wider context has received little attention so far.

The inception of critical design took place in the United Kingdom of the 1990s. Tony Blair's New Labour government had led the country into an era of unprecedented wealth and growth, while at the same time getting rid of many of socialism's old skeletons in the closet. The welfare state was redressing into a "jet age" technocratic behemoth for everyone—the ends of that endeavor weren't intended all that bad, if we understand its main ideologist and "Blair's favorite intellectual," Anthony Giddens, correctly. The catch was in the "means"—the "design" of the Third Way, the recipe for a politics beyond conflict.

Conflict, for the Third Way, was unnecessary, and, for the first time in history, avoidable. The new welfare state would always rebalance individual freedom against collective risk, personal opportunity against social vulnerability.

In drafting the Third Way, Giddens relied on the work of the German sociologist Ulrich Beck. As early as in 1987, Beck had coined the term "Risk Society"—*Risikogesellschaft*. In a radical departure from the fixed hierarchies of family, work, and state, Beck put the individual citizen in charge of designing his own biography—a kind of "existentialist" remix of liberalism. As Giddens quotes, "[the new individualism] is *not* Thatcherism, not market individualism, not atomization. On the contrary, it means 'institutionalized individualism.' Most of the rights and entitlements of the welfare state, for example, are designed for individuals rather than for families. In many cases they presuppose employment. Employment in turn implies education and both of these imply mobility. By all these requirements people are invited to constitute themselves as individuals; to plan, understand, design themselves as individuals."[10]

Giddens hoped to rebalance social democracy, the market, and individualism. Like Beck, he paid extensive attention to risks that came from modernity itself. Giddens asserted that "science and technology used to be seen as outside of politics, but this view has become obsolete"; "[D]ecision-making … cannot be left to the 'experts,' but has to involve politicians and citizens. In short, science and technology cannot stay outside democratic processes."[11] Such a statement may be considered the socio-political blueprint for Dunne and Raby's "design for debate"—which in turn contends that science and technology's ultimate translation into consumer products presents a moment of public scrutiny, not bland acceptance of accomplished facts.

The Risk Society hypothesis, and its subsequent transition to public policies, calculated their likelihood of potential future uncertainties. A fine-grained and adaptive management system would provide every consumer with just the right dose of prêt-à-porter self-governance and life (in)security. An individually catered polity, data mined for its own good. Art historian John Welchman summarizes: "[I]n this regimen, human activities are contained by techniques of social control which identify the potentials of disruption to the system —those threats and dangers that put it at risk or threaten its equilibrium. Since the rise of risk-based tools of governance, the operating system of power has shifted from the maintenance of a single, consistent rationale for the establishment of rules and boundaries, to the continuous, almost instantaneous, adjustment of its metrics in dialogue with the incremental availability of data."[12]

The environmental, social and political risks that stem from the modernization process are not ultimately contained by established political agents. They

10. U. Beck, "The Cosmopolitan Manifesto," *New Statesman*, March 20, 1998, quoted in A. Giddens, *The Third Way. The Renewal of Social Democracy*, Polity, Cambridge 1998, p. 36.

11. Giddens, Ibid., p. 59.

12. J.C. Welchman (ed.), *The Aesthetics of Risk*, JRP Ringier, Zurich 2008, p. 11.

boomerang back to the people themselves. This is much more so the case for Beck than for Giddens, who would have liked to subject science and technology to democratic control. As Welchman reminds us, Beck assumed that the "techno-economic superstructure is quasi-autonomous and cannot easily be challenged or realigned: while this structure accrues the benefits of development, it is insulated from the social costs, which individuals and communities experience directly as increased risks." Beck, in conclusion, "claims that responsibility for the maintenance of social systems has shifted from the state to its citizens."[13]

6. Skinny jeans and the Apocalypse

The near future is a contested site, a battle zone, and a foggy horizon. But there are no white Formica spaceships or aliens dressed in tight pajamas in this future world. Instead there are t-shirt wearing Marxist academics, and trend scouts in skinny jeans. Slovenian philosopher Slavoj Žižek clearly belongs to the first category. Exceptionally, he finds many of his admirers in the second. A celebrated author and avid commentator on current affairs, Žižek popularizes philosophy and is a philosophizer of pop culture (he is equally known for his analysis of the "ideologies" of toilets, or the politics of *The Sound of Music*, as for his takes on Sarah Palin and Donald Rumsfeld). More than anyone, Žižek has extracted intellectual value out of the geopolitical turmoil following September 11, 2001.

Recently Žižek has commented on social and environmental urgencies, but with different outcomes. The philosopher sees little viable policy solutions for the crisis—especially not through liberal consent. The self-politization of the situation will be immediate and irreversible. This view Žižek shares, on different premises, with Ulrich Beck, who foresaw a "sub-politics" consequential to the techno-scientific regime of late modernity (leading to its self-politicizing). Žižek presents an end game of sorts for the Risk Society hypothesis; he situates it in the indeterminate future.

"[T]he new emancipator politics will no longer be the act of a particular social agent, but an explosive combination of different agents. What unites us is that, in contrast to the classic image of proletarians who have 'nothing to lose but their chains,' we are in danger of losing all: the threat is that we will be reduced to an abstract empty Cartesian subject deprived of all substantial

---

13. Welchman, *The Aesthetics of Risk*, p. 12.

content, dispossessed of our symbolic substance, with our genetic base manipulated, vegetating in an unlivable environment. ... If this sounds apocalyptic, one should retort that we effectively live in an apocalyptic time—it is easy to note how each of the three processes of proletarization refer to an apocalyptic point: ecological breakdown, biogenetic reduction of humans to manipulable machines, total digital control over our lives... At all these levels, things are approaching a zero point, the end of time is near."[14]

Žižek's philosophy always skillfully and humorously mocks the liberal dream of civic consent to arrange for organic and painless social change (such as Western countries "fluidly" switching to green energy). Žižek has argued that in China capitalism works even better with autocratic rule behind it. Žižek has a long-standing love for Stalin, of whom he keeps a portrait in his Ljubljana apartment. Change, for Žižek, will be either ordered from above, or forced by a popular revolution. Yet when it comes to the more recent "end times" hypothesis, it clearly goes beyond the capacities of speculative design to visualize it—for this would equal designing an apocalypse of sorts. As comedian John Stewart noted, "we live in hard times, but we don't live in end times."[15] Such a careful balance was recently put in the most elegant terms of "prophecy" and "proposal" by New York-based artist Carol Bove, in her discussion on the work of the 1970s "radical architecture" group Superstudio, a noted precursor of critical design: "[T]he prophetic images and text often function as warning or have a negative connotation, and the proposal images and text often have a more positive or utopian ideal. Yet there is a great deal of overlap in both."[16] Consequently, speculative design embraces the prospective outlook not to state absolute end points, but to balance the negative with the positive.

7. Vanilla to Chocolate

Modern design shares a common anthology with art and architecture from the early 20th century avant-gardes. In general, the tendency has been to

---

14. S. Žižek, "Living in the End Times," *Polygraph*, no. 22, 2010, Duke University, Durham, NC, p. 244.

15. J. Stewart at the "Rally to Restore Sanity And/Or Fear," Washington, DC, October 30, 2010. See www.comedycentral.com/shows/rally_to_restore_sanity_and_or_fear/index.jhtml, retrieved November 1, 2010.

16. From Carol Bove's interview with Superstudio members in *Nothing Up My Sleeve, An exhibition based on the work of Stuart Sherman*, curated by Jonathan Berger, Regency Arts Press, 2010.

look back at this affiliation and overstate its explanatory value; any strategic thought about the future is automatically framed as a repetition of earlier artistic avant-garde movements. But the given that designers are citizens, who live and work in societies shaped by a variety of forces, potentially opens the field to a much wider set of influences. There are a variety of different "avant-gardes" which are not part of art history, yet to be considered influential to design practice—especially to the speculative kind.

One such school of thought is Game Theory. Originating in the later part of WWII, it structured competition and coordination between actors as economic games of strategy. With Game Theory in hand, the RAND corporation (Research And Development), a non-profit institution based in Santa Monica, theorized the "unthinkable"—the improbable, but not impossible, scenario of military conflict between the Soviet Union and the USA. It was considered that both opponents would prefer to avoid such a course of events, given the fact that nuclear war would be disastrous to both. RAND tried to popularize the genre by publishing popular science titles aimed at a wider readership. The corporation's long time senior analyst was Albert Wohlstetter, an Austrian-born mathematician who had before served at the General Panel Corporation, producing prefabricated housing based on Bauhaus ideas. While at RAND in the 1950s, Wohlstetter contributed to the theory of decision making. He questioned the idea that we always know from the outset what our preferences are, instead arguing that we build and adjust them on the go. Wohlstetter drew an early blueprint for Risk Society and, by extension, critical design: "Given any two alternatives, you either prefer one or you are indifferent. ... For a variety of reasons I think that [the axiom] that you can make that judgment about any two alternatives, is very implausible and wrong. If you think about preferences not as simple sensuous pleasures like preferring vanilla to chocolate, but complex alternatives, in many cases you just don't know how to compare them at all. You don't know whether you are indifferent or prefer one or the other, and when you think about how you make decisions, that part of your job is that you construct an order as you find out about things, so that you are always in the process of constructing your preferences."[17]

---

17. J. Digby, J. Goldhamer, "The Development of Strategic Thinking at RAND, 1948–63: A Mathematical Logician's View – An Interview with Albert Wohlstetter," July 5, 1985, p. 19, citation from J. Stevenson, *Thinking Beyond the Unthinkable*, Viking Press, New York 2008, p. 48.

Traditional game theory has focused on "zero sum games," where one player wins what his opponent loses. But there are many situations where opponents are mutually dependent, for example in "wars and threats of war, strikes, negotiations, criminal deterrence, class war, race war, price war, and blackmail; maneuvering in a bureaucracy or in a traffic jam," as Nobel Prize-winning economist Thomas Schelling put it. "[T]hese are the games in which, though the element of conflict provides the dramatic interest, mutual dependence is part of the logical structure and demands some kind of collaboration or mutual accommodation—tacit, if not explicit—even if only in the avoidance of mutual disaster."[18] Schelling assumed that the conditions of the "pure-collaboration" were not fundamentally different from those of conflict, because players have to understand each other and find patterns of behavior that make the other's actions predictable. Such factors count for conflict and collaboration. "They must communicate by hint and by suggestive behavior. Two vehicles trying to avoid collision, two people dancing together to unfamiliar music," or "the applauding members of a concert audience, who must at some point 'agree' on whether to press for an encore or to taper off together."[19]

Game Theory is a set of observed rules enabling the assessment of future scenarios. And though the perspective of binary conflict is no longer useful, games of strategy may still be considered a source of influence for speculative design, especially when it is about coordination and collaboration between actors—for example, in an online social network.

8. Prime Ministers and Taxi Drivers

In "futuring," or "future studies," a combination of forecasting and insight is used to predict trends. There may be stellar economic value to such predictions when they are endowed with enough authority—like, for example, the work of Paris-based trend forecaster Li Edelkoort ("Grey, grey, grey… how many times can you say grey…? As Li puts it, we are in a time of indecision and we are 'ready to embrace a time of hope and well being.' Black and white are neither and thus grey is the perfect positive balance.")[20]

---

18. T.C. Schelling, *The Strategy of Conflict*, Harvard University Press, Cambridge 1980 (1960), p. 83.

19. Schelling, *The Strategy of Conflict*, p. 85.

20. See http://thewrendesign.com/li-elderkoorts-trend-forecast-2010-2050/, retrieved November 29, 2010.

A futurologist should be an avid interpreter of reality, picking up so-called "weak signals." Such indicators are supposed to hold critical information with regard to the future; they are precursors to the more important "wildcards"—"sudden and unique incidents that can constitute turning points in the evolution of a certain trend." A wildcard is "an occurrence that is assumed to be improbable, but which would have large and immediate consequences."[21] Failure to interpret weak signals will make wildcards seem like a surprise—but there is no way one can ensure an event actually *is* a weak signal. All kinds of random events may qualify, without there being a way to determine what they do and do not foreshadow.

The more ambitious the hypothesis, the more diverse the actual "evidence," the more grandiose the forecast. The "method" becomes clever mash-up—instead of approaching the issue at hand from a self-contained set of doctrinal instruments, all emphasis is put on weaving the story.

Elina Hiltunen, a Finnish futurist, has a blog page full of pictures of mundane surroundings, all of which she has tagged as a "weak signal." One picture has the following caption: "In Helsinki there were mystery laminated book pages attached to the fence. What is this about? A new guerrilla marketing campaign, perhaps?"[22]

The synthesis of weak signals into a future scenario can serve many purposes. Critically it is about the near future; how do you as a forecaster assist organizations in adapting to the "massive change" at hand? From trend-watching hipsters and their preferred gluten-free snacks in Brooklyn or Copenhagen, to Power Pointing the conclusions to grey-suited, balding men in Stuttgart or Shanghai.

In the case of futuring, no one has gone quite as far as its most prominent practitioner—former *Fortune* editor Alvin Toffler, together with his wife, Heidi, responsible for a host of books of which the most well-known ones are *Future Shock* and *The Third Wave* (not to be confused with Giddens' *Third Way*). The world's premier futurologists, the Tofflers have coined now-commonplace neologisms, like "information overload," or "prosumer," and they have at considerable fees, helped corporations and organizations adapt to the

---

21. See L. Botterhuis *et al.*, "Monitoring the Future. Building an Early Warning System for the Dutch Ministry of Justice," *Futures*, vol. 42, no. 5, June 2010, pp. 454–65.

22. See www.future.vuodatus.net/, retrieved October 15, 2010.

changes they forecast. At a crossroads of media philosophy, popular science and corporate consultancy, Alvin Toffler is a dexterous provider of "memes" —cultural genes that multiply by imitation. The obvious power of their work is not scientific, but, in a weird sense—*artistic*; it is the mastery of narrative and rhetoric which matters more than methodological accuracy. In the acknowledgments to *The Third Wave* (1980), exploring the arrival of information society and the knowledge economy, Toffler explains his way of working: "… I have drawn on several streams of information. The first and most conventional comes from the reading of books, journals, newspapers, reports, documents, magazines, and monographs from many countries. The second has its source in interviews with change-makers around the world. I have visited them in their laboratories, executive suites, schoolrooms and studios, and they have been generous with their time and ideas. They range from family experts and physicists to Cabinet members and prime ministers. … Finally, in traveling I have relied on what I trust is an alert eye and ear. Often, firsthand experience or chance conversation sheds a revealing light on abstraction. A taxi driver in a Latin American capital told me more than all his government's cheery statistics: when I asked him why his people were not doing something to protest a soaring inflation rate, he simply imitated the stuttering of a machine gun."[23]

Note that Toffler does not reveal any particular method on his part. On the contrary, he obfuscates it by referring to both the "high" (prime ministers) and "low" (taxi drivers) status of his sources, the author posing both as a high society insider *and* a man of the people. All these sources together "should" amount to a viable and tested hypothesis, but there is no methodological assertion, other than the author's phenomenal sense of "insight." Futuring, once again, is a doctrine or practice which should be included among the set of "unrecognized avant-gardes." The work of the German author Ingo Niermann stands as a contemporary example. Niermann has recently bridged futuring with critical design by his *Solution* books, a series of small volumes each devoted to "solving" a particular set of particular social and political issues. Niermann proposed, for example, to create a giant pyramid in the German hinterland where the dead could be buried. The proposal combines the architectural megalomania of the neo-avant-gardes with a socio-political analysis that borders on trend forecasting.

---

23. A. Toffler, *The Third Wave*, William Morrow and Company, New York 1980, p. 461.

9. Social Networks and Risk Society

As Marina Vishmidt states in a brilliant essay, *The Mirror of the Network*, "risk becomes a secularized theology of appeasement of the unknown."[24] After the 2008 financial crisis, the credit crisis, and the bank bailouts, European governments have speeded their dismantling of social benefits and public goods. With the simultaneous advent of online social networks like Facebook, the technocratic specter of "Risk Society" becomes more fully visible in its social dimension. Again, the United Kingdom is the laboratory here with its Conservative-Liberal Democrat coalition government that took office in 2010. From the outset the Conservatives—under their leader David Cameron—have used social media and the idea of "crowdsourcing" in their campaign for a smaller government. Replacing public services like schools or post offices, communities are "empowered" to take over the tasks of government—while having the burden, the costs and the risks transferred from the collective, political body of the public state to the private, social body of the people. Effectively it is a transfer mainly of cost—not of power. The Conservative Manifesto that was the masthead of the campaign, promised to return former state assets "to the people." This manifesto was "not a traditional manifesto," which, if it were, indeed would fall prey to predictable criticisms of being utopian; instead, the manifesto was deeply rooted in the conservative tradition of going with the grain of human nature. Appreciated by *The Guardian* as a veil for "deep cuts, lower taxes for the rich and sweeping Thatcherite privatization," Big Society is the latest brand of neoliberalism. Author Mark Fisher notes that the crisis, caused to a large extent by neoliberal policies, is used to "electro-shock" the neoliberal program back into life.[25] Perhaps after all there is a common ground between David Cameron and Cameron Sinclair. The first, Britain's Prime Minister, accused the State of unnecessarily interrupting in the social field. The latter, a successful architect, accused architecture of vanity, breaking up the urban fabric. Both evoke pastoral impressions of community.

---

24. M. Vishmidt, "The Mirror of the Network," in Metahaven, *Uncorporate Identity*, Lars Müller, Baden 2010, p. 156.

25. See M. Fisher, "The Great Bullingdon Club Swindle," October 22, 2010, at http://k-punk. abstractdynamics.org/archives/2010_10.html, retrieved November 5, 2010.

10. Imaginative counterculture
If there is anything speculative design may contribute, it is to de-bunk the new, austerity-driven myths of the Risk Society. The consequences of advanced modernity are no longer debated as consumer lifestyle options, but as political and social scenarios with immediate relevance. Being counter-*establishment* is not enough. The "proposal" of speculative design is not another technocratic utopia, but an imaginative counter*culture*, alert of its own pitfalls, while making life more lively. Its "prophecy" is a playful analysis of the hard times we live in.

M/M (PARIS)

How did M/M start, how have you built your world? **M/M (Paris)** When we finished our studies and began to act within the real world, it was clear to us that we had to set up a production unit that would allow us to formalize and disseminate our ideas. Opening a graphic design studio seemed to be the best solution. It was our reaction to what was happening in the art world, which was, in our opinion, too far removed from reality—by this we mean people having a workshop, producing objects and eventually selling them to someone. In our mind a graphic design studio should be a workshop plugged directly into reality, as it operates in relation to commissioned works. This production unit would allow us to produce utopias and eventually see our dreams "alter" the world around us.

Then you had a background in the arts and specialized in graphic design? **M/M** Basically we were art students who studied graphic design to learn more about sign-making because we were surrounded by media networks at the time. We knew that if we had something important to say, it would be fundamental to be excellent at sign-making. We went through a post-Bauhaus program and learned all the techniques in order to be able to give any kind of materiality to our signs from an image (still and moving) to space. To be "fluent" with all media was a strategy we adopted since we were students. So when we started to work, at the beginning of the 1990s, we were fully operational—on many different levels—to express our convictions through posters, television, cinema, records, exhibitions, books, and then the web. We are now living in a so-called "multimedia world.; we personally don't like this term, but what it really means is that there are a variety of media that can provide different life and scale to an idea so that it is easier to "infect" reality with this idea. If we had started two hundred years ago, then maybe we would have had a painting studio because that was the most efficient medium at the time.

You once said that when you started you could set the rules of being graphic designers, also, in a way, because you were in France and there was much to be done. **M/M** The intuition that we had in art school was that it was possible to build within the reality of the French territory because there were no rules at all in the field of graphic design in France at the time. It is always the same, when there is a territory with no historical rules no one really cares, no one says you shouldn't do things like this or that. In being extremely well equipped in the field of graphic design, at the beginning of the 1990s we were somehow pioneers in a France that was completely deserted and uncreative. It seemed that the world belonged to us. Our dream was also economically feasible. Michaël's father is a dentist and he had a small spare room where we could set up a "nano" graphic workshop; it was a tiny corridor, so we bought a computer, a scanner, a printer, paper, pencils and there we started, working in a digitally equipped microscopic space. At the age of forty-nine M/M (Paris) (Michaël was twenty-four then and Mathias was twenty-five) was a fully professional and operational graphic design studio. We were impatient to be part of the world and to be involved in its construction. We did not want to be removed from it, in painting, drawing, writing or making something endlessly and then being anxiously for our ideas to be bought and consumed. We were eager to be activists within reality and the present. Affecting reality with the idea of art was our secret mission. The history of art during the entire 20th century is about the relationship between art and life. The context from which we were sharing and distributing our art was the innovation in our work. Basically when we started in 1991, through the context of graphic design, you could say "we have an idea about the world, and our point of view about the world is as interesting as you contemporary artists, you architects, you filmmakers, you writers or you musicians, the difference being that we are expressing ourselves through our field and that is perfectly valid as a strategy." It was a provocation, indeed, but that was the idea. Maybe the big shift then was not being afraid to be artists using graphic design as an extended medium. By commissioning M/M (Paris) you would tacitly accept that you would go through a creative conversation that would lead to the creation of an artwork anchored within reality. Of course, at the beginning our work was very aggressive and maybe chaotic, because we were simultaneously trying to take an articulated artistic stand and define our own activity. We cherish our early pieces, as they have the truly monstrous vitality that only teenagers can have.

How has the workshop developed since then? **M/M** We can say at present that our work has entered a phase of maturity. M/M (Paris) is now a clearly identifiable production unit; it has become a brand that has a self-contained vibrancy. Our projection is anchored within reality. Nevertheless, the size of the studio is somehow the same, M/M (Paris) has not put on weight. We have been working in the same space for about sixteen years. Originally M/M (Paris) started with two people: Michaël and Mathias. Now four others are working in the studio: an archivist who also answers the phone, and three assistants who deal with several different projects at the same time. The idea is to keep the studio in scale with our thoughts. This is why we describe our studio as a workshop, a research unit directly plugged into reality that produces working prototypes at scale 1. Some projects exist as singular and autonomous pieces but most of the time, even if they are autonomous pieces, they are connected to one another through different and various commissions. For instance, you may see the beginning of a piece starting within one project and then evolving into another project and so on—that makes our work evolutive, so it has the quality of a performance. It can be rethought or resized according to the events surrounding us. All together these elements form a cosmogony at the scale of M/M (Paris) through which the viewer, the spectator, the audience is invited to travel in order to participate in a nourishing experience. This is why the format of our work varies greatly in size and in aspect: there are signs that can be 2D, 3D, moving or even immaterial ones.

Using different media and working in different dimensions implies collaboration with other people. Then your studio is six people but you do collaborate with others when necessary? **M/M** Since we started we always thought that our studio should also be a "connecting" unit that can articulate itself with other creative and connecting units. Instead of being able to cover every practice in the field, providing average quality work, we decided that our studio would specialize. We decided to be experts. By being experts we can then collaborate with other experts so that we can really produce "a work of expertise" among experts. We hold the strong belief that by widely extending our knowledge in the area of signs, we will be able to have meaningful creative conversations with experts from other fields such as contemporary art, filmmaking, mathematics, politics, architecture, poetry, cookery... Sharing expertise means that you have spent time reducing your practice to its essence, to its smallest constituent (monad). Only when this is achieved is it possible to build an essential and universal conversation with another expert. It seems obvious that a generic conversation is a waste of time. So, since we started we have developed strong creative relationships with people such as Inez van Lamsweerde and Vinoodh Matadin, Philippe Parreno, Pierre Huyghe, Sarah Morris, Liam Gillick, Björk or Nicolas Ghesquière at Balenciaga, among others, in order to build strong conversational creative procedures. We can use a metaphor drawn from cinema: One can choose to do a film with things around and a portable digital camera, a kind of self-made "home cinema." One can also produce a movie with an extended team that includes a cinematographer, a set designer, actors... It is impossible to say one scenario is better than another. What counts is to use the appropriate scale according to what needs to be said. It's more like this that we approach our practice according to the scale of the piece we have to produce. We put together a team that allows us to reach the size and the audience we are aiming for.

But then you are still "graphic designers," we mean, is it important to be acknowledged as such? **M/M** When we are invited to graphic design conferences we are introduced as people "working in the graphic design field..." and then suddenly the word "artists" pops out of the blue. This happens when people no longer know how to classify your professional existence. For those people it is disturbing that one does not follow the rules of the profession in which one is supposed to be quietly involved because one is constantly reassessing his own activity by reprogramming the reality around him. Those people "slot" you into art without thinking about what it really means to be an artist. To be an artist is not a profession as such. Strangely enough these days one can be a garage owner, or a football player and be an artist, and one can be a professional contemporary artist and not be an artist. Of course, statistically it is more probable to find an artist in the contemporary art world. At the end of the day we are artists who are professional graphic designers, and we are impassioned by signs at any scale or state. We approach reality through the prism of signs. For instance, when we do work in (or with) space, we do not define ourselves as "architects," because for us working with space means experimenting on how a sign affects a space. The same thing applies to the stools, chairs, lamps, or tables we have designed— all these are 3D images representing reality. The working table displayed at the Triennale Design Museum [in the *Graphic Design Worlds* exhibition] is not a real piece of furniture, even though this table might be one of the most functional tables that could ever be used in a work place. This is the art of illusion.

Would you work on architecture, on buildings? **M/M** We somehow just started to answer that question five minutes ago. To make ourselves more clear, yes, we would work on architecture or buildings if the commission makes sense according to our expertise. As we live in a world of images, we think it is possible that a graphic designer is capable of designing a building that could be as good as a building designed by a contemporary professional architect. For example, Zaha Hadid's buildings are 3D images. This is the reason why they are interesting in the context of the present time. We don't want to discuss the quality of her images here, but at least what we can reckon is that she is not dealing with architectural problems, she is dealing with images in 3D that are shaping the contemporary visual architectural landscape.

What interests you most about the reality you want to be "plugged into," as you say? **M/M** Reality is pure fantasy produced by human beings—that is why it is fascinating. We like the idea that reality is a collective dream structured by a succession of negotiating acts so that every member of the group is able to participate—even with a tiny piece—in a collective dream. Every aspect of this extremely human mechanism is inspiring, so we do have an "ethnological" approach. That is why we like pop culture that circulates through music, cinema, television, literature, fashion, and art. We don't want to just comment on this or be spectators; we really want to be active within it. We do not want to be vampires, using pop culture as an easy edible substance. We are promoting and defending the idea of "an ecology of signs" within pop culture. Our idea is to create a sort of "eco system" based on the idea that if someone takes something out of pop culture, one has to produce something active and inject it back within this culture in order that pop culture does not consume itself and keeps being regenerated. Pop culture belongs to everyone and everyone should take care of it. Returning to the beginning of the answer, our studio is outside reality but it is completely plugged into it. We used to call our space an "office," *bureau*, not a "studio," so that we feel we are operating within a working reality. From that clear position we are then able to produce a truly effective image which, due to its distorting and reflective quality, may offer a different angle from which the world can be reflected: It enables the viewer to reconsider it. In the end we want the viewer to be active in his/her relation to our production.

You mean that your work is not sign-making for its own sake, and that your signs can enhance an awareness about the context in which they intervene? **M/M** Exactly. We think this is an important dimension of our work. We are constantly shifting the perception of collective reality within a social, economical, historical and geographical context by implanting signs that are articulating the perception of the world differently, in order to constantly reprogram it where we think it is needed. Those intelligent visual agents can strongly and deeply impact the viewer in order to make him change his preconceived perception of what surrounds him as reality. That's why most of the time the projects we have been working on there are some kind of layers of stories and the history surrounding them. For instance, we have been working for a theater for fifteen years, producing more than fifty posters for it; we decided on the rules for creating these posters fifteen years ago, and we are still working within the frame of the same rules. But the images produced are more and more complex because they are gaining psychological depth with time; like human beings, those images are aging and are affected by all the situations they are experiencing. In the end, the idea of longevity and continuity is affecting a context; the trajectory, the destiny of images is considered.

This links to the idea of the "archive of signs," that you once stated in an interview: that is, an archive of signs that exists in your work, through all your projects. Is this what you mean? **M/M** Each work created in our office is conceived so that it can be attached, anchored to reality. If a poster, a movie, an alphabet or an exhibition is successful, basically if it is a good sign, it automatically becomes real and turns into an event; then it exists by itself because people remember it. It is archived within the collective consciousness. As we produce work we are also archiving it within the world around us. By linking together a chain of things we produce, it becomes a kind of web, which archives itself within the world. You always find a link from one piece of work to another, not just in terms of look but in terms of meaning. That is why the notion of each piece being performative is very important. It can't just be the idea of a sign, it has to be a self-sufficient object, a kind of autonomous living entity.

This is an interesting reading of your work, and of graphic designers' work. Usually graphic designers feel their work and their position is almost invisible to people in general, or that people do not acknowledge them. What is your opinion about this? **M/M** We think it should be clearly stated that the graphic designer is not just providing a service any more, and that those days are over. Today machines and software are doing this, much better and faster than human beings: They are over-efficient in this sense. To survive and to be competitive with machines, a contemporary graphic designer has to be an author, a thinker, a poet, a journalist, a philosopher... I think that all the people who are promoting the idea of providing a service should no longer call themselves "graphic designers," as they are actually software operators. We don't mind them doing so, but then it is important to find another definition for what they do so that there is no further confusion, in order to keep promoting and teaching graphic design for its own particular strength. "Graphic design" is a great and practical term for us because we can invent ourselves, and this is what we did and what we still do. We think that a great graphic designer should engineer the spare and the wasted time of our contemporary world.

So some of these aspects of graphic design—like providing solutions or researching legibility—are just like small bricks in a wider discourse? **M/M** For us this is very basic, it is a kind of level one reaches within the thinking design process. Before even thinking of being a writer one has to learn how to draw the complete alphabet around the age of five. All the legibility obsession is evidence that is not worth discussing. It is part of the learning process not the creative process. Graphic design is not a science. We are not interested in graphic design, which is self-centered. For us graphic design is a powerful contemporary medium, and it is vital for us to be able to use this medium adequately because we want to make ourselves clearly understood. We want to share our views on the world with the other inhabitants of the world. But how does design affect reality? This is more the question. Some graphic design proposals (there are not that many) deeply affect reality and some don't, as they are only promoting the everyday life or more precisely accelerating its crassness... It is extremely complicated to produce an affecting sign. It is a true act of creation. There is no science that leads you to it. It is the same thing in the art world: some contemporary artists are just producing objects to furbish museums, public spaces, houses or gardens that need some gentle decorative devices. It is rare to encounter a piece that truly affects reality. The same principle also applies to architecture. One can imagine a truly performative and significant piece produced in collaboration with an architect, a contemporary artist, a philosopher, a sociologist, a poet or a filmmaker. It would be a kind of dream team in which the graphic designer takes on the role of translator with greatness.

Do you think that people who are making decisions and who are in charge of choosing whether or not to involve figures from different fields actually acknowledge the position of graphic designers? Does this happen in France? **M/M** No. There is no consideration for the crucial role of graphic designers in our contemporary society. Basically creative-minded people in France such as dancers, painters, photographers, or writers may gain official recognition by the State. But we don't know of any graphic designer who ever received such recognition. We really think graphic designers have a very important role to play within the cultural organization of a social group such as a city. A good example of this is when Peter Saville was appointed art director of the city of Manchester. A graphic designer could also be appointed director of a museum. Wim Crouwel has been the director of the Museum Boijmans Van Beuningen in Rotterdam for eight years.

[Giorgio Camuffo] *I totally agree. We have great potential. In our job we meet a lot of people, and as we explore and absorb lots of different bits of information, we grow, we gain an awareness of the world we live in. But then, of course, it is not just because we are graphic designers. You have to be smart...* **M/M** At some point you can go beyond your field. The same is true with architecture. When you say "this architect is great" you are acknowledging the fact that he is somehow superior in his field. If architects only talk to architects, at some point no one cares. The same thing with art. What is good about art, architecture, and cinema, is that they have invented tools that enable them to expose their ideas to the others. Then one reaches a kind of spiritual dimension under those circumstances. Maybe graphic designers should think about that fact too.

Then how do you feel about the growing interest that some graphic designers show in discussing their work, through conferences, exhibitions, and publications? **M/M** It really depends on how it is done. For instance I think what is really unproductive is when a graphic design exhibition is just about posters because it seems natural to do so, without even questioning the meaning of a poster as a medium and what it means to express ideas through this medium. For example, an artist who uses graphic design as a tool has the opportunity to scale, adapt and articulate the medium in relation to his ideas. Therefore, when you are dealing with an exhibition you have to be at the level of the art world, where there is already a long history of exhibitions that started at the beginning of the 20th century. One can see that the tools used by some of the artists of the last century were the ones used or invented by graphic designers, but those artists were not calling themselves "graphic designers," even though in effect they were doing graphic design. Think of a work by Marcel Duchamp: it's now called an artwork but it has the effect of a sign, it is somehow a truly intelligent logotype. It could be a graphic design piece. It is a decontextualized object put in a museum space in order to articulate a visual message. So it is basically like a word or a sign at the scale of the world. Nothing more than that. We wish that there were more design critics. Let's take the example of Italy: in Venice there are three events promoting art, architecture, and cinema. So why doesn't a strong cultural bridge with graphic design exist in any of them? It is urgent to build new cultural connections to promote the history of graphic design and its contemporary practice.

Speaking about signs, there is one thing we are curious to know: why do you design a lot of alphabets? Is it a way to reflect on your job and position? **M/M** Designing and building an extended collection of alphabets was a way for us to clearly tell the world that our specialism is sign-making and that we started as sign-makers. As we have already stated, maybe a hundred or two hundred years ago we would have been painters... The alphabetical tool is a kind of grammar for us; it is like playing the piano every day. Also it is a way for us to build a vocabulary that we can use extensively throughout our language. Within the alphabetical classification we like the notion of the series, the multiple—is everything the same or different? We are fascinated by the idea of one self-standing, independent item relating to twenty-six others so that at the end they are all linked to one another to build a group, a family. As we see it, it has a kind of political or sociological scale, somehow, in the sense that it reflects the way some group of strong individualities are building communities of thoughts. We think that the alphabet sums up many of our obsessions.

But then the other signs that you produce and use in your work are also like an alphabet? **M/M** Yes, they have the quality of an alphabet. They are individual but part of a group or a family. This relates to the self-archival idea we were describing earlier. Each of our projects is self-sufficient, but they all contain a part of a project to come or are part of an existing one. All our projects are delicately and intricately connected to one another so that in the end we can look at them in a wider realm; they somehow form an alphabet of projects all together. This is what we meant when we said that we believe that when we make an image it always exists between a previous one and the one that will follow. We like the idea that a sign is between two images. You understand now why the idea of history in its many dimensions is so important for us.

Just one last question that deals with education. Do you feel there is something missing in the contemporary scenario of graphic design education? **M/M** We think there is a very big problem in education, full stop. Whether it is graphic design, or art, or architecture. Since you or we were students, the world has completely changed. However, we don't see people teaching that change. We think the main problem in education is that no time is allowed to teach students to look at the world properly, and they do not know how to read it. Students have to be productive immediately; there is no longer time for failure, so right away they are forced to reproduce the world, where instead they should be thinking of how to produce reality.

NORM

We would like to start from your "world," its story, that means your background, your education, how you met and how you decided to set up Norm. **Dimitri Bruni** We met in Bienne, a small town north of Bern, at a really small graphic design school. I was born there. Manuel is from Bern. We met in the Vorkurs, the one-year preliminary course before you can enter the actual graphic design class. For me, as I remember, I didn't want to do anything else. I was focused on going to this design school and I think Manuel was also. **Manuel Krebs** I think it was about the school and the people who were there. It was very familiar, small, with very few people. **DB** The first year we had access to a lot of creativity, to every medium: photography, painting, drawing... Then we passed the exam for the professional class. We began this class together in 1992 and finished in 1996. It was such a small class.

Was it because it was a very exclusive and selective school? **MK** It was not so easy to be admitted. It was difficult but not impossible. **DB** But it was not the high school system. It was rather about professional training. **MK** It was also very classic, like the Bauhaus system. It was really based on skills. The funny thing was that the graphic design teachers were not so good. But there were other students and that was very important: we discovered graphic design together. We were a little bit like in the former Soviet Union; we were a bit disconnected. I remember once we came to visit a school in Zurich, and here they had a very modern building and computers in the classroom. We were very impressed—we thought "this is the real world." We were very provincial. **DB** Anyway, there was a kind of synergy with other students. We set up a lot of things at that time like *Silex*.[1] When we finished school we decided that we wanted to work together. **MK** But we needed money. I think it was, and it is, a good thing to gain some experience and to work for somebody after school, because you understand what you like and what you do not. We both worked for agencies, medium-sized, me in Geneva and Dimitri in Zurich. We realized that it was not what we wanted. We have always been in touch. Then one day, during a phone call, Dimitri said: "We have to go to Zurich now, it's very lively." So I also moved to Zurich and we rented a place that was, at the time, much too expensive for us, because nobody knew us. We lived in a garage without anything, but we had a very nice space in which to work.

So you lived together at the time that you set up the studio? **DB** Yes, we lived together. **MK** I would like to add something funny again about school, just to give you an idea about the context we came from, and how it was disconnected. We often were taken to the Museum für Gestaltung in Zurich to see exhibitions. And once there was an exhibition called the *99 Worst Posters*, the worst posters ever in history. And, you know, three of them were posters from teachers of ours. It is funny. But I think this had an influence on how we work: We felt that the input from the teachers was not to be taken seriously, somehow. We were very much looking at things. This is something that we still do a lot: we discuss the things we see, what is good, or what is not...

It seems you have a very close relationship with each other, and understanding. Then we wonder if this is a decision to keep the team like this, and to have a small studio. **MK** We don't see ourselves in a studio with twenty people; maybe it could be interesting... I don't know. However, we are now three actually, as Ludovic [Varone] joined us in 2005. **DB** It depends on the opportunities. **MK** Also this relates to the design process, you know. I am a little bit of a perfectionist but Dimitri is really extreme. And we feel that many things happen while you are doing them.

But you have relationships with other designers, for instance here in Zurich, like Cornel Windlin. Is it important for Norm to collaborate with other professionals? **DB** In that way we don't collaborate so directly. We never

---

1. Underground fanzine dedicated to the art of drawing; it started in 1994 and ended in 2004.

collaborate on one project together, but maybe the collaboration starts in sharing or looking at what the other people do. We know a lot of people, other graphic designers, but it is more like private, we have lunch together and we talk about whatever. We are not really interested in collaborating, or it has never happened that we collaborate directly on producing something. With Cornel maybe it is more of a collaboration through Lineto [digital font foundry], because we discuss certain typefaces, he would give his opinion, which we would of course not consider [laughter]. I think we have a very close collaboration inside the studio. It is not like Cornel, who often invites more people and they really do a project together. We don't do this.

So far we have not asked what graphic design is for you: how do you read graphic design as Norm? **MK** We see it, so to speak, as craftsmanship. We think there is a very technical side and we think graphic design is the skin of information somehow. **DB** Also, the graphic design world is a really, really, tiny world, so we consider our work or ourselves as sort of specialists in this field. It is something very small. **MK** We would like it to be something technical. We see ourselves as engineering information, not as artists of something. We would rather say it is not so much about creativity but more about structuring things.

We once read an interview with you, where you said that you would recommend students to decide quite early what kind of area of graphic design they would like to work in. Would you still say so? **DB** This point is in relation to education, though. A Korean guy came here and asked us this last question: "What do you judge as a good education?" This is not such an easy question but maybe an answer could be that within a school a good education would be that—when  they are finished with studies—students concerned know what they want to do, that they have an opinion on graphic design and not just follow a certain style. Maybe this is also a part of the teachers' job, to canalize the students so that at the end they know what they want to do, that they can have a personal approach. It is not just about tools, it is also about an attitude, the way of working.

Another quotation we have found about you is from Cornel Windlin, who once said that through your work you are creating your cosmos, like "Norm cosmos" with their preferences and rules.[2] *We wonder if you really feel this, and what are these rules?* **MK** Very honestly all this has an aesthetic side and it has a lot to do with how we started. Also with the two books that we published in 2000 and 2002—*Norm: Introduction* and *Norm: The Things*—they were statements and all the material that we used had to be filtered and to have a certain aesthetic. For instance it was really important that we mainly, or almost only, use our own typefaces, as long as the typeface will tell you how the work will look. So, in a way, we do not question certain things so much anymore because there are rules: I mean how we do things and how we don't. The longer you work with someone the more you have definite things on which you agree. Every designer has rules. You cannot design without rules. You cannot design a typeface without rules. Some people do not like the word "rule" because they think that there is a system. But they do follow rules. Even the wildest book will have a rule. We want to be very conscious of that. One of the big questions in graphic design is when your work is done, when it is finished, when it is good. So we tried to solve this question by saying "this is how we do it, we do this like *that* and *that* and *that*." And when we have done all of this, the work is done. Thus we don't have to question it anymore. The rules are the concepts somehow. Maybe instead of "rules" we can say "standards" or "concepts." We try to set them up at the beginning of the project. **DB** Then, when you are doing the work, you also have to change the rules... **MK** It is like in a zoo in Zurich, the tigers got really bored because they were always doing the same thing. So the zoo keepers started hiding their food in different places in their cages so they didn't know where the food was... **DB** ... to make it more interesting.

You mean that you have to move, to shift? **MK** Yes, to check where it is. This is something we try to do now, we try to change the approach sometimes, in a way that you can be curious, that you are interested in the subject. Also the subject has become more important to us, it is something that stimulates us more.

---

2. Quoted by L. Farrelly, "Buying into the Norm Cosmos," *Eye*, no. 70, 2008.

In your work, commissioned work is the main part? **DB** Yes, at the moment. **MK** Well, for example the *Replica* typeface that was a commission of the studio. In these cases there is always a risk. Pure designing of a typeface can take perhaps a year, so the office would advance the money, but this has to have a return, the typeface must sell.

So Replica *was the first typeface you specifically designed to be sold?* **MK** Really commercially, somehow yes. And this is quite difficult nowadays, because there are so many new typefaces being produced. It is like music, you can't be sure it is going to sell. But with the collaboration with Lineto it is good, because this a very small foundry, there are few typefaces coming out, and there is a good network of people interested in what it is doing.

What was the starting point for Replica? *You had an idea for a typeface or you needed a new font for some works?* **MK** Basically, we needed a new typeface. We used *Normetica* to work for some projects and then we did the *Simple* font, which has been very important for us to work on projects. But then, at some point, we found ourselves sort of in a hole: we somehow lost our identity because *Simple* was already bit old and *Replica* wasn't ready yet.

You use only Replica *for all your commercial work?* **MK** For everything. We almost only use *Replica*. It is only recently that, for example, for Swatch Company we designed another typeface, *Swatch CT*, because it could not be the same.

Then typeface has a crucial role in your design work? **MK** We say the typeface is the core or the molecule for the design.

Like the heart of your cosmos? **DB** Yes. We are not typographers, we are graphic designers who also do type design. This makes a difference.

How important are printing and printed matter for you, especially in this age, when people talk more and more about digital books? **DB** I think it is a question of value, value that we want to give. We feel very close to printing. **MK** We are also really interested in the mechanical process. To us physical presence is something that is really important. If you look at screen printing, the colors are so intense, and you can feel that it can only be done like this. It is very present, or "real" in a way, more than something digital. You can touch it. **DB** It gets closer to materiality. **MK** We are not nostalgic about books at all. We totally see and appreciate all the possibilities that come with the iPad or the digital book. We think this can be very good for many things. But of course a book like that of the photographer Miroslav Tichý,[3] with pictures in it, or art catalogues, cannot be the same on a screen. Because, somehow, with the printed book, I can "have" the picture. It is like possessing something. As long as the thing is digital or virtual I don't have it. And if it is printed I can have it. Also we give much importance to printing because a printed book will be around for a while. Sometimes you get a book that is ten or twenty years old, and there is such a pleasure in having it.

Speaking about books, is there any difference between designing books for others and designing your own books which you once defined as "visual essays"? **DB** The difference is maybe that it is much more difficult to design books, to give the content by yourself, to decide, because you have to define a lot of things, to be clear about what you want to publish. In publishing by yourself you are totally exposed on what is going out. If it is wrong it is not the fault of the lithographer or the person who wrote the text. You are totally exposed. It is a nice risk. For us the books we have published have also been related to a kind of statement or something we wanted to talk about. You have another responsibility in a way.

Are your editorial projects a way of designing and displaying your world? **DB** They are also a comment about graphic design, maybe reflecting on what we are doing, what the job of graphic design is. Probably you can also do that in a commission but it depends on the collaboration.

With these projects are you trying to address other designers or a broader public? **MK** We don't think about the target... **DB** For us it is important that the content is exactly what we want to say and if it is accessible that's nice and good. Of course we are trying our best to make it understandable.

---

3.   Designed by Norm, ICP/Steidl, New York 2010.

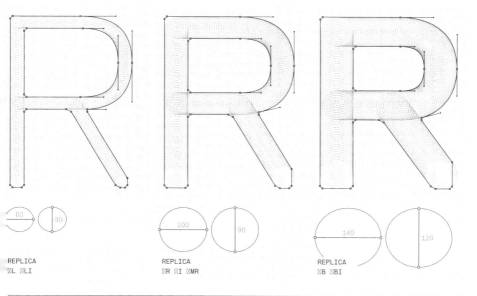

REPLICA
⊠L ⊠LI

REPLICA
⊠R ⊠I ⊠MR

REPLICA
⊠B ⊠BI

CIMAL GRID /■WIDTH /■SIDE BEARINGS /■KERNING

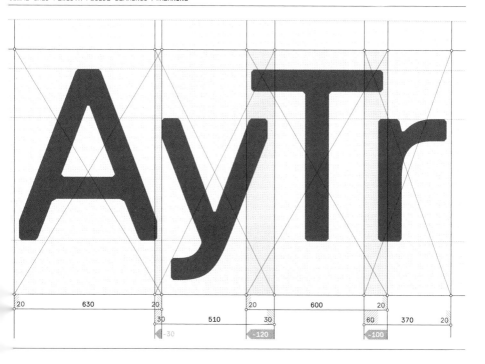

RADIM PEŠKO

Where did you start and how did you decide to move away from the Czech Republic? **Radim Peško** As for my background and "journey," I studied at the Academy of Arts, Architecture and Design in Prague, and the final year I found myself a bit tired of the academic environment and with an absolute lack of interest of building a career as a graphic designer—to establish a studio there, search for clients and so on. I felt that something was missing, some kind of essence, in the things that I was doing. Moreover, being educated in a post-Communist country meant (and it does even today) a lot of cultural isolation and disconnection from the rest of the world. So looking around and thinking what would be the next step, I discovered, through the work of Karel Martens—that I saw at an exhibition about Dutch graphic design—, a school based in Arnhem: the Werkplaats Typografie. Its model, based on practical assignments on one hand and the focus on development of individual voice, on the other, "fit" exactly into the gap I felt I was in after finishing my studies. So I moved to the Netherlands. Here I had the opportunity to meet new people and designers I had read about and admired. Meeting them was a great experience, which certainly opened my eyes and pushed me to move to Amsterdam and allowed things to happen.

How would you describe the world of graphic design today and your position in it? **RP** I am afraid I cannot offer any general descriptions. At best I can say that I am interested in how people interact with their habitat, in their relationship with technologies, language, or communication, if you like... A more precise answer to this question can only be the work itself. In the end I accept the definition under which this modern profession was established

and has developed through the years; to me there doesn't seem to be much to discuss about it. If we felt now that terms like "design" or "graphic design" do not really fit to describe some activities, I guess we might use some other terms. Let's just call it "work"—be it a book, a typeface, an exhibition or a workshop in the school.

How important are relationships and collaborations with other people for you, having a "network"? RP Connections happen naturally and inevitably as long as working as a designer you are always part of some team—one part of the whole. So it is not that such a network is a principal vehicle for making things; on the contrary, it feels more like a kind of a side product to me. But certainly it is a valuable one and quite essential in many cases. In fact, projects that give me the greatest satisfaction are those where I can work with people I have known for a long time—in a way we have already built up sort of bridges between our minds. Then each following work is a continuation of an ongoing discussion, a new conclusion, maybe.

Would you say that you create design "worlds," or that you participate in building worlds in some way, through graphic design? RP I think that any work comes from observation and some kind of creative input into the stream of things; so I would say that designing nowadays is perhaps more like channeling than building.

In 2009 you launched your own foundry. We know that in the past you preferred not to sell some of your fonts. Then, what motivated you to start RP Foundry? RP Starting my own foundry seemed like a good idea to me at the point when I realized that I had plenty of sketched out and unused typefaces in my drawer. Since I am an autodidact in type design, it took me years and years of trials and failures before my technical skills matched my expectations. As soon as this happened, and at the point in which I had clearer idea on how to do it, I decided to put some things online. Anyway, I still do not sell typefaces that were designed for very specific projects.

The field of graphic design appears to be broadening more and more. From your perspective, how do you read this phenomenon? RP Considering the "liquidity" of our time and society, it is very natural.

What is your position on the issues of designers' responsibilities, their social and cultural role? RP I don't know... I think that especially designers should be aware of any kind of ideology—be it artistic or political, or be it the ideology of "the good"—and act responsibly according to their best intentions and motivations at any given time and place. But this is valid for anyone else, I guess.

What do you think about graphic design education? What do you ask and expect from students when you teach? RP As a teacher I am hopefully succeeding in trying to pass on some of my experience, opening eyes, broadening perspectives, points of view perhaps. Schools are institutions and I never expected that much from them as a student. They can serve well in delivering some common knowledge, meeting people and giving you space, time and facilities for experimenting—all great opportunities, indeed. This incubation period is very important for every person who aims at working in the creative field, yet I feel that schools are rather like greenhouses, and I think the most important things happen outside of them—in the jungle.

MATHIAS SCHWEIZER

Could you give us a brief description of your "world" and work environment as an independent graphic designer: your training, your decision to work as a graphic designer, to work in Paris, etc.? **Mathias Schweizer** I came to Paris in 1998, after leaving school, to work with Graphistes Associés. After a short return to Switzerland in 2000, I came back here without really knowing why... and since then I have been working as an independent graphic designer. These twelve years in Paris have required me to make certain choices, to adopt a style of life that allows no concessions, at either the personal or professional level. Far from resulting in greater serenity, Paris has actually accentuated my desire for revolt. Like most big cities, it is visually polluted; as I see it, this is the perfect terrain in which to try out visual experiences with public spaces (if that term still makes sense). That is why Paris itself has inspired most of my images.

Is it important for you to establish links and relations with other people —We mean, other graphic designers and those working in related areas? Is collaboration an important part of your work? **MS** Certain collaborations have been fundamental in deciding how my work developed—in particular, my collaboration with Jean-Marc Ballée, a graphic designer for whom I have the highest respect. Most notably, we collaborated for several years on the communication for the "Rencontres Chorégraphiques Internationales de Seine-Saint-Denis." Each year we approached this commission by questioning the images that had been produced in previous years, all with the aim of evoking the presence of the human body without actually showing it. We shared this whole experience with Anita Mathieu, the Director of the Festival, who regularly made her own contribution to the final result. Treating the same theme every year is a very difficult exercise, but it was also a very enriching one; it influenced the way I approach subjects and the manner in which I work with my clients. After this experience I felt the need to approach commissions on my own, taking it as a principle that the client should always be brought into the creative process.

In your opinion, what is graphic design? In your professional activity, how do you interpret it as a discipline? What are your main objectives? **MS** Graphic design strives to initiate a relation; to create within someone the desire to continue along a course that was first revealed by the discovery of an image or a publication...

You work with different printing techniques and your posters always have a certain material quality. How important is the very physicality of your work? What is the importance of the physical senses? **MS** The attention paid to the very quality of production means that I can heighten the physical—carnal— quality of my images. It is something which allows me to develop an interaction with all the physical senses, at the same time as conveying a message.

The images you create can be very different: certain are illustrations that make reference to contemporary visual culture, others seem to be drawn from the natural world while they still carry references to the way the modern eye sees the world. How would you explain that? What is the fil rouge *that runs through all your work?* **MS** To start with, I always go with what the clients tell me about the subject; so it is inevitable that my responses to each project are different. That is the very basis of my method. Then I bring my own past to bear; striving to reach my own point of view with regard to the subject. I am someone who is very attracted by the idea of feeding off the public space, of proposing a rediscovery of that space through signs and codes that are shared by all of us. I like purloining a city's stigmata, to then put them to another purpose. Once digested, an image—by the very nature of things—has to share the stage with other images; it is re-introduced into the urban space as a desirable and/or monstrous "family relation."

Many of your posters seem to take graphic design to its limit, to engage with other fields of activity, especially art—like your Le Travail de Rivière *poster.*

How would you interpret your relation with art, both as a source of inspiration and with respect to your position as a graphic designer? **MS** I work in contexts which are heaving with responses and solutions. I like to disturb this situation by creating images that sometimes require the viewer to make an effort, to be attentive. But they always pose questions, while leaving the spectator free to follow his/her own course. One has to take time to learn the world, and it is the same with images (and all other forms of creation). My images may appear extreme, aggressive and sometimes gratuitous, but they are always a response to a subject, offering a different way of understanding it.

Do you think that, as a designer, you have a responsibility towards society, a responsibility within the space of public life? **MS** Given the previous questions/answers, I would say yes. I always act and work with the idea that my interlocutor is capable of interpreting what I propose in his own way, thus developing a rare sensation of freedom.

How would you describe yourself in your relation with your clients? **MS** As mentioned above, my clients have a very important place within the creative process itself. I share most of my questions with them. I like long working relationships, because—over time—they give you the chance to approach subjects in a more intimate and sincere manner. This is real work, requiring the clients to make an additional effort on top of their everyday problems —while, by definition, they should be the ones expecting solutions. I do not offer them any; I simply work together with them in trying to imagine the best way of talking about them.

You have taken part in various graphic design exhibitions and festivals. How do such events help the development of a culture of graphic design? Is there a risk that they make graphic design too inward-looking, with no connection with the real world? **MS** The problem with this kind of event is that often graphic design is dealt with as an end unto itself, without any reference to the problems associated with the context of creation itself. And this leaves it rather sad and lifeless, alone with those who practice it. It is a bit like the dog biting its own tail: it starts off chewing on its bone, and then ends up completely devouring itself.

THOMAS WIDDERSHOVEN
Thonik

As you may know, we have chosen the notion of "worlds" as a key to investigating graphic design and to present different stories and a variety of approaches, hopefully to address a wide public. What do you think about this? **Thomas Widdershoven** To me, the concept of world is something that is familiar—I would not use that word, but it is close to the way I think of how we work, because we intervene in social structures. As far as graphic design and the public is concerned, in the visual culture 3D designers have really become stars, and the 2D designers or the graphic designers seem to be very anonymous for the larger audience. But the reason is simple: we as graphic designers work for client business-to-business, while 3D designers work for the consumers, that is the public domain, and consumers want more information about the products to choose among them. So they get involved. Also, in 3D you get really beautiful magazines for almost no money, because it is full of advertising, because of the consumer. While in 2D, it is very hard to get interesting graphic design magazines, because we always work for clients and, of course, they do not buy magazines: we can just tell them about what we do, maybe we do books or websites, but it is not the same. So, yes, we really believe that graphic design is at the center—and, of course, this is also because we are graphic designers. But you are invisible in that center for the general audience. This can be very good by the way, and very handy, because you can act much faster and be more effective if you do not stand in the very center of the light. This is one of the reasons why we interact so easily with our clients: we do not take their light away. We are anonymous, and they take a lot of the credit, almost all the credit.

[Giorgio Camuffo] *What I am interested in, though, is not really just being under the light. In my office, in my work I can talk with clients, artists, musicians, with very different people, and all these relationships inevitably affect my work. My world is made up of the people I work and connect with. We graphic designers get contaminated by other people, fields, disciplines, and we can contaminate them. Then, of course, I also want to put a light on graphic designers and graphic design, especially in Italy. Probably also other fields, like industrial design, are not so well understood or considered. But I am now concerned with graphic design, because I feel that the cultural and social role of graphic designers often remains unnoticed and misunderstood.* TW Then you act as an ambassador for our trade, and this is also how I feel. We have to come out of our enclosure. This situation also reflects the way a career moves. You start in an art school, and you interact only with art, with designers who have very small yet very high quality practice for a very limited number of clients, in the cultural sector. This is when you really get an interest in your work, and where you get a feel for it, where people really understand what you add to this world. But if you start stepping out of this territory, then basically what you are doing is explaining to each new group of people what the quality of our work and approach is, the quality of design vs. non-design. When you step further into society you meet an increasingly economic sense of thinking, and then you have to counterbalance that with the cultural sense of thinking and with the quality sense of thinking. So all the time, you are not only educating new clients and groups but they are also educating us, because we come from this narrow area of society. The way I see it, at the heart of our business it is really graphic design, which is typography at the very core. That is what we are experts in and where we graphic designers understand each other. But the audience is uneducated, so sometimes they fall for real quality, they understand it, but sometimes they all just go for an overload of signs, just because they feel overly impressed by them. I think that people are really interested in type, in the visual aspect of text, it is a big part of our society, especially if you move a little bit from text to symbols—a letter is also a symbol—you see that people are immediately attracted to this; they are also very attracted to logos and identity... So these things influence people quite easily.

You mentioned education when speaking about your relationship with clients. How do you usually proceed with them? TW We listen very carefully to our clients, we take the brief very seriously, and we have a discussion. And then we filter from this brief things that can be effective, or not. Then we often just throw away the brief and make something that is a strong image or concept, or idea, and we blend it again with the analysis of our briefing. Then we use the client's words very literally, and we say, "you asked exactly for this." In a way we do filter a lot, we edit the brief, we are very strong editors, and in the end we bring what we think is the core, quite nude and powerful.

Is there also a kind of participation or collaboration with commissioners in the design process? **TW** Somehow we have a lively interaction and then at some point we retreat because we need to focus on what we are going to add to the project. We take a step back and we concentrate in the studio, and then we come out of the studio again with a proposal. So we do work together a lot, but at some point we also have to make sure that we remain an external force: these clients have worlds of their own, and the way people interact within them sometimes becomes quite narrow and they need an external force to shake everything up. One of the reasons why institutions need a new identity is because they have come to a standstill, in a social sense, so they not only want to tell a new story to their audience but they also want to reposition themselves. Although you can become really friendly with your clients, it is very important that you keep a certain distance from them, that you go back to your own space, and that you come up with a plan. And this plan will be something they can embrace but will also shock them in a way. That is what they want from you. In order to do that, you have to maintain a distance, a perspective.

We read an article about you where your approach is described as "strategic branding."[1] Is this a proper description of your approach, considering that you frequently work with institutions and in the cultural sector? **TW** Well, this is difficult. Because we are never really in the commercial field; we are always in a field that is public domain. At the very beginning we were in the art domain and in the cultural field, because that is where we found an interesting space for our design and interesting clients who liked design. Then we moved on and started educating people outside that area,

---

1.   N. Kawakami, *Thonik, the Desire to Communicate and Visual Expression: Bold Trials that Respect History*, www.thonik.com/read.php?sub=19.

but we stayed within the public domain: for instance we worked for the City of Amsterdam, a political party, intellectual newspapers, and now we are working with a broadcasting company, but again it is artistic and intellectual broadcasting. And what we say to these clients is that we address their clients, their audience, as civilians and not as consumers. So we see them as a group of people who share values; we don't see them as a group who wants to consume more. But then the communication world is 99 percent commercial. So we try to educate the people, but of course commercial people also do that and they have a vaster media, they control the signs that people react to. Then you have to get close to those signs but make a difference: we do apply branding—which is now the new thing in commercial communication—, we do apply strategies from the commercial area, because people are tuned into that kind of way of becoming attracted and then having their attention taken away. But then we have to be careful in how we put it, because if you put it like that, "strategic branding," it looks as if we are actually doing commercial design and we are not. You have to be careful with words.

So you do not have many commercial clients... **TW** That's it. I would not mind working with a commercial client, it is not something I am against. But somehow when we start to talk, we don't seem to understand one another. We work for a bank, a commercial bank, but it is the most green bank in the world...

Then you are suggesting that in a way you "choose" your clients, or there is a kind of mutual selection? **TW** There has to be a match. But we wait for clients to call us. We never call anyone because we don't think that is very fruitful. People have to have a first idea, then we always hope that they will visit five other agencies, to have a good comparison; and if they don't do that we tell them to do it, and we give them the names... of De Designpolitie and KesselsKramer! Only then can you start to talk. If we consider our portfolio it looks as if we choose our clients, but we are more pragmatic. If you come to us as a new client, the first conversation will be quite skeptical from our side; if you are able to get through that, then you will find us also eager to please.

Just to provide us with some background, can you tell us something about how you and Nikki [Gonnissen] met and decided to work together as Thonik? **TW** Nikki and I are also partners in life, so that is a very simple reason to start working together. We met in a park and we started talking.

We were still at school; she was studying art in Utrecht while I was studying in Amsterdam. At some point in the conversation we discovered that we were both graphic designers. Then she said "What do you do?" and I replied "I am designing a poetry magazine that is in the shops now"; and she said "Oh, my mother gave one to me"—it was a very famous but very small poetry magazine. She said she liked it very much. Of course her mother is quite important in our life! Then we finished school and somehow we just started working together, and found that we work together very easily. We also immediately started interacting with our clients, which already makes us different from a lot of designers. The moment we get a client we are very interested in his whole world and how we can change it, or enter into it, and how design can function for it. All these things were not so typical then, because in the cultural field at that time the designers were really like artists—so you gave them a job and never heard from them until they came with the finished product and then you had to be happy as a client. We started asking questions: "What do you want to achieve? Who do you want to reach? Why do you do this?, and Why shouldn't we do something totally different"?

Did this approach come from your education or was it just something that you felt you had to do? **TW** It was something that we immediately had in common. Also, I studied philosophy for a long time in the 1980s when there were no jobs and I did not know what to do. The nice thing about this is that I was educated at the same level as my clients, although I have never been able to do something effectively with it.

Do you feel there is a sort of balance between you and Nikki? **TW** Nikki is a very strong-willed woman, has a very strong personality. She positions herself very fast, she knows what she wants. I am more like a fish in the water. I can drift and she can be more focused. From the beginning it was a very good collaboration. Of course there is a stress factor, being together all the time.

"Position" is an interesting word: it means that you understand what is around you, what are your references, the directions that you want to take... **TW** You want to achieve a higher level. However, what I also think is very important is that you go back to your core and do your little things. For instance we have been very successful in other media now; we made viral movies for the Socialist Party, and we had a lot of people come here

THE WORLDS OF GRAPHIC DESIGNERS

and ask "Can you do viral movie"? But when we started talking with these potential clients about identity, quality of design, positioning and aims, they just didn't understand what we were talking about; they really just wanted a viral movie, but this is not our core medium. In this world where everybody is interacting and everybody is networked, I think we can achieve much more but it also means that you have to be careful that you really are expert at least in one thing, in one medium. And I feel that is one of the problems we have now with education: either educational institutions will open students up to the whole world and to all media, or they will narrow them down, to being experts in one small field. Somehow I think you have to find the right balance, because your career will only be propelled if you become an expert and still have the ability to be open. This is logical, but it also means that five-year courses are not enough and that you have to keep on learning.

voorsprong
ik denk **nrc**>

tegenwicht
ik denk **nrc**>

scherpte
ik denk **nrc**>

richting
ik denk **nrc**>

"——— —— —— —— —— —— —— —— — ———— —— —— —— —— —— —— —— ———— —— — ———— —— —— —— —— —— —— —— —— —— (—— —— —— — —— — —— —— ——) —— —— ——— —— ———— ——, —— —— —— — ——: "There is no such thing as Graphic Design. There are only graphic designers."[1]

————— —— —— —— —— —— —— —— —— —— — ——— "————— ——" —— —— — —— — —— —— —— —— —— —— —— —— ———: "——— —— —— —— —— ——, —— —— —— —— —— —— ... —— —— —— —— —— —— —— —— —— ——. —— —— —— —— ———— —— —— —— ——, —— —— —— ——, —— —— —— —— —— ——— —— —— —— — —— ——. —— —— —— —— ... —— —— —— — ——— —— —— —— —— — —— —— —— — ——, —— —— —— —— —— ——. —— —— ——, —— —— —— —— ——— ——."[2]

—— —— —— —— ——, —— —— —— ——, —— —— —— —— — ——. — —— ——, —— —— —— —— —— —— ——, —— —— —— —— ——. —— —— —— —— —— ——: —— —— —— ——, —— —— —— ——.

1. "—— —— —— —— —— —— ——. —— —— —— —— ——" —— —— —— — — —— —— —— —— —— ——, —— ——, —— —— —.

2. "———— ——," —— —— —— (—— —— ——), —— "—— —— ——, —— —— —— —— ——, —— —— —— —— ——, —— —— ——-—— —— ——.

Viva WAD!
The Inventor of the Graphic Design World

SERGIO POLANO

This book and the installations of its twin exhibition show a wide range of "Graphic Design Worlds" interpretations. A fair and square approach to the whole issue might be a paraphrase of the words (and purposes—*si parva licet*) which open Ernst Gombrich's *The Story of Art*: "There is no such thing as Graphic Design. There are only graphic designers."[1]

Proof of the unhelpful vagueness of a term such as "Graphic Design" can be read under the same entry in a recent *Design Dictionary*: "During the shift from the mechanical to digital, the tools of graphic design production … became freely available and relatively cheap. This demystified the notion of graphic design and, by extension, questioned both the professional standing and relevance of the graphic designer. Like many media roles, graphic design is now characterized by this uncertain identity … As these two aspects of graphic design—the overtly commercial and the overtly marginal—grow increasingly distinct, this schizophrenia renders the term increasingly vague and useless. At best, this implies that the term ought always to be distinctly qualified by the context of its use."[2]

So one might, just this once, give up to the anguish of definitions. It is better a lay, patient listening to a full chorus of voices, not always consonant. Anathemas are of little use here. Eschewing bias, one should try to grasp the

---

1.   "There is no such thing as Art. There are only artists" says Ernst Gombrich in the Introduction to his *The Story of Art*, Phaidon, London 1950.

2.   "Graphic Design," entry written by SBA (Stuart Bailey), in *Design Dictionary. Perspectives on Design Terminology*, edited by Michael Erlhoff and Tim Marshall, Birkhäuser, Basel-Boston-Berlin 2008.

meaning of the varied trace evidences, and to work towards an understanding of the phenomenon as a whole. Such attention to evidences may at least prove useful to those who consciously strive to cross the orthodoxy of the "Graphic Design" tangled matter.

It is the reader/visitor who is the ultimate judge of the issues raised by *Graphic Design Worlds*. Indeed, it is also true that, like it or not, we all share the denotations of the (healthy carrier) adjective "graphic"; at the same time, we learned from the etymology of "graphic" that its connotations range from write/trace to carve/paint. And we all know from Roland Barthes that "in the Orient, an ideographic civilization, it is 'traced out' what lies between painting and writing, without one practice becoming subsumed by the other. This makes it possible to avoid our wrecked law of filiation, a fatherly, civil, mental, scientific Law. A discriminating law, under which we put on the one side the graphic artists and on the other side the painters; on the one side the poets, and on the other side the novelists."[3]

Perhaps there is still some understandable uncertainty with regard to the widespread use of "design," a confusing term without qualifiers. As Simon Jervis has observed: "The English word 'design' became part of the French, German and Italian language as a term for 'industrial design' … This use is ironic in the case of Italy, given that the word 'design'—in the sense of a drawing intended to serve as a model and, therefore, to regulate the production of designs—derives from the Italian word *disegno*. A designer is someone who makes such drawings. This use of 'design' was current in English from at least as early as the 17th century … There is no doubt that, after the first Schools of Design were set up in 1836, the areas to which the terms 'designer' and 'design' apply have become more restricted, particularly within the institutional world of 'design.' However, there is no reason to abandon or erase their wider general meaning."[4]

Perhaps the best way to briefly support and confirm the above stated approach is to look at the emblematic career of an exceptional personality: William Addison Dwiggins (1880–1956), the very first one to refer to himself as a "graphic designer."

---

3. Comment written by Roland Barthes in 1970, and published in the 1993 edition of Robert Massin, *La Lettre et l'Image*, Gallimard, Paris (1st ed. 1970).

4. S. Jervis, Introduction to *The Penguin Dictionary of Design and Designers,* edited by Simon Jervis, Penguin Books, Harmondsworth 1984.

WAD[5] (as he liked to sign himself) coined the term "graphic design" in 1922—even if it did not gain currency until the middle of the 20th century—for the essay "A New Kind of Printing Calls for New Design," where he wrote: "Advertising design is the only form of *graphic design* that gets home to everybody" (our italics).[6]

The range of WAD's career—his many interests and passions coexisted without contradiction, fostered by a biting sense of humor—is captured in the subtitle to the 1957 *Memorial Exhibition William Addison Dwiggins 1880 – 1956* exhibition held in New York: *Calligrapher, Type Designer, Layout Artist, Illustrator, Book Designer, Mural Painter, Sculptor, Playwright, Puppeteer,[7] Costume Designer, Satirist, Thinker, Poet in Prose;*

---

5. On WAD, see: *WAD: The Work of W.A. Dwiggins*, The American Institute of Graphic Arts, New York 1937; *In Memory of William A. Dwiggins,* monographic issue of *Typographer*, XIX, 1958, spring, 1; D. Abbe, *William Addison Dwiggins*, Boston Public Library, Boston 1974, reprint with the title *William Addison Dwiggins: An Essay by Dorothy Abbe*, Pacific Center for the Book Arts, San Francisco 1987; D. Agner, *The Books of Wad*, Alan Wofsy Fine Arts, San Francisco 1977; the collection *A Tribute to William Addison Dwiggins, 1880-1956, on the Hundredth Anniversary of his Birth, privately printed for the Friends of Hermann Püterschein*, The Inkwell Press, New York 1980; P. Shaw, "Tradition and Innovation: The Design Work of William Addison Dwiggins," *Design Issues*, I, 1984, fall, 2, now in *Design History: An Anthology*, edited by Dennis P. Doordan, MIT Press, Cambridge 1995; W. Tracy, *Letters of Credit: A View of Type Design*, Gordon Fraser, London 1986; W. Tracy, *The Typographic Scene*, Gordon Fraser, London 1988; S. Carter, *William Addison Dwiggins*, in the collection *Twentieth Century Type Designers*, Lund Humphries, London 1995; the chapters on WAD in the various editions of Steven Heller, *Design literacy: understanding graphic design*, Allworth Press, New York 1997; V. Connare, *The Type Designs of William Addison Dwiggins*, May 2000, www.connare.com/essays.htm; P. Shaw, "The Life & Work of William Addison Dwiggins," *Linotype Matrix*, IV, (2006), 2; P. Shaw, "The Long And Complicated Saga Of W. A. Dwiggins' Design Of The Lakeside Press Edition Of Tales By Edgar Allan Poe," *Bibliologia*, 2007, 1 (tdc.org/news/2007-Shaw-WAD-Poe-Bibliologia.pdf), and 2009, 4. On the puppets in particular, see D. Abbe, *The Dwiggins Marionettes: A Complete Experimental Theatre in Miniature*, Harry N. Abrams, New York [1969]. A special thank to Paul Shaw for his kind help, and corrections to my text.

6. WAD, "A New Kind of Printing Calls for New Design," in a supplement to the *Boston Evening Transcript*, August 29, 1922, now in appendix B of Ellen Mazur Thomson, *The Origins of Graphic Design in America 1870-1920*, Yale University Press, New Haven-London 1997, and in the collection *Looking Closer 3: Classic Writings on Graphic Design*, Allworth Press, New York 1999.

7. For the puppets (including one of himself, to take curtain calls), WAD created a small thirty-seat home theater; complete with advertising posters and admission tickets, the shows were devised by him.

and, on top of all that, he was also a happy kite-builder.

Born in 1880,[8] WAD was nineteen years old when he moved from his native town to Chicago to study at the Frank Holme School of Illustration. There he would learn the bases of lettering under the still young—but soon renowned—designer of typefaces, Frederick W. Goudy (1865–1947); a fellow student was Oswald "Oz" Bruce Cooper (1879–1940), who was destined for a similar career (even if Oz judged himself "no good at drawing pictures"). After the unsuccessful launch of the Guernsey Printing Shop in Cambridge (Ohio) in 1903, WAD would move for good to Hingham (near Boston, Massachusetts) in 1904; he was following Goudy, who had already set up the Village Press, which would then move to New York in 1906. For fifteen years, WAD enjoyed increasing success as a "commercial artist" in advertising. At the same time, he printed a seriocomic magazine entitled *The Fabulist* headed the Harvard University Press (1917–18) and in 1919 founded the Boston Society of Calligraphers, of which he was President, Secretary and sole Member. An established figure in the world of advertising, he would—as a skilled writer—then publish blunt criticism of the low quality of contemporary printing in the 1919 *Extracts from an Investigation into the Physical Properties of Books as They Are At Present Published*: a small book written together with his cousin Laurence B. Siegfried (who over a decade after the *Extracts* would edit *The American Printer*), this was published by the Boston Society of Calligraphers. The *Extracts* gave the unanimous and stinging verdict of a Special Committee within the Society, which after studying the books printed in America since 1910 declared: "All Books of the present day are Badly Made." Later, the publisher Alfred A. Knopf would commission WAD to design on almost three hundred books, occasionally from 1926, continuously from 1934 to the 1950s. This undertaking shifted WAD's main interest from advertising, with which he was already dissatisfied, to the new challenges of graphic design, focusing primarily on illustration and editorial design. Two years after the beginning of the collaboration with Knopf, WAD published a book that soon became a standard: *Layout in Advertising*, a title that does not fully reflect the content. That work would be followed by a series of significant publications, as: *22 Printers' Marks and*

8.　WAD was born on June 19, 1880 in Martinsville, Ohio (in the middle of the state), but he lived much of his childhood in Richmond, Indiana (on the border with Ohio) and his teenage years in Cambridge, Ohio.

Seals Designed or Redrawn, Form Letters: Illustrator to Author, Towards a Reform of the Paper Currency, Particularly in Point of its Design for the imaginary land of The Antipodes, *Marionette in Motion, WAD to RR: A Letter About Designing Type, A Technique for Dealing with Artists, The Structure of a Book* and a collection of his numerous essays in *MSS. by WAD*.[9]
Incapable of turning his back on a design challenge, WAD would begin working on the design of typefaces in 1928; the challenge in question had been launched by Harry Gage of Mergenthaler-Linotype, who was himself reacting to WAD's criticism regarding the lack of a good sans serif (aka gothic in Usa) text typeface for the mechanical composition. Thus, almost in spite of himself, WAD designed his first typeface (Metroblack, which went on the market in 1929), starting a collaboration with Mergenthaler Linotype that would last for more than a quarter of a century and see him design about fifteen typefaces, accomplishing the families of Metro (1929–37), Electra (1935–49) and Caledonia (1938–40), which enjoyed great success in the Usa. After WWII, at home in Hingham, WAD not only managed puppets but also launched the refined Puterschein-Hingham Press,[10] working in collaboration with Dorothy Abbe from 1947 to the Christmas of 1956 (the day of his own death).

---

9. *Extracts from an Investigation into the Physical Properties of Books as They Are At Present Published,* The Society of Calligraphers, Boston 1919; *Layout in Advertising,* Harper & Brothers, New York 1928, rev. ed. 1948; *22 Printers' Marks and Seals Designed or Redrawn,* William Edwin Rudge, New York 1929; *Form Letters: Illustrator to Author,* William Edwin Rudge, New York 1930, to illustrate "the proper function of illustration and the relation between pictures and text"; *Towards a Reform of the Paper Currency, Particularly in Point of its Design,* The Limited Editions Club, New York 1932; *Marionette in Motion,* Puppetry Imprints, Detroit 1939; *WAD to RR: A Letter About Designing Type,* Harvard College Library, Cambridge 1940; *A Technique for Dealing with Artists,* Press of the Woolly Whale, New York 1941; *The Structure of a Book,* The Typophiles, New York 1945, formerly *Notes on the Structure of a Book,* introduction to the American Institute of Graphic Arts (ed.), *...Fifty Books, exhibited by the Institute, 1926,* Day, New York 1927; *MSS. by WAD,* The Typophiles, New York 1947. Among his most famous books, even if not published by Alfred A. Knopf: H.G. Wells, *The Time Machine,* Random House, New York 1931. The Special Collections at the University of Maryland (www.lib.umd.edu) include the William Addison Dwiggins Collection, with an on-line Annotated Inventory; the main archive on WAD is the William Addison Dwiggins Collection of the Rare Books Department at the Boston Public Library (www.bpl.org)—two puppets rooms—, where is also housed the Dorothy Abbe Collection.

10. Dr. Hermann Püterschein (a German pun) was the name WAD chose for his self-ironic literary alter-ego, who also ran Püterschein Authority responsible for the puppet theater.

If it were true that *ab uno disce omnis*, one might conclude that the Worlds of Graphic Design crowd in a galactical nebula.

P.S. "History is a magic mirror: those who look into it see their own image in the form of events and developments. It never stops. It is in continual movement, like the generations that look into it. It is never possible to grasp its full complexity. All it reveals to us are fragments, in relation to the moment from which it is viewed ... What we are dealing with here are things that are of little apparent importance; things that usually are not taken seriously—at least, as far as history is concerned. But just like in painting, what counts in history is not the importance of the material itself. Even a coffee spoon can reflect the sun. Overall, modest things—the things we are talking about—have burrowed right down to the very foundations of our life. These small daily objects accumulate, to the point that they generate energies which seize upon all of those who move within the circle of our civilization ... For the historian, nothing is banal. Just like the scientist, he cannot afford to accept anything as simply natural. He cannot allow himself to see objects with the eyes of someone who uses them everyday; he must bring to bear the eyes of the inventor, as if he were seeing them for the first time. He must have the fresh eyes of the inventor's contemporary, for whom such things seem marvelous and terrifying ... The decisive step is taken within the reader. In him, the partial meanings, which we are spelling out here, take on life as part of a whole."[11]

---

11. S. Giedion, *Mechanization Takes Command: A Contribution To Anonymous History*, Oxford University Press, New York 1948.

BIOGRAPHIES

Åbäke is a collective of four graphic designers—Patrick Lacey from the UK, Kajsa Ståhl from Sweden, Benjamin Reichen and Maki Suzuki from France—who decided to work together in the summer of 2000. Much of their work concentrates on the social aspect of design and on collaborative projects. Åbäke has twelve aliases in the form of associations created to enable projects such as a record label and a publishing house. To name a few: Kitsuné, Sexymachinery and Dent De Leone. a.b.a.k.e@free.fr

Giovanni Anceschi, artist and designer, design historian and theorist, focuses on visual culture and design research. He graduated from the Hochschule für Gestaltung in Ulm and has taught at various institutions. He is professor of Communication Design, Information Design and Basic Design and is coordinator of the doctoral research program in Design Sciences at the University IUAV of Venice. Anceschi is working to draft a revision of the discipline of communication design towards "multimodal direction." Among his publications: *Monogrammi e figure* (1988) and *L'oggetto della raffigurazione* (1992). www.newbasicdesign.it

Andrew Blauvelt is Curator of Architecture and Design and Chief of Communications and Audience Engagement at the Walker Art Center in Minneapolis, where he served as Design Director from 1998 to 2010. As Curator of Architecture and Design, Blauvelt has organized several design exhibitions at the Walker. He writes about design and culture for various publications and is a contributing writer for Design Observer (www.designobserver.com). A practicing graphic designer, his work has received more than one hundred design awards. www.walkerart.org/index.wac

Brave New Alps are Bianca Elzenbaumer and Fabio Franz. Since 2005 they work together focusing on communication design. Having graduated in 2006 from the Faculty of Design and Art of the Free University of Bozen-Bolzano, in 2010 they received their MA in Communication Art and Design from the Royal College of Art, London. Brave New Alps are interested in the cultural value of design and in its capacity of questioning and interpreting the contexts where it intervenes, and of actively suggesting a change in the ways of thinking and operating. www.brave-new-alps.com

Max Bruinsma is editor-in-chief of *Items*, the Dutch design magazine, supervising editor of *Iridescent*, Icograda's online journal of design research, and former editor-in-chief of *Eye*, the international magazine of graphic design. Since 1985, his critical writings have featured in major Dutch and international design magazines. In 2005, he received the Dutch Pierre Bayle Award for Design Criticism. Bruinsma currently teaches Design Writing at the Sandberg Institute's MA Design and at VU University's MA Design Cultures, both in Amsterdam. www.maxbruinsma.nl

Anthony Burrill is an English graphic designer and illustrator. After studying Graphic Design at the Leeds Polytechnic he completed a MA in Graphic Design at the Royal College of Art, London. He works across a range of media, including posters, moving image and 3D work. His illustrations and designs have been commissioned by cultural, social, and commercial

clients around the world. He regularly collaborates with musicians and animators to make films, music promos, and animations.
www.anthonyburrill.com

Charlotte Cheetham is the founder and author of Manystuff, an internationally renown blog about graphic design, started in 2007. Based in Paris, she is also a curator, editor and lecturer, involved in promoting the culture of graphic design. In 2008 Cheetham launched the printed magazine *Manystuff*, a laboratory of experiments and meditations, featuring contributions from graphic designers, authors and critics on relevant issues for contemporary culture.
www.manystuff.org

Andrea Codolo is a free-lance graphic designer who lives and works in Venice. Having taken his degree in Industrial Design at the University IUAV of Venice, he then gained experience at the Studio Camuffo, where he worked from 2004 to 2009. His work concentrates on visual identity, exhibition and editorial design, collaborating with various cultural institutions and foundations.
www.codolo.com

Giacomo Covacich graduated in Visual and Multi-Media Communication at the University IUAV of Venice. Since 2001 he has combined study and work, focusing particularly on communication in the widest sense of the term. Together with Morris Granzotto, he founded in 2007 WOW, a graphic design studio in Treviso.
http://wowowow.it

Nazareno Crea was born in Calabria and grew up in Rome, beginning his work experience within the world of visual communications and graphic design in Milan. Subsequently he moved to Switzerland, studying at the École Cantonale d'Art de Lausanne, where he then became an assistant and lecturer. In 2008 he moved to London, where he now lives and works after receiving a MA in Communication Art and Design from the Royal College of Art. He alternates commercial work with self-initi-

ated projects that explore the use of images and the written word within contemporary society.
www.nazareno.co.uk

Benedetta Crippa, a free-lance graphic designer, graduated in Communication Design at the Politecnico di Milano and is currently completing her graduate degree in Visual and Multimedia Communication at the University IUAV of Venice. Since 2009 she has worked with Studio Camuffo. She is interested in graphic design criticism, collaborating with various independent Italian publications.
www.benecrippa.com

De Designpolitie is a graphic design studio, founded by Richard van der Laken and Pepijn Zurburg in 1995, and based in Amsterdam. De Designpolitie works for various small and big clients in the non-profit and commercial sectors. The team also initiates exhibitions, festivals, books, lectures and workshops. Among other projects, since 2006 De Designpolitie (together with Lesley Moore and Herman van Bostelen) is behind the multi-awarded visual column Gorilla, that comments on current affairs through words and images.
www.designpolitie.nl

Dexter Sinister is something between a publishing imprint, a just-in-time-workshop and occasional bookstore, and a pseudonym co-operated by Stuart Bailey and David Reinfurt from the basement at 38 Ludlow Street, on the Lower East Side in New York City. Established in 2006, the project was originally set up to model a just-in-time economy of print production, running counter to the contemporary assembly-line realities of large-scale publishing. Since then, Dexter Sinister's work has branched haphazardly into many different contexts and venues, most recently galleries and museums.
www.dextersinister.org

Valerio Di Lucente, Italian graphic designer, is co-founder of Julia together with Erwan Lhuissier (France) and Hugo Timm (Brazil). The studio was founded in 2008 upon graduation from the Royal College of Art, London. The team works on books, typefaces, posters, websites, identities and exhibition design. www.julia.uk.com

Elliott Earls is a graphic designer and an Artist-in-Residence at Cranbrook Academy of Art in Bloomfield Hills, Michigan. Earls' work is represented in numerous museum collections and has been featured in countless books and publications. The writer Rick Poynor has once written of Earls: "If ever a designer seemed like a certified oddball, pursuing a trajectory far removed from the obligations of institutional life, it is Earls. He is one of those unclassifiable, mutant blooms thrown up by the fractured landscape of 1990s graphic design." www.theapolloprogram.com

Daniel Eatock is a London-based artist who uses graphic design methods and languages striving for objective and rational solutions to problems that cannot be formulated before they have been solved. He graduated from the Royal College of Art, London, in 1998, was part of the design staff at the Walker Art Center in Minneapolis. In 1999 he returned to UK where he began the Foundation 33 multi-disciplinary design studio. Since 2004 Eatock has maintained an independent studio practice. In 2008 *Imprint*, a monograph on his practice, was published by Princeton Architectural Press. www.eatock.com

Experimental Jetset is an Amsterdam-based graphic design studio founded in 1997 by Marieke Stolk, Erwin Brinkers and Danny van den Dungen. Focusing mainly on printed matter, they have worked on projects for national and international clients such as Stedelijk Museum CS in Amsterdam, Centre Georges Pompidou in Paris, and Japanese t-shirt labels 2K/Gingham and Publik. In 2007, a large selection of their work was acquired by the Museum of Modern Art in New York, for inclusion in the permanent collection. Between 2000 and 2009, Experimental Jetset have been teaching at the Gerrit Rietveld Academy, Amsterdam. www.experimentaljetset.nl

FF3300 was founded in 2006 as a free, independent bi-lingual magazine that discussed themes relating to design, communication and the visual arts. In 2008–09, the project developed into the creation of a communication design studio made up of Alessandro Tartaglia, Carlotta Latessa and Nicolò Loprieno. FF3300 designs "identity systems," communications strategies and products for the web and for traditional publishing. Tartaglia, Latessa and Loprieno are also active in education, teaching at various Italian universities. www.ff3300.com

Fuel is a design group founded at the Royal College of Art, London, in 1991 by Damon Murray and Stephen Sorrell. From the outset, they worked commercially for a variety of clients in the areas of fashion, art and film. They combined these commissions with projects of their own, producing a magazine also entitled *Fuel*, as well as producing and directing short films, idents, film titles and TV commercials. In 2005 they formed an independent publishing company within the group, Fuel Publishing. www.fuel-design.com

Tommaso Garner is a graphic designer who works with artists, art galleries, critics and curators on the creation of catalogues, artist books as well as on corporate identiy. He is art director of various magazines in the fields of art, fashion and contemporary culture—among them, *THE/END*, which he co-founded in 2006. Since 2008 he has been art director for the Kaleidoscope publishing house and art magazine based in Milan. www.tommasogarner.com

Mieke Gerritzen is a designer and currently the director of the Graphic Design Museum in Breda. In the early 1990s Gerritzen was one of

the first designers involved in the development of digital media in the Netherlands. She creates designs for all media and works with many different designers, writers and artists. Among her publications: *Catalogue of Strategy* (2001), *Everyone is a Designer* (2000, 2010), *Mobile Minded* (with G. Lovink, 2002) and *Next Nature* (editor with K. van Mensvoort, 2005).
www.all-media.info

Steven Heller is an American art director, journalist, critic, author, and editor who specializes on topics related to graphic design. He is the author, co-author, and/or editor of over 130 books on design and popular culture. Currently, he is co-chair of the MFA Designer as Author Department, Special Consultant to the President of the School of Visual Arts, New York, and writes the Visuals column for the *New York Times Book Review*.
www.hellerbooks.com

Invernomuto was founded in the Piacenza area in 2003, when Simone Bertuzzi and Simone Trabucchi came together to form a group engaged in audio-visual experimentation. Focusing upon mixing different types of languages, their research often takes the form of projects which break format boundaries; one such is the publishing project *ffwd_mag* (initiated in 2003), which also includes the production of videos and performances and the curating of events. Invernomuto's work has been included in individual and collective exhibitions in Italy and abroad.
www.invernomuto.info

Christophe Jacquet (Toffe) is a graphic designer, an artist "activist graphique." Based in Paris, his work encompasses a range of fields including visual identity for cultural institutions, corporate identity and visual communication systems. He had different artistic commands for the French Ministry of Culture. Since its foundation, he is the art director of Poptronics. fr, a website devoted to electronic cultures. He has curated exhibitions and his work has been exhibited at diverse venues. He is Visiting Pro-

fessor at the most prestigious universities, and teaches graphic design at the École Supérieure des Arts Décoratifs in Strasbourg.
www.productiongenerale.fr

Manuel Joseph is a French poet who was born in 1965 to a father and a mother—his father gaped at the Ash Wednesday supper while his mother stammered at the feast of the sentimental—on the 22nd [twenty plus two] of the month that has three letters.

Erik Kessels is a founding partner and creative director of KesselsKramer, an independent international communications agency located in Amsterdam. The agency expanded into London in 2008 where they set up KK Outlet, a combined exhibition space, gallery and communications agency in Hoxton Square. Kessels is an avid photography collector and has published several books of vernacular images through KesselsKramer Publishing including the series *In Almost Every Picture*. Since 2000, he has been one of the editors of the alternative photography magazine *Useful Photography*. He has curated numerous exhibitions including most recently *Use me Abuse me* at the New York Photo Festival in 2010.
www.kesselskramer.com
www.kesselskramerpublishing.com
www.kkoutlet.com

Na Kim is a South-Korean-born graphic designer based in Amsterdam. After studying product design at the Korea Advanced Institute of Science and Technology, Daejon, and graphic design at the Hongik University, Seoul, from 2006 to 2008 she studied at the Werkplaats Typografie in Arnhem, The Netherlands. In 2008 she organized in Seoul *Starting from Zero*, the ten years exhibition of the Werkplaats Typografie. Since 2009 she has been the art director of *Graphic* magazine. She also works on self-initiated projects, such as the independent magazine *umool umool*. Her work is featured in various publications and she participates in international exhibitions.
www.ynkim.com

Emily King is a London-based design historian who concentrates on writing and curating. Her books include *Robert Brownjohn: Sex and Typography* (2005) and *C/ID: Visual Identity and Branding for the Arts* (2006), and in 2003 she edited the Peter Saville monograph *Designed by Peter Saville*. She has curated a number of exhibitions and contributes to an eclectic selection of international magazines including *Frieze*, *The Gentlewoman* and *Apartamento*.

Kasia Korczak is a Polish-born graphic designer. She completed a BA in Fine Arts at London Metropolitan University and a MA residency program at the Werkplaats Typografie in Arnhem, the Netherlands. Interested in design as a vehicle for producing and distributing content, she works primarily with printed matter and specializes in artist books. In 2005, Korczak co-founded Slavs and Tatars, an artists' collective that works across several media, disciplines, and registers of culture, with a common thread in the stories —both political and personal—of Eurasia. http://kasia-korczak.blogspot.com www.slavsandtatars.com

Zak Kyes is a Swiss-American graphic designer based in London whose practice encompasses editing, publishing and curating. Kyes joined the Architectural Association in London as Art Director in September 2006. He curated the touring exhibition *Forms of Inquiry: The Architecture of Critical Graphic Design* and is the co-editor of the accompanying catalogue (with M. Owens, 2007). His books include *The Reader: Iaspis Forum on Design and Critical Practice* (with M. Ericson et al., 2009), *Exhibition Prosthetics* (with J. Grigely, 2010), and *Cosey Complex Reader* (with M. Fusco, R. Birkett, 2010). In 2008 he co-founded Bedford Press, a private press and imprint of AA Publications. He currently teaches at the Architectural Association School of Architecture, London, and at the École cantonale d'art de Lausanne. www.zak.to

Harmen Liemburg is a Dutch graphic artist. En route to becoming an artist and design journalist, he started his career as an academic cartographer. In 1998 he graduated from the Gerrit Rietveld Academie, Amsterdam, and became a member of a new breed of designers, one that is closely linked to the world of art, education and museums. Obsessed with screen printing, his style emphasizes the narrative aspect of images and the occasional beauty of everyday vernacular. He is also a design journalist, mainly for the Dutch magazine *Items*. www.harmenliemburg.nl

Mario Lupano, a historian and critic of contemporary architecture, is a professor at the Arts and Design Faculty of the University IUAV of Venice. His work has focused particularly on Italian architecture of the first half of the 20th century, exploring the relationship between Modernism and Fascism. He is interested in the mutual interaction of design and the arts and the process of curating. He has curated various exhibitions intended as space for critical discourse and instruments of vision, and has worked on editorial projects in which the action of criticism finds expression in the montage of various kinds of image and text. Together with Luca Emanueli and Marco Navarra, he is the curator of the *Lo-fi Architecture* project, which aims to champion awareness of a "low definition" approach to design disciplines.

Lupo&Burtscher is a design studio that was founded in Bolzano in 2004 by Angelika Burtscher and Daniele Lupo. The studio works on editorial projects, visual communication, product design, interior design and exhibit design, operating mainly in the arts and culture sector. In 2003 Burtscher and Lupo also launched **Lungomare**, which offers space for research into the very culture of design, exploring the relations between various disciplines via different formats: conferences, discussions, publications, exhibitions or other forms of intervention within public spaces. www.lupoburtscher.it www.lungomare.org

Ellen Lupton is curator of contemporary design at Cooper-Hewitt, National Design Museum, Smithsonian Institution, in New York City. She is director of the Graphic Design MFA program at Maryland Institute College of Art (Mica) in Baltimore. She is the author of numerous books about design, including *Design Your Life* (2009), *Graphic Design: The New Basics* (2008), *DIY: Design It Yourself* (2006), and *Thinking with Type* (2004).
http://elupton.com

Geoff McFetridge is an artist and graphic designer based in Los Angeles, California. Born in Canada, he was schooled at the Alberta College of Art and Design and the California Institute of the Arts. From 1996 to 1998, he was art director of the underground Beastie Boys magazine *Grand Royal*. He then founded the design studio Champion Graphics with which he has serviced for numerous international clients and won countless international awards. Instinctively ignoring creative boundaries, McFetridge is a multidisciplinary artist and designer, making the convergence of disciplines central to his work—encompassing logos, poetry, animation, graphics, sculpture, textile and wallpaper and paintings.
www.championdontstop.com

Metahaven (Vinca Kruk, Daniel van der Velden) is a studio for critical graphic design with a focus on visual identity. They are based in Amsterdam. From research projects, such as the *Sealand Identity Project* (2004), *Museum of Conflict* (2006), and *Quaero* (2007), the group has moved into installation making and speculative design projects, such as *Affiche Frontière* (CAPC musée d'art contemporain de Bordeaux, 2008), *Stadtstaat* (Künstlerhaus Stuttgart and Casco Utrecht, 2009) and Manifesta 8 (Murcia and Cartagena, 2010). Metahaven also produces commissioned work for clients, such as the Antennae paperback series for publishing house Valiz. Metahaven's work has been included in various group exhibitions. Their book *Uncorporate Identity* was published in 2010 by Lars Müller.
www.metahaven.net

Joseph Miceli is a graphic designer and typographer. Born in Sicily, he spent his formative years in New York City, doing graffiti and infiltrating American society. In 1999 he returned to Europe and studied graphic design and typography at the Gerrit Rietveld Academie, Amsterdam. He currently lives between Vilnius, Turin and Rome as an independent graphic designer, and typographer, working since 2005 under the name Alfa60 together with designer Lina Ozerkina.
www.alfa60.com/joe

M/M (Paris) is an art and design partnership consisting of Mathias Augustyniak and Michaël Amzalag, established in Paris in 1992. They have defined their practice as a strategic position within the landscape of contemporary culture. Their production—as much commissioned as self initiated—has been featured in numerous museums around the world such as the Tate Modern, Solomon R. Guggenheim Museum, Drawing Center, Palais de Tokyo and Centre Pompidou. Their clients and collaborators reflect their multi-dimensional activities across the fields of music (Björk, Kanye West, Benjamin Biolay), fashion (Balenciaga, Givenchy, Yohji Yamamoto, *Vogue Paris*), art (Pierre Huyghe, Sarah Morris, Philippe Parreno, Liam Gillick), photography (Inez van Lamsweerde & Vinoodh Matadin, Craig McDean, Bruce Weber) or design (Café Etienne Marcel, Hotel Thoumieux)
www.mmparis.com

Norm was founded in Zurich on January 1, 1999, by Dimitri Bruni and Manuel Krebs, and expanded with Ludovic Varone in 2005. Norm is an office that works with all aspects of graphic design. It is also a project in itself, a platform for research and reflections on visual communication, publishing books and typefaces.
www.norm.to

Radim Peško is a graphic designer based in Amsterdam. Born in Kyjov, in the former Czechoslovakia, after studying at the Academy of Arts, Architecture and Design in Prague he completed his postgraduate program at the Werkplaats Typografie in Arnhem, The Netherlands, in 2004. He has worked for and collaborates with many cultural institutions. He teaches at the Gerrit Rietveld Academie in Amsterdam and is visiting lecturer at the École cantonale d'art de Lausanne. In 2009 he launched the digital type foundry RP Foundry. A collection of his photographs, *Informal Meetings*, was published in 2010 (Bedford Press).
www.radimpesko.com

Sergio Polano graduated in Architecture in 1974, studying under Manfredo Tafuri at the IUAV Architecture Institute University of Venice, where he would eventually become Full Professor of History of Contemporary Art and where he concluded his academic career in 2008. He is the author of fifteen books and more than three hundred articles in magazines and periodicals regarding contemporary architecture, event design, industrial design and applied graphics.
www.polano.eu

Mathias Schweizer, a Swiss-French graphic designer, lives and works in Paris. After studying at the art school in La Chaux-de-Fonds, Switzerland, he joined the Paris studio Graphistes Associés in 1998, and set up his own studio in 1999. His work as a graphic designer constantly shifts between different means of expression, combining video art, typographical conceptions, image and music. This is especially true of Rolax®, a record label he founded in 2003 together with Léonard de Léonard, Seep and Komori.
http://weizer.ch

Silvia Sfligiotti is a graphic designer, teacher and design critic, and co-founder (with Raffaella Colutto) of Alizarina, a visual communication studio based in Milan. She

regularly writes, teaches and holds lectures at international conferences and several Italian universities and design schools. She is co-author of four books on visual communication and typography, curator of design exhibitions, and member of the editorial board of the magazine *Progetto Grafico*. Since 2008 she represents Italy on the jury of the European Design Awards.
www.alizarina.net

Studio Temp is a graphic design studio founded in Bergamo in 2007 by Fausto Giliberti, Guido Gregorio Daminelli and Marco Fasolini. With a focus on printed media —books, magazines, visual identity—the studio also works on web design, motion graphics, and interactive installations. Other than working on commission, Studio Temp has also initiated various independent projects.
www.madeintemp.com

Tankboys is an independent graphic studio founded by Lorenzo Mason and Marco Campardo in 2005, and based in Venice. Tankboys deals with arts and communication design, focusing mainly on print and editorial projects, working for companies as well as for cultural institutions. In 2008 they co-founded with others XYZ, a non-profit gallery for the applied arts (graphics, photography, design) based in Treviso. In 2009, together with illustrator Elena Xausa, they initiated Automatic Books, an independent publishing house.
www.tankboys.biz

Thonik is a studio founded in 1993 by Nikki Gonnissen and Thomas Widdershoven. Specializing in visual communication with an emphasis on graphic design, Thonik uses a strategic approach through a broad array of media, regarding each project as a chance to experiment. The studio works primarily in the cultural, political and social field. Among its clients, the Museum Boijmans Van Beuningen in The Netherlands, Museum Marta Herford in Germany, the Venice Architecture Biennale and the Dutch Socialist Party. Over the last few years Thonik had several solo exhibitions in The Netherlands, Shanghai, Tokyo and Paris. www.thonik.com

Alice Twemlow is the co-founder and chair of a two-year graduate program in Design Criticism at the School of Visual Arts in New York City. She is also a PhD candidate in the History of Design department at the Royal College of Art, London; her research examines the changing relationship of design criticism to its publics in the UK and the US since the 1950s. Twemlow is a contributing editor to *Design Observer* (www.designobserver.com) and her essays are included in many magazines and books. She is the author of *What is Graphic Design For?* (2006).

Francesco Valtolina is a free-lance graphic designer based in Milan; his work focuses on editorial design and identity design. Since 2008 he has been art director of Mousse Publishing and of the magazine *Mousse*; in that same year he co-founded, together with Edoardo Bonaspetti, the design and communication studio of the same name which operates primarily in the cultural field, working on commissioned or self-initiated editorial projects as well as on the development of web and new media content. His work has been published in various international magazines, and he has taken part in a number of conferences and round-tables on contemporary publishing. http://moussepublishing.com

Carlo Vinti is a critic and historian of design and visual communication. Having received a PhD in Arts Theory and History, he has since 2005 taught History of Graphic Design and Visual Communication at the Faculty of Art and Design of the University IUAV of Venice. His publications include: *Gli anni dello stile industriale 1948–1965. Immagine e politica culturale nella grande impresa italiana* (2007) and *Mark McGinnis* (2010).

Giorgio Camuffo, graphic designer, art director and curator, is the founder of Studio Camuffo (Venice), a design team and creative lab in the field of visual communication. Engaged in promoting the culture of graphic design since the 1980s, he collaborates with important institutions, organizing workshops, conferences and exhibitions. He has taught and has been a tutor at diverse universities. In 2006–09 he was the director of the master degree program in Visual and Multimedia Communication at the University IUAV of Venice. He has curated many publications focused on contemporary graphic design; among them: *Grafici italiani* (1995), *Communication What* (2002), *Red Wine and Green* (2004) and *Teach me, Please* (2005). www.studiocamuffo.com

Maddalena Dalla Mura is a free-lance editor and curator. She graduated in 2000 in Conservation of the Cultural Heritage and in 2010 received her PhD degree in Design Sciences from the University IUAV of Venice. Her research interests concentrate on design history and museum studies. www.maddamura.eu

INDEX OF NAMES

CREDITS

Editorial Coordination
Cristina Garbagna

Editing
Gail Swerling
Valeria Perenze

Graphic Coordination
Angelo Galiotto

Technical Coordination
Andrea Panozzo

Quality Control
Giancarlo Berti

Translations
Jeremy Scott
Sylvia Notini

www.electaweb.com

© 2011 by La Triennale di Milano
Triennale Design Museum
by Mondadori Electa S.p.A., Milan

This volume was printed by Mondadori Electa S.p.A.
at Mondadori Printing S.p.A. Verona in 2011